A
Rage
FOR
ORDER

A

Rage

FOR

ORDER

POETRY OF THE
NORTHERN IRELAND
TROUBLES

■

EDITED BY

FRANK ORMSBY

THE
BLACKSTAFF
PRESS

ACKNOWLEDGEMENT

The editor gratefully acknowledges the financial help
of The Arts Council of Northern Ireland

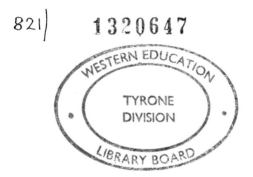
First published in 1992 by
The Blackstaff Press Limited
3 Galway Park, Dundonald, Belfast BT16 0AN, Northern Ireland
with the assistance of
The Arts Council of Northern Ireland

Typeset by Textflow Services Limited

Printed by The Guernsey Press Company Limited

British Library Cataloguing in Publication Data
Rage for Order: Poetry of the Northern
Ireland Troubles
I. Ormsby, Frank
821.91408

ISBN 0-85640-490-X

The blood-dimmed tide is loosed, and everywhere
The ceremony of innocence is drowned;
The best lack all conviction, while the worst
Are full of passionate intensity.

W.B. Yeats, 'The second coming'

We had fed the heart on fantasies,
The heart's grown brutal from the fare;
More substance in our enmities
Than in our love; O honey-bees,
Come build in the empty house of the stare.

W.B. Yeats, 'Meditations in time of civil war'

CONTENTS

2
'Close one eye and be king . . .'

5
'To the other shore . . . '

6

'And hope and history rhyme . . . '

PREFACE

> Somewhere beyond the scorched gable end and the burnt-out buses
>   there is a poet indulging
>   his wretched rage for order –
> or not as the case may be; for his
>   is a dying art,
>   an eddy of semantic scruples
>   in an unstructurable sea.

This anthology celebrates what the speaker in Derek Mahon's poem at first dismisses or underestimates but later concedes – the values of art in times of violence. In particular, though not exclusively, it celebrates the poetry written during the phase of Northern Ireland's Troubles which began in 1968.

The current poetry revival in the North had its immediate origins some years before that date, in the early and mid-1960s. Many of the emerging poets were 'scholarship' children, beneficiaries of the Education Act of 1947 (an act which also, by making further education more widely available to the Catholic minority, paved the way for the Northern Ireland Civil Rights Association, the People's Democracy movement and the Social Democratic and Labour Party), beginning to find their voices at Queen's University Belfast, Trinity College Dublin and elsewhere at a time of intense cultural activity in the North. At the start of the decade the English poet Philip Hobsbaum, then a lecturer at Queen's, founded a writers' group at which young poets such as Seamus Heaney, Michael Longley, Seamus Deane and James Simmons read their work and which continued to meet for several years after Hobsbaum's departure from Belfast. The *Belfast Telegraph* and magazines such as Harry Chambers's *Phoenix*, *Threshold* and the *Northern Review* provided early outlets for these poets, until, in 1965, the Queen's University Festival (later the Belfast Festival at Queen's) promoted a series of Festival Publications, the first pamphlet collections of, among others, Heaney, Longley, Simmons, Deane and Mahon. The process of consolidation continued when, in 1966, Heaney's *Death of a Naturalist* was published to immediate acclaim, followed by Simmons's *Late but in Earnest* and John Montague's *A Chosen Light* (both in 1967), Mahon's *Night-Crossing* (1968), Longley's *No Continuing City*, Heaney's *Door into the Dark*, Simmons's *In the Wilderness and Other Poems* and Padraic Fiacc's *By the Black Stream* (all in 1969). By the end of the decade, yet another generation of Northern Irish poets, those whose first collections appeared in the 1970s, had begun to publish in the *Honest Ulsterman* magazine, founded by James Simmons in 1968.

A number of other poetic milestones of the 1960s should be mentioned here. The appearance of Louis MacNeice's *Collected Poems* (1966) and John Hewitt's *Collected Poems 1932–1967* (1968) confirmed these poets as exemplars and influences. Hewitt's book also prefigured the re-emergence in the 1970s of poets such as Roy McFadden and Robert Greacen, whose first collections had been published in the 1940s. The work of all four serves as a reminder that Troubles poetry (like the Troubles themselves) did not originate in 1968. The sixteenth section of MacNeice's 'Autumn journal' (1939), for example, which makes direct reference to earlier Troubles incidents in the York Street district of Belfast, has a remarkably contemporary ring: its themes of sectarian division and intransigence, the fear, suspicion and violence that Irish children are heir to, the complex, turbulent relationship between Ireland and Britain, the Irishman's love–hate engagement with his country, the artist's (in this case ironic) 'envy' of the man of 'action'; its depiction of a society where free speech is 'nipped in the bud' and the 'minority always guilty'; its imagery of drums, bombs, banners, sectarian graffiti and of Belfast as a 'city built upon mud', make it a source poem for much of this anthology. John Hewitt, too, in poems such as *Freehold*, 'The colony' and 'Once alien here' (all written in the 1940s) and in many of his Glens of Antrim poems, had focused on the descendants of the English and Scottish settlers who had colonised Ulster in the early seventeenth century and he attempted to express their dilemmas. Indeed, his use of historical perspective and parallel in 'The colony', in which the speaker is a Roman colonist, may have served as a model for younger poets of how to address the Troubles obliquely with a dynamic balance of involvement and restraint; and the reservation he himself expresses about this approach, in a poem called 'Parallels never meet' (1969), his fear that the 'coarser texture' of reality in the north of Ireland may be sanitised or lost among the classical associations and resonances, anticipate a recurrent concern among Northern Irish poets generally.

So, when the most recent phase of Troubles erupted in 1968–9, it was inevitable that an already vigorous poetic community should reflect the crisis. Initially, the response was cautious. Although there was some journalistic pressure to produce a kind of war poetry, and although a number of poets engaged in the poetry of the latest atrocity (to adapt Conor Cruise O'Brien's phrase about instant politics), the majority, while recognising the need for response, were more circumspect. Seamus Heaney writes that for Northern Irish poets at that time 'the problems of poetry moved from being simply a matter of achieving the satisfactory verbal icon to being a search for images and symbols adequate to our predicament' and described the urgent necessity 'to discover a field of force in which, without abandoning fidelity to the processes and experience of poetry . . . it would be possible to encompass the perspectives of a humane reason and at the same time to grant the religious intensity of the violence its deplorable authenticity and complexity' ('Feeling into words', from *Preoccupations: Selected Prose 1968–1978*, 1980). Michael Longley records how Northern Irish writers in the late 1960s and early 1970s were sometimes accused of exploitation if they wrote about the Troubles and evasion if they did not, concedes that the poet 'would be inhuman if he did not respond to tragic events in his own community and a poor artist if he did not seek to endorse that response imaginatively', but also states his conviction that 'the artist needs time in which to allow the raw material of experience to settle to an imaginative depth' ('Preview', *Radio Times*, 20–6 October 1979). The northern poets have continued, in reviews and criticism as well as poetry, to weigh and scrutinise the relationship between art and politics and the nature of artistic responsibility. Far from being cripplingly self-conscious – Seamus Deane has noted that artists 'can often be more troubled by the idea that they should be troubled by a crisis than they are by the crisis itself' ('The artist and the Troubles', *Ireland and the Arts*, 1983) – this preoccupation has proved enabling, underpinning and balancing the rich body of Troubles poetry of the last twenty-five years. It has neither stifled the cry of protest nor frozen the spring of compassion and in itself constitutes a valuable, challenging examination of the whole nature of 'response'.

This is, perhaps, a suitable point to raise the question of what makes a Troubles poem. There is no simple answer and I have tried not to be prescriptive. It would, after all, be possible to compile a 'relevant' anthology of great political poems and elegies from world literature of all ages, and it is with the timelessness and universal application of such poetry (and painting) in mind, as the poets themselves had, that I have included, fully or in extract, Heaney's *The Cure at Troy* (after Sophocles), Longley's 'The butchers' (after Homer) and 'Peace' (after Tibullus), Mahon's 'Courtyards in Delft' (after Pieter de Hooch) and Tom

Paulin's 'A nation, yet again' (after Pushkin), to mention some obvious examples. More problematically for the anthologist, it is arguable that *any* poem by a Northern Irish poet since 1968, on whatever subject, could be termed a Troubles poem, in that it may, consciously or unconsciously, reflect the context in which it was written. The unconscious element can only be matter for speculation, but there is interesting evidence of poets' awareness of how the Troubles shadow their poems on other subjects. Montague's highly personal collection *The Great Cloak* (1978), about the disintegration of a marriage and the growth of a new relationship, has the epigraph,

> As my Province burns
> I sing of love,
> Hoping to give that fiery
> Wheel a shove.

Montague has described the book as 'a political statement . . . for love poetry is a form of political poetry' ('Beyond the Planter and the Gael', *Crane Bag*, vol. 4 no. 2, 1980–1). The domestic and love poems of Michael Longley have a similar conscious dimension, as do his poems about the flora and fauna of County Mayo; these, as Peter McDonald remarks, 'are not simply idyllic retreats from "the nightmare ground", but oblique ways of understanding it'.

Given also the extent to which the Troubles permeate entire booklength collections by Northern Irish poets – among them *The Rough Field* (1972) by John Montague, *An Exploded View* (1973) by Michael Longley, *North* (1975) by Seamus Heaney, *Liberty Tree* (1983) by Tom Paulin, *Missa Terribilis* (1986) by Padraic Fiacc, *Meeting the British* (1987) by Paul Muldoon, *The Irish for No* (1987) and *Belfast Confetti* (1989) by Ciaran Carson – it has proved difficult to select adequately from work that has radiated so widely and profoundly from its central concern.

The Troubles poems reprinted here are chosen from some twelve hundred I have read on the subject. Many of those omitted were worthy, heartfelt and sincere, but had little else to recommend them as poems. Many more were propagandist exercises – depressingly instructive but more likely (in Mahon's words) to 'perpetuate/The barbarous cycle' than help (in Montague's) to 'give that fiery/Wheel a shove'. The poets represented are predominantly from the north of Ireland, the Republic of Ireland, and England, but there is also work by a Scot, a New Zealander, two Americans and two Russians. Three contributors

– Arthur McVeigh, Kerry Carson and Conor Carson – were still schoolchildren when their poems were written. I have taken the opportunity to reprint in full a number of relevant longer poems, among them Hewitt's 'The colony', already mentioned; Simmons's 'Lament for a dead policeman', modelled on Eibhlín Dhubh Ní Chonaill's eighteenth-century Gaelic poem 'The lament for Art Ó Laoghaire'; Longley's sequence 'Letters' (to three Irish poets); and Muldoon's elusive, fractured narrative 'The more a man has the more a man wants'.

The content, which includes some fifty poems already anthologised in the precursor to this volume, Padraic Fiacc's *The Wearing of the Black: An Anthology of Contemporary Ulster Poetry* (1974), is organised in six sections. The first ranges over the historical origins of the Troubles, the clash and blend of different traditions in the North, the endless interaction, for better or worse, of past and present. The second focuses on the dangerous undercurrents of injustice and resentment, complacency and discontent, particularly in the period between the establishment of the Northern Ireland state in 1921 and the turmoil of 1968. The third is a sustained elegy for the casualties and victims: civilians, policemen, soldiers, hunger strikers, internees. In section four the predominant subjects are art and politics, the ways in which men of 'action' and, more especially, men of 'words', make, or fail to make, or might make 'things happen', artistic obligation, the centrality and/or marginality of the artist in times of violence, the search for artistic models, and the problems of reaction and response. Section five returns, in a more concentrated way, to the relationship between Northern Ireland and Britain, mainly as experienced by a number of writers who have lived in, or visited, the North; I have broadened the section to include poems by Northern Irish writers that depict the role and plight of the British soldier in the North and a number that portray Northern Ireland as a casualty of colonialism, abandoned or manipulated from outside by unscrupulous politicians and civil servants. The final grouping of poems begins with a reacknowledgement of the '*odi atque amo*' impulses recorded in MacNeice's 'Autumn Journal XVI' (section one) and the perpetually unfinished business of learning 'what is meant by home' (Mahon); its images of healing, peace, normality, have an appropriately vulnerable ring; potential and aspiration are constantly affirmed, their fragility constantly recognised.

Poetry is not, of course, so easily categorised, and while I am confident that individual sections of the anthology are coherent, I recognise that many of the poems included would fit comfortably into more than one section. It seems to me that imaginative relocations and permutations are among a reader's creative pleasures in a collection of this nature.

Seamus Deane has written of the work of Heaney and Mahon that in their efforts 'to come to grips with destructive energies, they attempt to demonstrate a way of turning them towards creativity. Their sponsorship is not simply for the sake of art; it is for the energies embodied in art which have been diminished or destroyed elsewhere.' Deane's comment sums up the affirmative thrust of the poetry collected here. The vitalities and humane perspectives of that poetry, its cumulative counterblasts to the reductive, lethal simplicities of the propagandist, its embodiment of 'semantic scruples' in a province where language is often a dangerous, sometimes a fatal, weapon, give it its own powerful 'field of force'. Its underlying 'rage for order', as the multiple ironies of Mahon's poem intimate, is much more than the wretched last throe of 'a dying art'. Somewhere close to the 'scorched gable end and the burnt-out buses' it is sturdily and enhancingly alive.

FRANK ORMSBY
BELFAST, JULY 1992

1

'In this Irish past I dwell . . . '

from 'Return'
SEAMUS DEANE

SEAMUS HEANEY

BOGLAND

for T.P. Flanagan

We have no prairies
To slice a big sun at evening –
Everywhere the eye concedes to
Encroaching horizon,

Is wooed into the cyclops' eye
Of a tarn. Our unfenced country
Is bog that keeps crusting
Between the sights of the sun.

They've taken the skeleton
Of the Great Irish Elk
Out of the peat, set it up
An astounding crate full of air.

Butter sunk under
More than a hundred years
Was recovered salty and white.
The ground itself is kind, black butter

Melting and opening underfoot,
Missing its last definition
By millions of years.
They'll never dig coal here,

Only the waterlogged trunks
Of great firs, soft as pulp.
Our pioneers keep striking
Inwards and downwards,

Every layer they strip
Seems camped on before.
The bogholes might be Atlantic seepage.
The wet centre is bottomless.

ROBINSON JEFFERS

SHANE O'NEILL'S CAIRN
to U.J.

When you and I on the Palos Verdes cliff
Found life more desperate than dear,
And when we hawked at it on the lake by Seattle,
In the west of the world, where hardly
Anything has died yet: we'd not have been sorry, Una,
But surprised, to foresee this gray
Coast in our days, the gray waters of the Moyle
Below us, and under our feet
The heavy black stones of the cairn of the lord of Ulster.
A man of blood who died bloodily
Four centuries ago: but death's nothing, and life,
From a high death-mark on a headland
Of this dim island of burials, is nothing either.
How beautiful are both these nothings.

JOHN MONTAGUE

from A SEVERED HEAD

And who ever heard
Such a sight unsung
As a severed head
With a grafted tongue?
Old rhyme

2

All around, shards of a lost tradition:
From the Rough Field I went to school
In the Glen of the Hazels. Close by
Was the bishopric of the Golden Stone;
The cairn of Carleton's homesick poem.

Scattered over the hills, tribal
And placenames, uncultivated pearls.
No rock or ruin, dun or dolmen
But showed memory defying cruelty
Through an image-encrusted name.

The heathery gap where the Rapparee,
Shane Barnagh, saw his brother die –
On a summer's day the dying sun
Stained its colours to crimson:
So breaks the heart, Brish-mo-Cree.

The whole landscape a manuscript
We had lost the skill to read,
A part of our past disinherited;
But fumbled, like a blind man,
Along the fingertips of instinct.

The last Gaelic speaker in the parish
When I stammered my school Irish
One Sunday after mass, crinkled
A rusty litany of praise:
Tá an Ghaedilg againn arís . . .

Tír Eoghain: Land of Owen,
Province of the O'Niall;
The ghostly tread of O'Hagan's
Barefoot gallowglasses marching
To merge forces in Dun Geanainn

Push southward to Kinsale!
Loudly the war-cry is swallowed
In swirls of black rain and fog
As Ulster's pride, Elizabeth's foemen,
Founder in a Munster bog.

. . . .

(Dumb,
bloodied, the severed
head now chokes to
speak another tongue:–

As in
a long suppressed dream,
some stuttering garb-
led ordeal of my own)

An Irish
child weeps at school
repeating its English.
After each mistake

The master
gouges another mark
on the tally stick
hung about its neck

Like a bell
on a cow, a hobble
on a straying goat.
To slur and stumble

In shame
the altered syllables
of your own name;
to stray sadly home

And find
the turf-cured width
of your parents' hearth
growing slowly alien:

In cabin
and field, they still
speak the old tongue.
You may greet no one.

To grow
a second tongue, as
harsh a humiliation
as twice to be born.

Decades later
that child's grandchild's
speech stumbles over lost
syllables of an old order.

6

Yet even English in these airts
Took a lawless turn, as who
Would not stroll by Bloody Brae
To Black Lough, or guddle trout
In a stream called the Routing Burn?

Or rest a while on Crooked Bridge
Up the path to Crow Hill;
Straight by Ania's Cove to Spur Royal,
Then round by Duck Island
To Green Mount and New Town Civil?

A last look over the dark ravine
Where that red-tufted rebel,
The Todd, out-leaped the pack;
Turning home by Favour Royal
And the forests of Dourless Black.

And what of stone-age Sess Kill Green
Tullycorker and Tullyglush?
Names twining braid Scots and Irish,
Like Fall Brae, springing native
As a whitethorn bush?

A high, stony place – bogstreams,
Not milk and honey – but our own:
From the Glen of the Hazels
To the Golden Stone may be
The longest journey
                         I have ever gone.

PAUL MULDOON

MEETING THE BRITISH

We met the British in the dead of winter.
The sky was lavender

and the snow lavender-blue.
I could hear, far below,

the sound of two streams coming together
(both were frozen over)

and, no less strange,
myself calling out in French

across that forest-
clearing. Neither General Jeffrey Amherst

nor Colonel Henry Bouquet
could stomach our willow-tobacco.

As for the unusual
scent when the Colonel shook out his hand-

kerchief: *C'est la lavande,
une fleur mauve comme le ciel.*

They gave us six fishhooks
and two blankets embroidered with smallpox.

JOSEPH CAMPBELL

THE PLANTER

The Celt, I say,
Has shown some artistry
In living; you, the Planter, none.
Under moon or sun
You are the same, a dull dog, countryless,
Traditionless and letterless;
Without a dance or song
To speed the time along;
Without a hint of who the Maker was
Who named your farm, or who
Lifted the cromleac in the twisted haws
Marching your barley-field. No clue
Is deigned you. The grey past is dead
For you, as Beauty is. Your head
Is but a block, your filmed eye
Blind to the vision and the mystery
Of Man's progression thro' the Northern Land
Since the first Niall threw the Bloody Hand.

JOHN HEWITT

ONCE ALIEN HERE

Once alien here my fathers built their house,
claimed, drained, and gave the land the shapes of use,
and for their urgent labour grudged no more
than shuffled pennies from the hoarded store
of well-rubbed words that had left their overtones
in the ripe England of the moulded downs.

The sullen Irish limping to the hills
bore with them the enchantments and the spells
that in the clans' free days hung gay and rich
on every twig of every thorny hedge,
and gave the rain-pocked stone a meaning past
the blurred engraving of the fibrous frost.

So I, because of all the buried men
in Ulster clay, because of rock and glen
and mist and cloud and quality of air
as native in my thought as any here,
who now would seek a native mode to tell
our stubborn wisdom individual,
yet lacking skill in either scale of song,
the graver English, lyric Irish tongue,
must let this rich earth so enhance the blood
with steady pulse where now is plunging mood
till thought and image may, identified,
find easy voice to utter each aright.

THE COLONY

First came the legions, then the colonists,
provincials, landless citizens, and some
camp-followers of restless generals
content now only with the least of wars.

Among this rabble, some to feel more free
beyond the ready whim of Caesar's fist;
for conscience' sake the best of these, but others
because their debts had tongues, one reckless man,
a tax absconder with a sack of coin.

With these, young law clerks skilled with chart and stylus,
their boxes crammed with lease-scrolls duly marked
with distances and names, to be defined
when all was mapped.
                    When they'd surveyed the land,
they gave the richer tillage, tract by tract,
from the great captains down to men-at-arms,
some of the sprawling rents to be retained
by Caesar's mistresses in their far villas.

We planted little towns to garrison
the heaving country, heaping walls of earth
and keeping all our cattle close at hand;
then, thrusting north and west, we felled the trees,
selling them off the foothills, at a stroke
making quick profits, smoking out the nests
of the barbarian tribesmen, clan by clan,
who hunkered in their blankets, biding chance,
till, unobserved, they slither down and run
with torch and blade among the frontier huts
when guards were nodding, or when shining corn
bade sword-hand grip the sickle. There was once
a terrible year when, huddled in our towns,
my people trembled as the beacons ran
from hill to hill across the countryside,
calling the dispossessed to lift their standards.
There was great slaughter then, man, woman, child,
with fire and pillage of our timbered houses;
we had to build in stone for ever after.

That terror dogs us; back of all our thought
the threat behind the dream, those beacons flare,
and we run headlong screaming in our fear;
fear quickened by the memory of guilt

for we began the plunder – naked men
still have their household gods and holy places,
and what a people loves it will defend.
We took their temples from them and forbade them,
for many years, to worship their strange idols.
They gathered secret, deep in the dripping glens,
chanting their prayers before a lichened rock.

We took the kindlier soils. It had been theirs,
this patient, temperate, slow, indifferent,
crop-yielding, crop-denying, in-neglect-
quickly-returning-to-the-nettle-and-bracken,
sodden and friendly land. We took it from them.
We laboured hard and stubborn, draining, planting,
till half the country took its shape from us.

Only among the hills with hare and kestrel,
will you observe what once this land was like
before we made it fat for human use –
all but the forests, all but the tall trees –
I could invent a legend of those trees,
and how their creatures, dryads, hamadryads,
fled from the copses, hid in thorny bushes,
and grew a crooked and malignant folk,
plotting and waiting for a bitter revenge
on their despoilers. So our troubled thought
is from enchantments of the old tree magic,
but I am not a sick and haunted man . . .

Teams of the tamer natives we employed
to hew and draw, but did not call them slaves.
Some say this was our error. Others claim
we were too slow to make them citizens;
we might have made them Caesar's bravest legions.
This is a matter for historians,
or old beards in the Senate to wag over,
not pertinent to us these many years.

But here and there the land was poor and starved,
which, though we mapped, we did not occupy,

leaving the natives, out of laziness
in our demanding it, to hold unleased
the marshy quarters, fens, the broken hills,
and all the rougher places where the whin
still thrust from limestone with its cracking pods.

They multiplied and came with open hands,
begging a crust because their land was poor,
and they were many; squatting at our gates,
till our towns grew and threw them hovelled lanes
which they inhabit still. You may distinguish,
if you were schooled with us, by pigmentation,
by cast of features or by turn of phrase,
or by the clan names on them which are they,
among the faces moving in the street.
They worship Heaven strangely, having rites
we snigger at, are known as superstitious,
cunning by nature, never to be trusted,
given to dancing and a kind of song
seductive to the ear, a whining sorrow.
Also they breed like flies. The danger's there;
when Caesar's old and lays his sceptre down,
we'll be a little people, well outnumbered.

Some of us think our leases have run out
but dig square heels in, keep the roads repaired;
and one or two loud voices would restore
the rack, the yellow patch, the curfewed ghetto.
Most try to ignore the question, going their way,
glad to be living, sure that Caesar's word
is Caesar's bond for legions in our need.
Among us, some, beguiled by their sad music,
make common cause with the natives, in their hearts
hoping to win a truce when the tribes assert
their ancient right and take what once was theirs.
Already from other lands the legions ebb
and men no longer know the Roman peace.

Alone, I have a harder row to hoe:
I think these natives human, think their code,

though strange to us, and farther from the truth,
only a little so – to be redeemed
if they themselves rise up against the spells
and fears their celibates surround them with.
I find their symbols good, as such, for me,
when I walk in dark places of the heart;
but name them not to be misunderstood.
I know no vices they monopolise,
if we allow the forms by hunger bred,
the sores of old oppression, the deep skill
in all evasive acts, the swaddled minds,
admit our load of guilt – I mourn the trees
more than as symbol – and would make amends
by fraternising, by small friendly gestures,
hoping by patient words I may convince
my people and this people we are changed
from the raw levies which usurped the land,
if not to kin, to co-inhabitants,
as goat and ox may graze in the same field
and each gain something from proximity;
for we have rights drawn from the soil and sky;
the use, the pace, the patient years of labour,
the rain against the lips, the changing light,
the heavy clay-sucked stride, have altered us;
we would be strangers in the Capitol;
this is our country also, nowhere else;
and we shall not be outcast on the world.

THE IRISH DIMENSION

With these folk gone, next door was tenanted
by a mild man, an Army Officer,
two girls, a boy, left in his quiet care,
his wife, their mother, being some years dead.
We shortly found that they were Catholics,
the very first I ever came to know.
To other friends they might be Teagues or Micks;
the lad I quickly found no sort of foe.

Just my own age. His Christian Brothers School
to me seemed cruel. As an altar boy
he served with dread. His magazines were full
of faces, places named, unknown to me.
Benburb, Wolfe Tone, Cuchullain, Fontenoy.
I still am grateful, Willie Morrissey.

BRENDAN KENNELLY

from CROMWELL

IN THE SEA

Big Island whispered to little island
'I'm right here at your back.
Shall I bugger you?
Shall I breathe down your neck?
Most of the time I hardly see you at all
You're so small, you're so small
And when you insist that you really exist
I can scarcely follow your voice.
Well, do you exist, you sea-shrouded mite?
Or are you a floating illusion
Invisible to all except me?'

Little island replied 'There is sea-light
Between us, and storms and countless drowned men.
Yes, I'm near you. Near. Right here. In the sea.'

A WOUND

Little island whispered over his shoulder
To Big Island who was reflecting on
The fact that there was no island more
Beautiful than himself, 'I'm here, and someone,

'Probably one of my aboriginals,
Has set out in a low boat bearing proof

Of this. You may boot him in the genitals,
Work him over, lock him up, but his love

'For me is such he believes I exist
And wishes to remind you of that truth.'
A bomb mashed Big Island in the side,

The aboriginal was duly booted and later lost.
'I'm here' said little island. 'I can see that'
Groaned Big, 'I must tend this wound before it goes bad.'

OFFENDERS

'Your aboriginals keep sticking thorns in my side'
Complained Big Island to little island.
'I'm sorry about that' said little island
'But what shall I do to stop them being bad?'
'My idea' said Big Island 'is to build
A prison big enough to house all offenders.
When they do wrong and I establish their guilt
I'll send them there for a chastening number of years.'

'And where will this prison be?' queried little island.
Big Island smiled, 'Close to your heart, of course.
Even the worst offenders will feel happy there
Listening in respectful loving silence
To the heartbeat every aboriginal heart adores.'

Little island thought 'Why do I feel like an offender?'

IT IS THE NEARNESS THAT KILLS

It is the nearness that kills, thought little island,
And Big Island is too near,
So near, it makes the sea a servant,
Calls rebellious waves to order
And eats me with its nearness.
And yet, it does not see me at all.
If I were farther away, if there were distance
Between us, Big Island might take a full
Look at me and see me for what I am.

15

But damn it, that's the prob, what am I?
Poisoned lake? Lost river? Buried forest? Bottomless bog?
People cry and die in me all the time,
Children change in me, birds eat me,
I am too far from myself, too near to Big.

SEAMUS HEANEY

TRADITIONS
for Tom Flanagan

I

Our guttural muse
was bulled long ago
by the alliterative tradition,
her uvula grows

vestigial, forgotten
like the coccyx
or a Brigid's Cross
yellowing in some outhouse

while custom, that 'most
sovereign mistress',
beds us down into
the British isles.

II

We are to be proud
of our Elizabethan English:
'varsity', for example,
is grass-roots stuff with us;

we 'deem' or we 'allow'
when we suppose

and some cherished archaisms
are correct Shakespearean.

Not to speak of the furled
consonants of lowlanders
shuttling obstinately
between bawn and mossland.

III

MacMorris, gallivanting
round the Globe, whinged
to courtier and groundling
who had heard tell of us

as going very bare
of learning, as wild hares,
as anatomies of death:
'What ish my nation?'

And sensibly, though so much
later, the wandering Bloom
replied, 'Ireland,' said Bloom,
'I was born here. Ireland.'

TOM PAULIN

UNDER CREON

Rhododendrons growing wild below a mountain
and no long high wall or trees either;
a humped road, bone-dry, with no one –
passing one lough and then another
where water-lilies glazed, primed like traps.

A neapish hour, I searched out gaps
in that imperial shrub: a free voice sang
dissenting green, and syllables spoke

holm oaks by a salt shore, their dark tangs
glistening like Nisus in a night attack.

The daylight gods were never in this place
and I had pressed beyond my usual dusk
to find a cadence for the dead: McCracken,
Hope, the northern starlight, a death mask
and the levelled grave that Biggar traced;

like an epic arming in an olive grove
this was a stringent grief and a form of love.
Maybe one day I'll get the hang of it
and find joy, not justice, in a snapped connection,
that Jacobin oath on the black mountain.

SEAMUS HEANEY

REQUIEM FOR THE CROPPIES

The pockets of our greatcoats full of barley –
No kitchens on the run, no striking camp –
We moved quick and sudden in our own country.
The priest lay behind ditches with the tramp.
A people, hardly marching – on the hike –
We found new tactics happening each day:
We'd cut through reins and rider with the pike
And stampede cattle into infantry,
Then retreat through hedges where cavalry must be
    thrown.
Until, on Vinegar Hill, the fatal conclave.
Terraced thousands died, shaking scythes at cannon.
The hillside blushed, soaked in our broken wave.
They buried us without shroud or coffin
And in August the barley grew up out of the grave.

LOUIS MACNEICE

CARRICKFERGUS

I was born in Belfast between the mountain and the gantries
   To the hooting of lost sirens and the clang of trams:
Thence to Smoky Carrick in County Antrim
   Where the bottle-neck harbour collects the mud which jams

The little boats beneath the Norman castle,
   The pier shining with lumps of crystal salt;
The Scotch Quarter was a line of residential houses
   But the Irish Quarter was a slum for the blind and halt.

The brook ran yellow from the factory stinking of chlorine,
   The yarn-mill called its funeral cry at noon;
Our lights looked over the lough to the lights of Bangor
   Under the peacock aura of a drowning moon.

The Norman walled this town against the country
   To stop his ears to the yelping of his slave
And built a church in the form of a cross but denoting
   The list of Christ on the cross in the angle of the nave.

I was the rector's son, born to the anglican order,
   Banned for ever from the candles of the Irish poor;
The Chichesters knelt in marble at the end of a transept
   With ruffs about their necks, their portion sure.

The war came and a huge camp of soldiers
   Grew from the ground in sight of our house with long
Dummies hanging from gibbets for bayonet practice
   And the sentry's challenge echoing all day long;

A Yorkshire terrier ran in and out by the gate-lodge
   Barred to civilians, yapping as if taking affront:
Marching at ease and singing 'Who Killed Cock Robin?'
   The troops went out by the lodge and off to the Front.

The steamer was camouflaged that took me to England –
  Sweat and khaki in the Carlisle train;
I thought that the war would last for ever and sugar
  Be always rationed and that never again

Would the weekly papers not have photos of sandbags
  And my governess not make bandages from moss
And people not have maps above the fireplace
  With flags on pins moving across and across –

Across the hawthorn hedge the noise of bugles,
  Flares across the night,
Somewhere on the lough was a prison ship for Germans,
  A cage across their sight.

I went to school in Dorset, the world of parents
  Contracted into a puppet world of sons
Far from the mill girls, the smell of porter, the salt-mines
  And the soldiers with their guns.

from AUTUMN JOURNAL

XVI

Nightmare leaves fatigue:
  We envy men of action
Who sleep and wake, murder and intrigue
  Without being doubtful, without being haunted.
And I envy the intransigence of my own
  Countrymen who shoot to kill and never
See the victim's face become their own
  Or find his motive sabotage their motives.
So reading the memoirs of Maud Gonne,
  Daughter of an English mother and a soldier father,
I note how a single purpose can be founded on
  A jumble of opposites:
Dublin Castle, the vice-regal ball,
  The embassies of Europe,

Hatred scribbled on a wall,
    Gaols and revolvers.
And I remember, when I was little, the fear
    Bandied among the servants
That Casement would land at the pier
    With a sword and a horde of rebels;
And how we used to expect, at a later date,
    When the wind blew from the west, the noise of shooting
Starting in the evening at eight
    In Belfast in the York Street district;
And the voodoo of the Orange bands
    Drawing an iron net through darkest Ulster,
Flailing the limbo lands –
    The linen mills, the long wet grass, the ragged hawthorn.
And one read black where the other read white, his hope
    The other man's damnation:
Up the Rebels, To Hell with the Pope,
    And God Save – as you prefer – the King or Ireland.
The land of scholars and saints:
    Scholars and saints my eye, the land of ambush,
Purblind manifestoes, never-ending complaints,
    The born martyr and the gallant ninny;
The grocer drunk with the drum,
    The land-owner shot in his bed, the angry voices
Piercing the broken fanlight in the slum,
    The shawled woman weeping at the garish altar.
Kathleen ni Houlihan! Why
    Must a country, like a ship or a car, be always female,
Mother or sweetheart? A woman passing by,
    We did but see her passing.
Passing like a patch of sun on the rainy hill
    And yet we love her for ever and hate our neighbour
And each one in his will
    Binds his heirs to continuance of hatred.
Drums on the haycock, drums on the harvest, black
    Drums in the night shaking the windows:
King William is riding his white horse back
    To the Boyne on a banner.
Thousands of banners, thousands of white
    Horses, thousands of Williams

Waving thousands of swords and ready to fight
  Till the blue sea turns to orange.
Such was my country and I thought I was well
  Out of it, educated and domiciled in England,
Though yet her name keeps ringing like a bell
  In an under-water belfry.
Why do we like being Irish? Partly because
  It gives us a hold on the sentimental English
As members of a world that never was,
  Baptized with fairy water;
And partly because Ireland is small enough
  To be still thought of with a family feeling,
And because the waves are rough
  That split her from a more commercial culture;
And because one feels that here at least one can
  Do local work which is not at the world's mercy
And that on this tiny stage with luck a man
  Might see the end of one particular action.
It is self-deception of course;
  There is no immunity in this island either;
A cart that is drawn by somebody else's horse
  And carrying goods to somebody else's market.
The bombs in the turnip sack, the sniper from the roof,
  Griffith, Connolly, Collins, where have they brought us?
Ourselves alone! Let the round tower stand aloof
  In a world of bursting mortar!
Let the school-children fumble their sums
  In a half-dead language;
Let the censor be busy on the books; pull down the Georgian slums;
  Let the games be played in Gaelic.
Let them grow beet-sugar; let them build
  A factory in every hamlet;
Let them pigeon-hole the souls of the killed
  Into sheep and goats, patriots and traitors.
And the North, where I was a boy,
  Is still the North, veneered with the grime of Glasgow,
Thousands of men whom nobody will employ
  Standing at the corners, coughing.
And the street-children play on the wet
  Pavement – hopscotch or marbles;

And each rich family boasts a sagging tennis-net
　　On a spongy lawn beside a dripping shrubbery.
The smoking chimneys hint
　　At prosperity round the corner
But they make their Ulster linen from foreign lint
　　And the money that comes in goes out to make more money.
A city built upon mud;
　　A culture built upon profit;
Free speech nipped in the bud,
　　The minority always guilty.
Why should I want to go back
　　To you, Ireland, my Ireland?
The blots on the page are so black
　　That they cannot be covered with shamrock.
I hate your grandiose airs,
　　Your sob-stuff, your laugh and your swagger,
Your assumption that everyone cares
　　Who is the king of your castle.
Castles are out of date,
　　The tide flows round the children's sandy fancy;
Put up what flag you like, it is too late
　　To save your soul with bunting.
Odi atque amo:
　　Shall we cut this name on trees with a rusty dagger?
Her mountains are still blue, her rivers flow
　　Bubbling over the boulders.
She is both a bore and a bitch;
　　Better close the horizon,
Send her no more fantasy, no more longings which
　　Are under a fatal tariff.
For common sense is the vogue
　　And she gives her children neither sense nor money
Who slouch around the world with a gesture and a brogue
　　And a faggot of useless memories.

W . R . RODGERS

EPILOGUE
to 'THE CHARACTER OF IRELAND'

I am Ulster, my people an abrupt people
Who like the spiky consonants in speech
And think the soft ones cissy; who dig
The *k* and *t* in orchestra, detect sin
In sinfonia, get a kick out of
Tin cans, fricatives, fornication, staccato talk,
Anything that gives or takes attack,
Like Micks, Tagues, tinkers' gets, Vatican.
An angular people, brusque and Protestant,
For whom the word is still a fighting word,
Who bristle into reticence at the sound
Of the round gift of the gab in Southern mouths.
Mine were not born with silver spoons in gob,
Nor would they thank you for the gift of tongues;
The dry riposte, the bitter repartee's
The Northman's bite and portion, his deep sup
Is silence; though, still within his shell,
He holds the old sea-roar and surge
Of rhetoric and Holy Writ.
Three hundred years ago our foundling fathers
With farthing fists and thistles in their eyes
Were planted on this foreshore,
Bibles for bibs and bloody pikes for rattles
And tombs for keeps. There was not time
To wade through wedding to a birth.
Calvin and culverin sang the cradle-song
And Cromwell made the bed.
Put to a frugal breast of swollen hopes
They did their levelling best and left it flat
As water. Winding-sheet and swaddling-band
Were one. Needle-flute and thimble-drum
Stitched the way to kingdom-come, to Derry,
Aughrim, Enniskillen, and the Boyne:
Rat-a-ta-ta, rat-a-ta-ta, rat-a-ta-ta,

Humdrummery of history.
And I, born to the purple passage,
Was heir to all that Adamnation
And hand-me-down of doom, the late comer
To the worn-out womb.
The apple blushed for me below Bellevue,
Lagan was my Jordan, Connswater
My washpot, and over Belfast
I cast out my shoe.

RUDYARD KIPLING

ULSTER 1912

Their webs shall not become garments, neither shall they cover
themselves with their works: their works are works of iniquity and
the act of violence is in their hands.

Isaiah 59:6

The dark eleventh hour
Draws on and sees us sold
To every evil power
We fought against of old.
Rebellion, rapine, hate,
Oppression, wrong and greed
Are loosed to rule our fate,
By England's act and deed.

The Faith in which we stand,
The laws we made and guard,
Our honour, lives, and land
Are given for reward
To Murder done by night,
To Treason taught by day,
To folly, sloth, and spite,
And we are thrust away.

The blood our fathers spilt,
Our love, our toils, our pains,

Are counted us for guilt,
And only bind our chains.
Before an Empire's eyes
The traitor claims his price.
What need of further lies?
We are the sacrifice.

We asked no more than leave
To reap where we had sown,
Through good and ill to cleave
To our own flag and throne.
Now England's shot and steel
Beneath that flag must show
How loyal hearts should kneel
To England's oldest foe.

We know the war prepared
On every peaceful home,
We know the hells declared
For such as serve not Rome –
The terror, threats, and dread
In market, hearth, and field –
We know, when all is said,
We perish if we yield.

Believe, we dare not boast,
Believe, we do not fear –
We stand to pay the cost
In all that men hold dear.
What answer from the North?
One Law, one Land, one Throne.
If England drive us forth
We shall not fall alone!

GERALD DAWE

A QUESTION OF COVENANTS
28 September 1913

The *Patriotic* turns to face
an invisible sea. From Castle Place
thousands swarm through side-streets
and along the unprotected quays just
to glimpse Carson, gaunt as usual,
who watches the surge of people
call, *'Don't leave us. You mustn't leave us'*,
and in the searchlight's beam,
his figure arched across the upper deck,
he shouts he will come back
and, if necessary, fight this time.

It is what they came to hear
in the dark September night.
As the *Patriotic* sails out
Union colours burst in rockets
and bonfires scar the hills
he departs from, a stranger to both sides
of the lough's widening mouth
and the crowd's distant singing
'Auld Lang Syne' and 'God Save the King'.

TOM PAULIN

SETTLERS

They cross from Glasgow to a black city
    Of gantries, mills and steeples. They begin to belong.
He manages the Iceworks, is an elder of the Kirk;
    She becomes, briefly, a cook in Carson's Army.
Some mornings, walking through the company gate,

27

He touches the bonnet of a brown lorry.
It is warm. The men watch and say nothing.
  'Queer, how it runs off in the night,'
He says to McCullough, then climbs to his office.
  He stores a warm knowledge on his palm.

  Nightlandings on the Antrim coast, the movement of guns
Now snug in their oiled paper below the floors
  Of sundry kirks and tabernacles in that county.

JOHN HEWITT

ENCOUNTER, NINETEEN TWENTY

Kicking a ragged ball from lamp to lamp,
in close November dusk, my head well down,
not yet aware the team had dribbled off,
I collided with a stiffly striding man.

He cursed. I stumbled, glimpsing his sharp face,
his coat brushed open and a rifle held
close to his side. That image has become
the shape of fear that waits each Irish child.

Shock sent each reeling from the light's pale cone;
in shadow since that man moves out to kill;
and I, with thumping heart, from lamp to lamp,
still race to score my sad unchallenged goal.

LOUIS MACNEICE

BELFAST

The hard cold fire of the northerner
Frozen into his blood from the fire in his basalt
Glares from behind the mica of his eyes
And the salt carrion water brings him wealth.

Down there at the end of the melancholy lough
Against the lurid sky over the stained water
Where hammers clang murderously on the girders
Like crucifixes the gantries stand.

And in the marble stores rubber gloves like polyps
Cluster; celluloid, painted ware, glaring
Metal patents, parchment lampshades, harsh
Attempts at buyable beauty.

In the porch of the chapel before the garish Virgin
A shawled factory-woman as if shipwrecked there
Lies a bunch of limbs glimpsed in the cave of gloom
By us who walk in the street so buoyantly and glib.

Over which country of cowled and haunted faces
The sun goes down with a banging of Orange drums
While the male kind murders each its woman
To whose prayer for oblivion answers no Madonna.

MAURICE JAMES CRAIG

BALLAD TO A TRADITIONAL REFRAIN

Red brick in the suburbs, white horse on the wall,
Eyetalian marbles in the City Hall:

O stranger from England, why stand so aghast?
May the Lord in His mercy be kind to Belfast.

This jewel that houses our hopes and our fears
Was knocked up from the swamp in the last hundred years;
But the last shall be first and the first shall be last;
May the Lord in His mercy be kind to Belfast.

We swore by King William there'd never be seen
An all-Irish Parliament at College Green,
So at Stormont we're nailing the flag to the mast:
May the Lord in His mercy be kind to Belfast.

O the bricks they will bleed and the rain it will weep,
And the damp Lagan fog lull the city to sleep;
It's to hell with the future and live in the past:
May the Lord in His mercy be kind to Belfast.

RICHARD MURPHY

from THE BATTLE OF AUGHRIM

In bowler hats and Sunday suits,
Orange sashes, polished boots,
Atavistic trainbands come
To blow the fife and beat the drum.

Apprentices uplift their banner
True-blue-dyed with 'No Surrender!'
Claiming Aughrim as if they'd won
Last year, not 1691.

On Belfast silk, Victoria gives
Bibles to kneeling Zulu chiefs.
Read the moral, note the date:
'The secret that made Britain great.'

Derry, oakwood of bright angels,
Londonderry, dingy walls
Chalked at night with 'Fuck the Queen!'
Bygone canon, bygone spleen.

DONALD DAVIE

BELFAST ON A SUNDAY AFTERNOON

Visiting Belfast at the end of June,
We found the Orange Lodge behind a band:
Sashes and bearskins in the afternoon,
White cotton gloves upon a crippled hand.

Pastmasters pale, elaborately grim,
Marched each alone, beneath a bowler hat:
And, catapulted on a crumpled limb,
A lame man leapt the tram-lines like a bat.

And first of all we tried to laugh it off,
Acting bemusement in the grimy sun;
But stayed to worry where we came to scoff,
As loud contingents followed, one by one.

Pipe bands, flute bands, brass bands and silver bands,
Presbyter's pibroch and the deacon's serge,
Came stamping where the iron Mænad stands,
Victoria, glum upon a grassy verge.

Some brawny striplings sprawled upon the lawn;
No man is really crippled by his hates.
Yet I remembered with a sudden scorn
Those 'passionate intensities' of Yeats.

ROY MCFADDEN

THOSE GLORIOUS TWELFTHS

At ten I saw exclamatory blood
On Earlswood Road, a cagecar and a beak-
Capped constable with crowblack gun. We went
To Portrush in July, the great event
Abstracted to indifferent gull and rock.

At twenty, reading law, I glimpsed a gun
Glint in the smile of D.I., former Tan,
War-hero who'd won fancy ribboned stuff
For gutting Germans. Dead Huns not enough,
He grilled halfbaked dissenting Irishmen.

At thirty, pigmy family nudging knee,
Wedged in a village dazed by roaring drums
That drowned my destination; trapped by tied
Tiers of faces blinding stonedeaf road:
Inactive, voiceless, I chewed famine crumbs

Like those who willed another hopeless day
Eyeing the shrivelled root and the stopped hand.
Now forty, knowing men in government,
And collared curs that bark down argument
And foul what they must fail to understand:

I hurry children from the bloodsmeared drums,
Myself from the Inspector. If I rein
My family back from rearing history,
The white horse on the wall, the ricochet,
It is to turn a corner, or else, say,
A new leaf that will dock the nettle's pain.

Project an image for this place and time –
Aloof from cheers and flags, the maddened gun –
Of one embarrassed, guilty monument
Leaving its plinth in the establishment
To smuggle flowers to graves it can't disown.

JOHN ENNIS

LONDONDERRY

As long as the Foyle rises, the eagle flies
and heather blooms for the late bell honey
this black acid soil is for living in.
Peninsulas are ample with their grain,
hazels with their catkins give us nuts.
We are afraid you will take them from us.
You do not have sole rental on these oaks
and that is why I close the gates on you.

Antrim, why do you think so bad of us?
Our hearts beat to the same rhythms,
our children go to school like yours
but you have cut them from our wombs,
served up young boys to their fathers
fed us in tears to the swollen rivers.
The same bad blood now races both our veins
and that is why I close the gates on you.

Was there not one corner you could have spared?
Was there not one field we could have bargained
shaking hands across wheat, wished a blessing
on like neighbours over intestate green fences?
If a forgotten polity brought our mothers
why grind on their sons such bitter querns?
Deep down you call on us little but evil
and that is why I close the gates on you.

Both our fathers, too, were once seafarers.
If we look to London, why do you rage?
'Irish', were you so planted from Adam?
Intruders, we both sailed west to furze-lit hills,
like you, we dug dykes, sowed corn, threw up roofs;
like you we had dreams, strong limbs, girls we craved.
I love the full harvest moon too over the Creggan
and that is why I close the gates on you.

I have no illusions,
the men I fight are young like me
goaded by old dotards and their bells.
You do not question,
you do not isolate the plumed wolves
you do not weep when my friends die
you do not
and that is why I close the gates on you.

Do not feed me with your dead heroes.
For me every perch of earth is sacred,
every rood is a bounty from creation.
If there were the sun, I would grow you figs.
If there were the sun, I would give you wine.
If there were the sun, I would sell you olives.
I'm not enchanted by your mythic vapours
and that is why I close the gates on you.

Old Windbags, do not treat us to your tares
for you have wiped us off this fair island.
Christ, at our backs lies the pirate fleet!
But I know you will be merciless and wind
our guts, like Brodar's, round your trees.
We have our stones and scythes and pikes
here for you have made of us the masters
and that is why I close the gates on you.

Daybreak, tomorrow, I'll eat the same gruel
back to the grind of the apprentice
hammering till the salt sweat trickles
as the frosty bosses lord it over our souls.
We are not the first, or the last poor
squabblers across white tussocks in the blood.
We have full right like you to this blue December sky
and that is why I close the gates on you.

JOHN MONTAGUE

A NEW SIEGE

for Bernadette Devlin

Once again, it happens.
Under a barrage of stones
and flaring petrol bombs
the blunt, squat shape of
an armoured car glides
into the narrow streets
of the Catholic quarter
leading a file of helmet-
ed, shielded riot police;
once again, it happens,
like an old Troubles film,
run for the last time . . .

Lines of history
　lines of power
the long sweep
　of the Bogside
under the walls
　up to Creggan
the black muzzle
　of Roaring Meg
staring dead on
　cramped houses
the jackal shapes
　of James's army
watching the city
　stiffen in siege

Lines of defiance
　lines of discord
near the Diamond
　brisk with guns
British soldiers
　patrol the walls
the gates between
　Ulster Catholic
Ulster Protestant
　a Saracen slides
past the Guildhall
　a black Cuchulain
bellowing against
　the Scarlet Whore
twin races petrified
　the volcanic ash
of religious hatred

SMALL SHOT HATH
    POURED LIKE HAIL
THE GREAT GUNS
    SHAKEN OUR WALLS
a spectral garrison
    no children left
sick from eating
    horseflesh, vermin
curs fattened on
    the slain Irish
still flaunting
    the bloody flag
of 'No Surrender'
    GOD HAS MADE US
AN IRON PILLAR
    AND BRAZEN WALLS
AGAINST THIS LAND.

Symbol of Ulster
    these sloping streets
blackened walls
    sick at heart and
seeking a sign
    the flaghung gloom
of St Columb's
    the brass eagle of
the lectern bearing
    the Sermon on the Mount
in its shoulders
    'A city that is
set on a hill
    cannot be hid.'

Columba's Derry!
    ledge of angels
radiant oakwood
    where the man dove
knelt to master
    his fiery temper
exile chastened
    the bright candle
of the Uí Néill
    burns from Iona
lightens Scotland
    with beehive huts
glittering manuscripts
    but he remembers
his secret name
    'He who set his
back on Ireland.'

Rearing westward
    the great sunroom
of Inis Eoghain
    coiling stones of
Aileach's hillfort
    higher than Tara
the Hy Niall
    dominating Uladh
the white cone
    of Sliabh Snacht
sorrow veiled
    the silent fjord
is uaigneach Eire
    as history's wind
plucks a dynasty
    from the ramparts
bids a rival
    settlement rise

Lines of leaving
  lines of returning
the long estuary
  of Lough Foyle, a
ship motionless
  in wet darkness
mournfully hooting
  as a tender creeps
to carry passengers
  back to Ireland
a child of four
  this sad sea city
my landing place
  the loneliness of
Lir's white daughter's
  ice crusted wings
forever spread
  at the harbour mouth.

Lines of suffering
  lines of defeat
under the walls
  ghetto terraces
sharp pallor of
  unemployed shades
slope shouldered
  broken bottles
pubs and bookies
  red brick walls
Falls or Shankill
  Lecky or Fountain
love's alleyway
  message scrawled
Popehead: Tague
  my own name
hatred's synonym

London's Derry!
  METHOUGHT I SAW
DIDOE'S COLONY
  BUILDING OF CARTHAGE
culverin and saker
  line strong walls
but local chiefs
  come raging in
O'Cahan, O'Doherty
  (a Ferrara sword
his visiting card)
  a New Plantation
a new mythology
  Lundy slides
down a peartree
  as drum and fife
trill ORANJE BOVEN!

Lines of protest
  lines of change
a drum beating
  across Berkeley
all that Spring
  invoking the new
Christ avatar
  of the Americas
running voices
  streets of Berlin
Paris, Chicago
  seismic waves
zigzagging through
  a faulty world

But will the meek
inherit the earth?
RELIGION POISONS US
NORTH AND SOUTH.
A SPECIAL FORCE OF
ANGELS WE'D NEED
TO PUT MANNERS ON US.
IF THE YOUNG WERE
HONEST, THEY'D ADMIT
THEY DON'T HOLD
WITH THE HALF OF IT.
THE SHOWBANDS
AND THE BORDER HALLS
THAT'S THE STUFF
Said the guardian
of the empty church
pale siege windows
shining behind us

Overflowing from
narrow streets
cramped fields
a pressure rising
to match it
tired marchers
nearing Burntollet
young arms linked
banners poled high
the baptism of
flying missiles
spiked clubs
Law and Order's
medieval armour
of glass shield
and dangling baton

Lines of action
lines of reaction
the white elephant
of Stormont, Carson's
raised right claw
a Protestant parliament
a Protestant people
major this and
captain that and
general nothing
the bland, pleasant
face of mediocrity
confronting in horror
its mirror image
bull-voiced bigotry

Lines of loss
lines of energy
always changing
always returning
A TIDE LIFTS
THE RELIEF SHIP
OFF THE MUD
OVER THE BOOM
the rough field
of the universe
growing, changing
a net of energies
crossing patterns
weaving towards
a new order
a new anarchy
always different
always the same

The emerging order
　of the poem invaded
by cries, protestations
　a people's pain
the defiant face
　of a young girl
campaigning against
　memory's mortmain
a blue banner
　lifting over a
broken province
　DRIVE YOUR PLOUGH
a yellow bulldozer
　raising the rubble
a humming factory
　a housing estate
hatreds sealed into
　a hygienic honeycomb

Across the border
　a dead man
drives to school
　past the fort
at Greene Castle
　a fury of love
for North, South
　eats his heart
on the far side
　a rocky promontory
his family name
　O'Cahan, O'Kane
my uncle watches
　sails upon Foyle
(a flock of swans)
　drives forward

PADRAIC FIACC

from THE HERO

*The phenomenon of the hero that, like the salmon,
he contributes to his own extinction*

II

The fiery salmon makes for himself a cold house – Ronan

His jaw is dark now and sets.

He's found a reason to kill, a 'cause'.

He's plotting murder, he forgets
Foot-free parish pantomime days

When he was the lad played Santa Claus.

JOHN MONTAGUE

HEROICS

In an odour of wet hawthorn
arm-swinging heroes march,
eyes chill with yearning.
They sport dark berets and
shoulder rifles as forthrightly
as spades. Spider webs
lace their sparbled boots.
A burst of automatic fire
solves the historical problem.
They drop to one knee.

MICHAEL LONGLEY

ON SLIEVE GULLION
for Douglas Carson

On Slieve Gullion 'men and mountain meet',
O'Hanlon's territory, the rapparee,
Home of gods, backdrop for a cattle raid,
The Lake of Cailleach Beara at the top
That slaked the severed head of Conor Mor:

To the south the Border and Ravensdale
Where the torturers of Nairac left
Not even an eyelash under the leaves
Or a tooth for MacCecht the cupbearer
To rinse, then wonder where the water went.

I watch now through a gap in the hazels
A blackened face, the disembodied head
Of a mummer who has lost his bearings

Or, from the garrison at Dromintee,
A paratrooper on reconnaissance.

He draws a helicopter after him,
His beret far below, a wine-red spot
Swallowed by heathery patches and ling
As he sweats up the slopes of Slieve Gullion
With forty pounds of history on his back.

Both strangers here, we pass in silence
For he and I have dried the lakes and streams
And Conor said too long ago: 'Noble
And valiant is MacCecht the cupbearer
Who brings water that a king may drink.'

JAMES SIMMONS

FROM THE IRISH

Most terrible was our hero in battle blows:
hands without fingers, shorn heads and toes
were scattered. That day there flew and fell
from astonished victims eyebrow, bone and entrail,
like stars in the sky, like snowflakes, like nuts in May,
like a meadow of daisies, like butts from an ashtray.

Familiar things, you might brush against or tread
upon in the daily round, were glistening red
with the slaughter the hero caused, though he had gone.
By proxy his bomb exploded, his valour shone.

SEAMUS HEANEY

THE TOLLUND MAN

I

Some day I will go to Aarhus
To see his peat-brown head,
The mild pods of his eye-lids,
His pointed skin cap.

In the flat country nearby
Where they dug him out,
His last gruel of winter seeds
Caked in his stomach,

Naked except for
The cap, noose and girdle,
I will stand a long time.
Bridegroom to the goddess,

She tightened her torc on him
And opened her fen,
Those dark juices working
Him to a saint's kept body,

Trove of the turfcutters'
Honeycombed workings.
Now his stained face
Reposes at Aarhus.

II

I could risk blasphemy,
Consecrate the cauldron bog
Our holy ground and pray
Him to make germinate

The scattered, ambushed
Flesh of labourers,

Stockinged corpses
Laid out in the farmyards,

Tell-tale skin and teeth
Flecking the sleepers
Of four young brothers, trailed
For miles along the lines.

III

Something of his sad freedom
As he rode the tumbril
Should come to me, driving,
Saying the names

Tollund, Grabaulle, Nebelgard,
Watching the pointing hands
Of country people,
Not knowing their tongue.

Out there in Jutland
In the old man-killing parishes
I will feel lost,
Unhappy and at home.

SEAMUS DEANE

RETURN

The train shot through the dark.
Hedges leapt across the window-pane.
Trees belled in foliage were stranded,
Inarticulate with rain.
A blur of lighted farm implied
The evacuated countryside.

I am appalled by its emptiness.
Every valley glows with pain

As we run like a current through;
Then the memories darken again.
In this Irish past I dwell
Like sound implicit in a bell.

The train curves round a river,
And how tenderly its gouts of steam
Contemplate the nodding moon
The waters from the clouds redeem.
Two hours from Belfast
I am snared in my past.

Crusts of light lie pulsing
Diamanté with the rain
At the track's end. Amazing!
I am in Derry once again.
Once more I turn to greet
Ground that flees from my feet.

ROBINSON JEFFERS

ANTRIM

No spot of earth where men have so fiercely for ages of time
Fought and survived and cancelled each other,
Pict and Gael and Dane, McQuillan, Clandonnel, O'Neill,
Savages, the Scot, the Norman, the English,
Here in the narrow passage and the pitiless north, perpetual
Betrayals, relentless resultless fighting.
A random fury of dirks in the dark: a struggle for survival
Of hungry blind cells of life in the womb.
But now the womb has grown old, her strength has gone forth;
  a few red carts in a fog creak flax to the dubs,
And sheep in the high heather cry hungrily that life is hard;
  a plaintive peace; shepherds and peasants.

We have felt the blades meet in the flesh in a hundred ambushes
And the groaning blood bubble in the throat;

In a hundred battles the heavy axes bite the deep bone,
The mountains suddenly stagger and be darkened.
Generation on generation we have seen the blood of boys
And heard the moaning of women massacred,
The passionate flesh and nerves have flamed like pitchpine and fallen
And lain in the earth softly dissolving.
I have lain and been humbled in all these graves, and mixed new flesh
　　with the old and filled the hollow of my mouth
With maggots and rotten dust and ages of repose. I lie here and plot
　　the agony of resurrection.

DEREK MAHON

RATHLIN ISLAND

A long time since the last scream cut short –
Then an unnatural silence; and then
A natural silence, slowly broken
By the shearwater, by the sporadic
Conversation of crickets, the bleak
Reminder of a metaphysical wind.
Ages of this, till the report
Of an outboard motor at the pier
Fractures the dream-time, and we land
As if we were the first visitors here.

The whole island a sanctuary where amazed
Oneiric species whistle and chatter,
Evacuating rock-face and cliff-top.
Cerulean distance, an oceanic haze –
Nothing but sea-smoke to the ice-cap
And the odd somnolent freighter.
Bombs doze in the housing estates
But here they are through with history –
Custodians of a lone light that repeats
One simple statement to the turbulent sea.

A long time since the unspeakable violence –
Since Somhairle Buidh, powerless on the mainland,
Heard the screams of the Rathlin women
Borne to him, seconds after, upon the wind.
Only the cry of the shearwater
And the roar of the outboard motor
Disturb the singular peace. Spray-blind,
We leave here the infancy of the race,
Unsure among the pitching surfaces
Whether the future lies before us or behind.

2

'Close one eye and be king . . . '

from 'Ecclesiastes'
DEREK MAHON

JOHN HEWITT

THE COASTERS

You coasted along
to larger houses, gadgets, more machines,
to golf and weekend bungalows,
caravans when the children were small,
the Mediterranean, later, with the wife.

You did not go to church often,
weddings were special;
but you kept your name on the books
against eventualities;
and the parson called, or the curate.

You showed a sense of responsibility,
with subscriptions to worthwhile causes
and service in voluntary organisations;
and, anyhow, this did the business no harm,
no harm at all.
Relations were improving. A good
useful life. You coasted along.

You even had a friend or two of the other sort,
coasting too: your ways ran parallel.
Their children and yours seldom met, though,
being at different schools.
You visited each other, decent folk with a sense
of humour. Introduced, even, to
one of their clergy. And then you smiled
in the looking glass, admiring, a
little moved by, your broadmindedness.
Your father would never have known
one of them. Come to think of it,
when you were young, your own home was never
visited by one of the other sort.

Relations were improving. The annual processions
began to look rather like folk festivals.

When that noisy preacher started,
he seemed old-fashioned, a survival.
Later you remarked on his vehemence,
a bit on the rough side.
But you said, admit it, you said in the club,
'You know, there's something in what he says.'

And you who seldom had time to read a book,
what with reports and the colour supplements,
denounced censorship.
And you who never had an adventurous thought
were positive that the church of the other sort
vetoes thought.
And you, who simply put up with marriage
for the children's sake, deplored
the attitude of the other sort
to divorce.
You coasted along.
And all the time, though you never noticed,
the old lies festered;
the ignorant became more thoroughly infected;
there were gains, of course;
you never saw any go barefoot.

The government permanent, sustained
by the regular plebiscites of loyalty.
You always voted but never
put a sticker on the car;
a card in the window
would not have been seen from the street.
Faces changed on the posters, names too, often,
but the same families, the same class of people.
A minister once called you by your first name.
You coasted along
and the sores suppurated and spread.

Now the fever is high and raging;
who would have guessed it, coasting along?
The ignorant-sick thresh about in delirium
and tear at the scabs with dirty fingernails.
The cloud of infection hangs over the city,
a quick change of wind and it
might spill over the leafy suburbs.
You coasted too long.

DEREK MAHON

GLENGORMLEY

'Wonders are many and none is more wonderful than man'
Who has tamed the terrier, trimmed the hedge
And grasped the principle of the watering-can.
Clothes-pegs litter the window ledge
And the long ships lie in clover. Washing lines
Shake out white linen over the chalk thanes.

Now we are safe from monsters, and the giants
Who tore up sods twelve miles by six
And hurled them out to sea to become islands
Can worry us no more. The sticks
And stones that once broke bones will not now harm
A generation of such sense and charm.

Only words hurt us now. No saint or hero,
Landing at night from the conspiring seas,
Brings dangerous tokens to the new era –
Their sad names linger in the histories.
The unreconciled, in their metaphysical pain,
Dangle from lamp-posts in the dawn rain;

And much dies with them. I should rather praise
A worldly time under this worldly sky –
The terrier-taming, garden-watering days

Those heroes pictured as they struggled through
The quick noose of their finite being. By
Necessity, if not choice, I live here too.

TOM PAULIN

IN THE LOST PROVINCE

As it comes back, brick by smoky brick,
I say to myself – strange I lived there
And walked those streets. It is the Ormeau Road
On a summer's evening, a haze of absence
Over the caked city, that slumped smell
From the blackened gasworks. Ah, those brick canyons
Where Brookeborough unsheathes a sabre,
Shouting 'No Surrender' from the back of a lorry.

And the sky is a dry purple, and men
Are talking politics in a back room.
Is it too early or too late for change?
Certainly the province is most peaceful.
Who would dream of necessity, the angers
Of Leviathan, or the years of judgement?

DEREK MAHON

ECCLESIASTES

God, you could grow to love it, God-fearing, God-
    chosen purist little puritan that,
for all your wiles and smiles, you are (the
    dank churches, the empty streets,
the shipyard silence, the tied-up swings) and
    shelter your cold heart from the heat

of the world, from woman-inquisition, from the
    bright eyes of children. Yes you could
wear black, drink water, nourish a fierce zeal
    with locusts and wild honey, and not
feel called upon to understand and forgive
    but only to speak with a bleak
afflatus, and love the January rains when they
    darken the dark doors and sink hard
into the Antrim hills, the bog meadows, the heaped
    graves of your fathers. Bury that red
bandana and stick, that banjo; this is your
    country, close one eye and be king.
Your people await you, their heavy washing
    flaps for you in the housing estates –
a credulous people. God, you could do it, God
    help you, stand on a corner stiff
with rhetoric, promising nothing under the sun.

GERALD DAWE

LITTLE PALACES
for Gerard Fanning

Donkey's Lane:
an orchard and allotments,
broken window-frames, pigeon-huts
on stilts, corrugated iron;
and blankets hung out
on the line to air.

A woman dusts the living room.
The Queen on horseback
smiles down upon tongues
of sprouting ivy. Everything
is right with the world;
even the kerbstones are painted.

JOHN MONTAGUE

STELE FOR A NORTHERN REPUBLICAN

Once again, with creased forehead
and trembling hands, my father calls
me from stifling darkness . . .
Little enough I know of your struggle,
although you come to me more and more,
free of that heavy body armour
you tried to dissolve with alcohol,
a pale face straining in dream light
like a fish's belly

               upward to life.
Hesitantly, I trace your part in
the holy war to restore our country,
slipping from home to smoke
an absentee's mansion, concoct
ambushes. Games turned serious
when the cross-fire at Falban
riddled the tender of policemen,
one bleeding badly

               stretched upon
the stone flags of our kitchen,
your sisters moving in a whisper
of blood and bandages. Strange war
when the patrol scouted bales
of fodder, stray timber, tar
to prepare those sheltering walls
for reprisal's savage flames
if he should die!

            That night
you booked into a Strabane hotel.
'Locals were rarely used for jobs:
orders of the Dublin organizer,
shot afterwards, by his own side.'
A generation later, the only sign
of your parochial struggle was
when the plough rooted rusty guns,

dull bayonets, in some rushy glen
for us to play with.
                    Although again
and again, the dregs of disillusion
churned in our Northern parents' guts
to set their children's teeth on edge;
my mother hobbling to the shed
to burn the Free State uniforms
her two brothers had thrown off
(frugal, she saved the buttons):
my father, home from the boat at Cobh,
staring in pale anger at a Redmond
Commemoration stamp
                    or tearing to
flitters the polite Masscard sent
by a Catholic policeman. But what if
you have no country to set before Christ,
only a broken province? No parades,
fierce medals, will mark Tyrone's re-birth
betrayed by both South and North;
so lie still, difficult old man,
you were right to choose a Brooklyn slum
rather than a half-life in this
by-passed and dying place.

SEAMUS HEANEY

SERVANT BOY

He is wintering out
the back-end of a bad year,
swinging a hurricane-lamp
through some outhouse;

a jobber among shadows.
Old work-whore, slave-

blood, who stepped fair-hills
under each bidder's eye

and kept your patience
and your counsel, how
you draw me into
your trail. Your trail

broken from haggard to stable,
a straggle of fodder
stiffened on snow,
comes first-footing

the back doors of the little
barons: resentful
and impenitent,
carrying the warm eggs.

from SINGING SCHOOL

1   THE MINISTRY OF FEAR
for Seamus Deane

Well, as Kavanagh said, we have lived
In important places. The lonely scarp
Of St Columb's College, where I billeted
For six years, overlooked your Bogside.
I gazed into new worlds: the inflamed throat
Of Brandywell, its floodlit dogtrack,
The throttle of the hare. In the first week
I was so homesick I couldn't even eat
The biscuits left to sweeten my exile.
I threw them over the fence one night
In September 1951
When the lights of houses in the Lecky Road
Were amber in the fog. It was an act
Of stealth.

Then Belfast, and then Berkeley.
Here's two on's are sophisticated,
Dabbling in verses till they have become
A life: from bulky envelopes arriving
In vacation time to slim volumes
Despatched 'with the author's compliments'.
Those poems in longhand, ripped from the wire spine
Of your exercise book, bewildered me –
Vowels and ideas bandied free
As the seed-pods blowing off our sycamores.
I tried to write about the sycamores
And innovated a South Derry rhyme
With *hushed* and *lulled* full chimes for *pushed* and *pulled*.
Those hobnailed boots from beyond the mountain
Were walking, by God, all over the fine
Lawns of elocution.

Have our accents
Changed? 'Catholics, in general, don't speak
As well as students from the Protestant schools.'
Remember that stuff? Inferiority
Complexes, stuff that dreams were made on.
'What's your name, Heaney?'

'Heaney, Father.'

'Fair
Enough.'

On my first day, the leather strap
Went epileptic in the Big Study,
Its echoes plashing over our bowed heads,
But I still wrote home that a boarder's life
Was not so bad, shying as usual.

On long vacations, then, I came to life
In the kissing seat of an Austin Sixteen
Parked at a gable, the engine running,
My fingers tight as ivy on her shoulders,
A light left burning for her in the kitchen.
And heading back for home, the summer's
Freedom dwindling night by night, the air
All moonlight and a scent of hay, policemen
Swung their crimson flashlamps, crowding round

The car like black cattle, snuffing and pointing
The muzzle of a sten-gun in my eye:
'What's your name, driver?'

                          'Seamus . . . '

                                    Seamus?

They once read my letters at a roadblock
And shone their torches on your hieroglyphics,
'Svelte dictions' in a very florid hand.

Ulster was British, but with no rights on
The English lyric: all around us, though
We hadn't named it, the ministry of fear.

2   A CONSTABLE CALLS

His bicycle stood at the window-sill,
The rubber cowl of a mud-splasher
Skirting the front mudguard,
Its fat black handlegrips

Heating in sunlight, the 'spud'
Of the dynamo gleaming and cocked back,
The pedal treads hanging relieved
Of the boot of the law.

His cap was upside down
On the floor, next his chair.
The line of its pressure ran like a bevel
In his slightly sweating hair.

He had unstrapped
The heavy ledger, and my father
Was making tillage returns
In acres, roods, and perches.

Arithmetic and fear.
I sat staring at the polished holster
With its buttoned flap, the braid cord
Looped into the revolver butt.

'Any other root crops?
Mangolds? Marrowstems? Anything like that?'
'No.' But was there not a line
Of turnips where the seed ran out

In the potato field? I assumed
Small guilts and sat
Imagining the black hole in the barracks.
He stood up, shifted the baton-case

Further round on his belt,
Closed the domesday book,
Fitted his cap back with two hands,
And looked at me as he said goodbye.

A shadow bobbed in the window.
He was snapping the carrier spring
Over the ledger. His boot pushed off
And the bicycle ticked, ticked, ticked.

SEAMUS DEANE

A SCHOOLING

Ice in the school-room, listen,
The high authority of the cold
On some November morning
Turning to fragile crystals
In the Government milk
I was drinking and my world
All frost and snow, chalk and ice;
Quadratic equations on the board
Shining and shifting in white
Isosceles steps. In that trance
What could I know of his labour?
I, in my infinitesimally perceptive dance,
Thought nothing of the harbour

Where, in his fifth hour,
Waist-deep in water,
He laid cables, rode the dour
Iron swell between his legs
And maybe thought what kind of son,
An aesthetician of this cold,
He had, in other warmth, begot?
But there's ice in the school-room,
Father. Listen. The harbour's empty.
The Government's milk has been drunk.
It lies on the stomach yet, freezing,
Its kindness, inhuman, has sunk
In where up starts the feeling
That pitches a cold in the thought
Of authority's broken milk crystals
On the lips of the son you begot.

THE BRETHREN

Arraigned by silence, I recall
The noise of lecture-rooms,
School refectories and dining hall,
A hundred faces in a hundred spoons,
Raised in laughter or in prayer bent,
Each distorted and each innocent.

Torrential sunshine falling through the slate
Made marquetries of light upon the floor.
I still recall those greasy Belfast flats
Where parties hit upon a steady roar
Of subdued violence and lent
Fury to the Sabbaths which we spent

Hung over empty streets where Jimmy Witherspoon
Sang under the needle old laments
Of careless love and shivered moon,
Evoked the whorish armpit scents
Of Negro brothels while the Plymouth Brethren
Two doors down sat sunk in heaven.

Stupor Sunday, stupor mundi. What was to come
If not the eyes that were growing
Above violent mouths in the light-in-dark aquarium
Of the Sunday's splashless, deep-sown
Peace? What if it were shattered?

Recently I found old photographs
Fallen behind the attic water-tank,
And saw my friends were now the staffs
Of great bureaucracies. Some frames stank
Of mildew, some were so defaced
That half the time I couldn't put a face

On half of them. Some were dead.
The water had seeped through a broken housing,
Had slowly savaged all those eyes and heads.
I felt its closing coldness dousing
Those black American and white hummed tunes,
The faces echoed in those hammered spoons.

JOHNSTON KIRKPATRICK

CATHOLICS

They left before the anthem,
out of seats and up the aisles,
the lights still down, in glow.

What did they miss, if anything?
Sometimes, the final embrace, the hero
riding away in a skitter of dust.

Perhaps, too, the fantastic sentiments
of a world in order where justice
works at last. Always,

the trusted music and the drawn
curtains bumping like two clowns
looking the wrong way.

FRANK ORMSBY

SHEEPMAN

Even the barflies move to corner tables,
Mouthing 'Sheepman'. The barman serves,
But grudgingly. Like Mexicans and half-
Breeds I must wear that special hangdog look,
Say nothing.

There is too much cattle country. The range
Is free in theory, cowmen find
Excuses to resent the different.
They claim that cows won't feed where sheep have fed.
Pathetic.

Don't say the outcast has his dignity.
Perhaps it's something not to thrive
On brawn, or trample those whose small stampedes
Hurt no one; such victories are thin, cold
Consolation.

Unbowed I claim my rights – to herd alone,
And be accepted. When I skirt
The rim of cattle drives, salute me,
And when I come to share your bunkhouse fire,
Make room.

PAUL MULDOON

THE INDIANS ON ALCATRAZ

Through time their sharp features
Have softened and blurred,
As if they still inhabited
The middle distances,
As if these people have never
Stopped riding hard

In an opposite direction,
The people of the shattered lanees
Who have seemed forever going back.
To have willed this reservation,
It is as if they are decided
To be islanders at heart,

As if this island
Has forever been the destination
Of all those dwindling bands.
After the newspaper and TV reports
I want to be glad that
Young Man Afraid Of His Horses Lives

As a brilliant guerrilla fighter,
The weight of his torque
Worn like the moon's last quarter,
Though only if he believes
As I believed of his fathers,
That they would not attack after dark.

PADRAIC FIACC

SANCTUS
for Gerald Dawe

Sinking on iron streets, the bin-lid-
shielded, battleship-grey-faced kids

Shinny up the lamppost, cannot tear
Themselves away, refuse to come in

From the dying lost day they douse
With petrol and set the town's holy

Cows on fire, as if the burning bus or car
Could light up their eyes ever, much less
The burning of our own kitchen houses

Coming over the TV screen had held
Any surprises, for really, we
Wallow in this old-time Western, where
The 'savages' are bad
And lost the war because the white men

Always have to be the Good Guys.

SEAMUS HEANEY

ACT OF UNION

I

Tonight, a first movement, a pulse,
As if the rain in bogland gathered head
To slip and flood: a bog-burst,
A gash breaking open the ferny bed.

Your back is a firm line of eastern coast
And arms and legs are thrown
Beyond your gradual hills. I caress
The heaving province where our past has grown.
I am the tall kingdom over your shoulder
That you would neither cajole nor ignore.
Conquest is a lie. I grow older
Conceding your half-independent shore
Within whose borders now my legacy
Culminates inexorably.

II

And I am still imperially
Male, leaving you with the pain,
The rending process in the colony,
The battering ram, the boom burst from within.
The act sprouted an obstinate fifth column
Whose stance is growing unilateral.
His heart beneath your heart is a wardrum
Mustering force. His parasitical
And ignorant little fists already
Beat at your borders and I know they're cocked
At me across the water. No treaty
I foresee will salve completely your tracked
And stretchmarked body, the big pain
That leaves you raw, like opened ground, again.

SEAMUS DEANE

DERRY

I

The unemployment in our bones
Erupting on our hands in stones;

The thought of violence a relief,
The act of violence a grief;

Our bitterness and love
Hand in glove.

II

At the very most
The mind's eye
Perceives the ghost
Of the hands try
To timidly knock
On the walled rock.
But nothing will come
And the hands become
As they insist
Mailed fists.

III

The Scots and English
Settling for the best.
The unfriendly natives
Ready for the worst.
It has been like this for years
Someone says,
It might be so forever, someone fears,
Or for days.

JOHN HEWITT

BOGSIDE, DERRY, 1971

Shielded, vague soldiers, visored, crouch alert:
between tall houses down the blackened street;
the hurled stones pour, hurt-instinct aims to hurt,
frustration spurts in flame about their feet.

Lads who at ease had tossed a laughing ball,
or, ganged in teams, pursued some shouting game,

beat angry fists against that stubborn wall
of faceless fears which now at last they name.

Night after night this city yields a stage
with peak of drama for the pointless day,
where shadows offer stature, roles to play,
urging the gestures which might purge in rage
the slights, the wrongs, the long indignities
the stubborn core within each heart defies.

PAUL MULDOON

THE HANDS

To the chopping-block, on which the farmer Sebastian split
logs against the Asturian cold,
the Guardia Civil would shove him and spit:
Now clench the fist with which you made so bold.

Four of them held him under.
He writhed and whimpered, in a state of shock.
The axe would fall, and sunder
the hands that had quarried rock.

With bloody stumps he loped across the land.
They laughed as they shot after him. And when he blared
one came over to stop his mouth with loam.

He lay dead in the field. But his far-fetched hands
would stir at night, and the villagers heard
the fists come blattering on their windows, looking for home.

after the German of Erich Arendt

JOHN HEWITT

THE GREEN SHOOT

In my harsh city, when a Catholic priest,
known by his collar, padded down our street,
I'd trot beside him, pull my schoolcap off
and fling it on the ground and stamp on it.

I'd catch my enemy, that errand boy,
grip his torn jersey and admonish him
first to admit his faith and, when he did,
repeatedly to curse the Pope of Rome;

schooled in such duties by my bolder friends;
yet not so many hurried years before,
when I slipped in from play one Christmas Eve
my mother bathed me at the kitchen fire,

and wrapped me in a blanket for the climb
up the long stairs; and suddenly we heard
the carol singers somewhere in the dark,
their voices sharper, for the frost was hard.

My mother carried me through the dim hall
into the parlour, where the only light
upon the patterned wall and furniture
came from the iron lamp across the street;

and there looped round the lamp the singers stood,
but not on snow in grocers' calendars,
singing a song I liked until I saw
my mother's lashes were all bright with tears.

Out of this mulch of ready sentiment,
gritty with threads of flinty violence,
I am the green shoot asking for the flower,
soft as the feathers of the snow's cold swans.

WES MAGEE

NO SURRENDER!

This was *the* catch-phrase around Ulster's farms
when I was a boy. It came with a smile,
a certain nod of the head, a raised fist.
I saw it on crumbling walls in Belfast,
and read it in warehouses at the docks.
Back in Sheffield I repeated it like
a charm. Teachers told me to keep quiet.

My father was always ready with his
stories of papes dumped in the village bog,
and I listened when he told how Fenians
crossed the border and rustled Armagh cows.
A cousin of mine stuck his head clean through
a window pane when he heard an Orange
flute band sashing its way up Duck Street.

Fenians, Orangemen, Black Saturday, prods,
the Twelfth, no surrender. Names and phrases
I can roll around my tongue like pebbles.
Solzhenitsyn tells how Russian soldiers
were *forbidden* to surrender. Capture,
then release, meant imprisonment back in
the Motherland. Catch-22, plus some.

The Irish, the Russians; no surrender.
Half a world lies between Tyrone's green fields
and the wind-ridden heights of Chelyabinsk,
yet the same phrase has been larynx tattooed.
It is croaked, a worry of syllables,
a constriction of sounds in thirsty throats.
In its noose men and women are throttled.

ROBERT JOHNSTONE

ME AS MOSES

That was me in the ark by the Nile;
it was for me the dark princess fell,
my northern colouring, my green eyes.

I could imagine a childhood in palaces
among bare-breasted servants,
wearing linen, my head shaved,

leading my people,
marching them through the sea,
making promises God would keep.

The force of my personality
would show my brother what to say.
They would remember me

pointing at hills and valleys,
pastures we'd never make home,
which we would never surrender.

SEAMUS DEANE

READING *PARADISE LOST* IN PROTESTANT ULSTER 1984

Should I give in to sleep? This fire's warm,
I know the story off by heart,
Was up so late last night and all the harm
That can be done is done. Far apart
From Milton's devils is the present crew
Of zombie soldiers and their spies,
Supergrasses in whose hiss

We hear the snake and sense the mist
Rise in dreams that crowd the new
Awaking with their demobbed cries.

In the old ground of apocalypse
I saw a broken church near where
Two lines of trees came to eclipse
The summer light. Beside the stair
A grey crow from an old estate
Gripped on the Book of Common Prayer,
A rope of mice hung on a strip
Of altar-cloth and a blurring date
Smeared the stone beneath the choir.

Awake again, I see the window take
An arc of rainbow and a fusing rain.
None should break the union of this State
Which God with Man conspired to ordain.
But the woe the long evening brings
To the mazy ambushes of streets
Marks us more deeply now than that bower
Of deepest Eden in our first parents' hour
Of sexual bliss and frail enamourings
Could ever do. Our 'sovran Planter' beats

Upon his breast, dyadic evil rules;
A syncope that stammers in our guns,
That forms and then reforms itself in schools
And in our daughters' couplings and our sons'!
We feel the fire's heat, Belial's doze;
A maiden city's burning on the plain;
Rebels surround us, Lord. Ah, whence arose
This dark damnation, this hot unrainbowed rain?

ROBERT JOHNSTONE

EDEN SAYS NO
graffito in Eden village, County Antrim

As a people favoured by the Almighty,
we discovered writing for ourselves
(we've got our own historians, and poets –
some have dubbed us handy with a phrase).
Hence that slogan daubed on the Garden wall.

A reptilian representative
from a firm of nurserymen
(not one of us, if you catch my meaning)
tried to induce us to turn commercial
with free samples of edible fruit
and all types of honeyed talk.

But we know what we've got in Eden
and we aren't about to throw it away.
The slogan reminds us, as much as them,
that our soil must stay pure and unsullied.
Within these walls fruit shall never grow
because Eden will always say No.

JAMES SIMMONS

ULSTER SAYS YES

One Protestant Ulsterman
wants to confess this:
we frightened you Catholics, we gerrymandered,
we applied injustice.

However, we weren't Nazis or Yanks,
so measure your fuss

who never suffered like Jews or Blacks,
not here, not with us;

but, since we didn't reform ourselves,
since we had to be caught
red-handed, justice is something
we have to be taught.

JOHN HEWITT

FROM THE TIBETAN

In my native province when I was young
the lamas were presumed to be dishonest,
not because they were more wicked than the rest
but their calling gave them more scope.

They were not expected to be philosophers
or poets, for they were not educated persons;
theories were as inconceivable as books
in their satchels. All they were asked
was to provide certain familiar noises
on fixed occasions of the calendar,
spinning the wheels with ritual fervour
and chanting of *The Emperor's Tunic*
and *The Great Wall of China*.

For the rest of their time it was anticipated
that they should work hard rewarding their families,
promoting their nephews, replenishing their stores,
and accepting presents from contractors.
Traditionally, all this was to be done with a show
of cordiality, with handclasps, salutes,
conspicuous finger-signals and audible passwords:
the effect which it was desired to produce
being that of reluctant necessity
for complicated manoeuvre.

Now I am older and live in the suburbs of the capital,
I find that the lamas here are very much the same,
save that the rewarding, promoting, replenishing, is
done on their behalf by a permanent secretariat,
leaving them more time to devote to the illusion
of exercising power: this forces them to acquire
a more sophisticated vocabulary; indeed,
one or two of them have written books:
in my native province this
would have been looked upon with disfavour,
for we are a simple people.

TOM PAULIN

OF DIFFERENCE DOES IT MAKE

*During the 51-year existence of the Northern Ireland Parliament
only one Bill sponsored by a non-Unionist member was ever passed.*

Among the plovers and the stonechats
protected by the Wild Birds Act
of nineteen-hundred-and-thirty-one,
there is a rare stint called the notawhit
that has a schisty flight-call, like the chough's.
Notawhit, notawhit, notawhit
– it raps out a sharp code-sign
like a mild and patient prisoner
pecking through granite with a teaspoon.

WITHOUT MERCY

He wakes, a traveller through the horny gates,
Safe with the luggage of himself.
With the freight of dreams, anger and stiff tissue.

To have struggled through the dark again,
Where he recognized that man, Aeneas,
Burdened with a father and all the guilts

Of ruined childhood, is to have won again
And found the state stable and enduring,
As hard and proud as the body of a man

Who has travelled to the middle years
And known them fixed and dull, a dry place
Where the weak scatter when he breathes.

And in this less-than-classic dawn he knows
That judges pray only to the law of men.
They are stretched even as the men they stretch.

FRANK ORMSBY

FLOODS

At high tide the sea is under the city,
A natural subversive. The Farset,
Forced underground, observes no curfew,
And, sleepless in their beds, the sullen drains
Move under manholes.

Blame fall on the builders, foolish men.
This strained civility of city, sea, breaks
Yearly, snapped by native rains,
Leaving in low streets the sandbagged doors,
The furnished pavements.

TOM PAULIN

A PARTIAL STATE

Intractable and northern,
dry in the sun when it shines,
otherwise rained on, justly.

White god to desert god, 'The
lines are open, what you do
to your helots is up to

'you, no concern of ours. Say
no if you like, but keep them
quiet. Never forget that

'irony is the weapon
of the disarmed, that yours are
blunter instruments, dourness.'

*

The chosen, having broken
their enemies, scattered them
in backstreets and tight estates.

Patriarch and matriarch,
industry and green hills, no
balance of power. Just safety.

Stillness, without history;
until leviathan spouts,
bursting through manhole covers

in the streets, making phones ring on
bare desks. 'The minister is
playing golf, please try later.'

*

Special constables train their
machine guns on council flats;
water-cannons, fire, darkness.

The clocks are bleeding now on
public buildings. Their mottoes,
emblems of failure, tell us:

What the wrong gods established
no army can ever save.

ROBERT JOHNSTONE

THE FRUIT OF KNOWLEDGE

In a wee, twee cul-de-sac
beside Kilroot
entitled the Garden of Eden,
a man on a kitchen chair
has placed himself in the sun
among grandchildren.

The last image of my dad
was in the rear-view mirror
of the car he'd given me,
my father and mother
on the Lisburn Road,
waving as I left for England.

But his hand raised
wishing good luck
also played an invisible line
to a fish tearing a hook:
in High Street now and Royal Avenue
I hear the waters under my feet.

Someday, to release the world
from the memory of what we were,
the wave of the past,
the wave of history,
will drown grave, field and thoroughfare
from the Garden of Eden to Edenderry.

TOM PAULIN

DESERTMARTIN

At noon, in the dead centre of a faith,
Between Draperstown and Magherafelt,
This bitter village shows the flag
In a baked absolute September light.
Here the Word has withered to a few
Parched certainties, and the charred stubble
Tightens like a black belt, a crop of Bibles.

Because this is the territory of the Law
I drive across it with a powerless knowledge –
The owl of Minerva in a hired car.
A Jock squaddy glances down the street
And grins, happy and expendable,
Like a brass cartridge. He is a useful thing,
Almost at home, and yet not quite, not quite.

It's a limed nest, this place. I see a plain
Presbyterian grace sour, then harden,
As a free strenuous spirit changes
To a servile defiance that whines and shrieks
For the bondage of the letter: it shouts
For the Big Man to lead his wee people
To a clean white prison, their scorched tomorrow.

Masculine Islam, the rule of the Just,
Egyptian sand dunes and geometry,

A theology of rifle-butts and executions:
These are the places where the spirit dies.
And now, in Desertmartin's sandy light,
I see a culture of twigs and bird-shit
Waving a gaudy flag it loves and curses.

CADAVER POLITIC

The grey hills of that country fall away
  Like folds of skin. There are some mountains somewhere
And public parks with metal fountains.
  Rains fall and then fogs freeze, drifting
Over empty stretches of water, forts
  With broken walls on small islands.
Rafted cities smoke in the rain and sharp posts
  Have been knocked deep into flabby ground,
Thin tatters of chicken wire strung to them.
  Coffins are moored in its bays and harbours.
A damp rag, it flies several flags –
  Bunting and boneyard streamers, the badges
Of territory. In the waste, silent valleys
  Clans are at their manoeuvres.
At the bottom of a cliff, on a tussock
  Of ground by a lean-to shed, a group
Of men and women huddle, watching a man
  Who tries, with damp matches, to light a board
Washed on that coast by the grey sea.

NORMAN DUGDALE

REASONS OF STATE

Mostly the butchery occurred elsewhere.
Someone was knifed among the shadows or
Garrotted at the dark turn of the stair –

A scuffle and groan, blood on the walls and floor,
Then silence. The courtiers smiled to hide their dread,
Being frightened of the truth and even more

Of being known to know. Though rumour spread
King kept his secrets, Council held their tongue
But thought it seemly they should mourn the dead

And quietly discouraged those among
The foreign embassies and fools who tried
To pry into the facts or right the wrong . . .

Half-crowns paid for entry, we join the guide
Or wander round in summer frocks and flannels,
Stare at the portraits stiff with ruffs and pride,

The armour, faded tapestries, enamels.
Inside, the rooms seem cramped and dark, lit by brief
Shafts of light, revealing the dust on panels

Sprung with damp or age. Emerging with relief
We start up children's games or make for tea
At tables on a terrace, we whose chief

Virtues are domestic, who disagree
With violence, tend our gardens, knit, provide
Against the future and do not think to see

Such evil in our world. Somewhere inside
The labyrinth men shift and calculate,
Huddle together where the ways divide

Or grope and stumble through the fog of hate
(Mouths choked with dust, eyes straining), long for ease,
An end of torment, treachery, debate,

Who murder innocence beneath the trees.

DEREK MAHON

POEM BEGINNING WITH A LINE BY CAVAFY

It is night and the barbarians have not come.
It was not always so hard;
When the great court flared
With gallowglasses and language difficulty
A man could be a wheelwright and die happy.

We remember oatmeal and mutton,
Harpsong, a fern table for
Wiping your hands on,
A candle of reeds and butter,
The distaste of the rheumatic chronicler,

A barbarous tongue, and herds like cloud-shadow
Roaming the wet hills
When the hills were young,
Whiskery pikemen and their spiky dogs
Preserved in woodcuts and card-catalogues.

Now it is night and the barbarians have not come.
Or if they have we only recognize,
Harsh as a bombed bathroom,
The frantic anthropologisms
And lazarous ironies behind their talk

Of fitted carpets, central heating
And automatic gear-change –
Like the bleached bones of a hare
Or a handful of spent
Cartridges on a deserted rifle range.

COURTYARDS IN DELFT
PIETER DE HOOCH, 1659
for Gordon Woods

Oblique light on the trite, on brick and tile –
Immaculate masonry, and everywhere that
Water tap, that broom and wooden pail
To keep it so. House-proud, the wives
Of artisans pursue their thrifty lives
Among scrubbed yards, modest but adequate.
Foliage is sparse, and clings. No breeze
Ruffles the trim composure of those trees.

No spinet-playing emblematic of
The harmonies and disharmonies of love;
No lewd fish, no fruit, no wide-eyed bird
About to fly its cage while a virgin
Listens to her seducer, mars the chaste
Precision of the thing and the thing made.
Nothing is random, nothing goes to waste:
We miss the dirty dog, the fiery gin.

That girl with her back to us who waits
For her man to come home for his tea
Will wait till the paint disintegrates
And ruined dykes admit the esurient sea;
Yet this is life too, and the cracked
Out-house door a verifiable fact
As vividly mnemonic as the sunlit
Railings that front the houses opposite.

I lived there as a boy and know the coal
Glittering in its shed, late-afternoon
Lambency informing the deal table,
The ceiling cradled in a radiant spoon.
I must be lying low in a room there,
A strange child with a taste for verse,
While my hard-nosed companions dream of war
On parched veldt and fields of rain-swept gorse;

For the pale light of that provincial town
Will spread itself, like ink or oil,
Over the not yet accurate linen
Map of the world which occupies one wall
And punish nature in the name of God.
If only, now, the Maenads, as of right,
Came smashing crockery, with fire and sword,
We could sleep easier in our beds at night.

DEATH AND THE SUN
(ALBERT CAMUS, 1913–1960)
Le soleil ni la mort ne se peuvent regarder fixement.
La Rochefoucauld

When the car spun from the road and your neck broke
I was hearing rain on the school bicycle shed
Or tracing the squeaky enumerations of chalk;
And later, while you lay in the *mairie*,
I pedalled home from Bab-el-Oued
To my mother silently making tea,
Bent to my homework in the firelight
Or watched an old film on television –
Gunfights under a blinding desert sun,
Bogartian urgencies in the Ulster night.

How we read you then, admiring the frank composure
Of a stranger bayed by dogs who could not hear
The interior dialogue of flesh and stone,
His life and death a work of art
Conceived in the silence of the heart.
Not that he would ever have said so, no,
He would merely have taken a rush-hour tram
To a hot beach white as a scream,
Stripped to a figure of skin and bone
And struck out, a back-stroke, as far as he could go.

Deprived though we were of his climatic privileges
And raised in a northern land of rain and murk,
We too knew the familiar foe, the blaze

Of headlights on a coast road, the cicadas
Chattering like watches in our sodden hedges;
Yet never imagined the plague to come,
So long had it crouched there in the dark –
The *cordon sanitaire*, the stricken home,
Rats on the pavement, rats in the mind,
'St James Infirmary' playing to the plague wind.

'An edifying abundance of funeral parlours',
The dead on holiday, cloth caps and curlers,
The shoe-shine and the thrice-combed wave
On Sunday morning and Saturday night;
Wee shadows fighting in a smoky cave
Who would one day be brought to light –
The modes of pain and pleasure,
These were the things to treasure
When times changed and your kind broke camp.
Diogenes in the dog-house, you carried a paraffin lamp.

Meanwhile in the night of Europe, the winter of faces,
Sex and opinion, a deft hand removes
The Just Judges from their rightful places
And hangs them behind a bar in Amsterdam –
A desert of fog and water, a cloudy dream
Where an antique Indonesian god grimaces
And relativity dawns like a host of doves;
Where the goalie who refused suicide
Trades solidarity for solitude,
A night watch, a self-portrait, supper at Emmaus.

The lights are going on in towns that no longer exist.
Night falls on Belfast, on the just and the unjust,
On its Augustinian austerities of sand and stone –
While Sisyphus' descendants, briefly content,
Stand in the dole queues and roll their own.
Malraux described these preterite to you
As no longer historically significant;
And certainly they are shrouded in white dust.
All souls leprous, blinded by truth, each ghost
Steams on the shore as if awaiting rescue.

One cannot stare for long at death or the sun.
Imagine Plato's neolithic troglodyte
Released from his dark cinema, released even
From the fire proper, so that he stands at last,
Absurd and anxious, out in the open air
And gazes, shading his eyes, at the world there –
Tangible fact ablaze in a clear light
That casts no shadow, where the vast
Sun gongs its lenity from a brazen heaven
Listening in silence to his rich despair.

JOHN HEWITT

from FREEHOLD II: THE LONELY HEART

Once in a seaside town with time to kill,
the windless winter-daylight ebbing chill,
the cafés shut till June, the shop blinds drawn,
only one pub yet open where a man
trundled his barrels off a dray with care,
and two men talking, small across the square,
I turned from broad street, down a redbrick row,
past prams in parlours and infrequent show
of thrusting bulbtips, till high steps and porch
and rigid statue signalised a church.
I climbed the granite past St Patrick's knees,
saw cross in stone, befingered, ringed with grease,
and water in a stoup with oily skin,
swung door on stall of booklets and went in
to the dim stained-glass cold interior
between low pews along a marble floor
to where the candles burned, still keeping pace
with ugly coloured Stations of the Cross.
Two children tiptoed in and prayed awhile.
A shabby woman in a faded shawl
came hirpling past me then, and crumpled down,
crossing herself and mumbling monotone.

I stood and gazed across the altar rail
at the tall windows, cold and winter pale;
Christ and His Mother, Christ and Lazarus,
Christ watching Martha bustle round the house,
Christ crowned, with sceptre and a blessing hand.
I counted seven candles on the stand;
a box of matches of familiar brand
lay on a tray. It somehow seemed my right
to pay my penny and set up my light,
not to this coloured Christ nor to His Mother,
but single flame to sway with all the other
small earnest flames against the crowding gloom
which seemed that year descending on our time,
suppressed the fancy, smiled a cynic thought,
turned clicking heel on marble and went out.

Not this my fathers' faith: their walls are bare;
their comfort's all within, if anywhere.
I had gone there a vacant hour to pass,
to see the sculpture and admire the glass,
but left as I had come, a protestant,
and all unconscious of my yawning want;
too much intent on what to criticise
to give my heart the room to realise
that which endures the tides of time so long
cannot be always absolutely wrong;
not even with a friendly thought or human
for the two children and the praying woman.
The years since then have proved I should have stayed
and mercy might have touched me till I prayed.

For now I scorn no man's or child's belief
in any symbol that may succour grief
if we remember whence life first arose
and how within us yet that river flows;
and how the fabled shapes in dream's deep sea
still evidence our continuity
with being's seamless garment, web and thread.

O windblown grass upon the mounded dead,
O seed in crevice of the frost-split rock,
the power that fixed your root shall take us back,
though endlessly through aeons we are thrust
as luminous or unreflecting dust.

JAMES SIMMONS

FOR JAN BETLEY

The sad river passes
through melancholy glades
where leaves are silenced. It is late.

Under damp grasses
under the mist and trees, grenades
are stored in boxes, and will wait.

3

'How many counties . . . ?'

from 'The Northern Ireland Question'
DESMOND EGAN

DESMOND EGAN

from POEMS FOR NORTHERN IRELAND

V: THE NORTHERN IRELAND QUESTION

two *wee girls*
were playing tig near a car . . .

how many counties would you say
are worth their scattered fingers?

PAUL DURCAN

IRELAND 1972

Next to the fresh grave of my beloved grandmother
The grave of my firstlove murdered by my brother

JOHN HEWITT

ULSTER NAMES

I take my stand by the Ulster names,
each clean hard name like a weathered stone;
Tyrella, Rostrevor, are flickering flames:
the names I mean are the Moy, Malone,
Strabane, Slieve Gullion and Portglenone.

Even suppose that each name were freed
from legend's ivy and history's moss,
there'd be music still in, say, Carrick-a-rede,
though men forget it's the rock across
the track of the salmon from Islay and Ross.

The names of a land show the heart of the race;
they move on the tongue like the lilt of a song.
You say the name and I see the place –
Drumbo, Dungannon, or Annalong.
Barony, townland, we cannot go wrong.

You say Armagh, and I see the hill
with the two tall spires or the square low tower;
the faith of Patrick is with us still;
his blessing falls in a moonlit hour,
when the apple orchards are all in flower.

You whisper Derry. Beyond the walls
and the crashing boom and the coiling smoke,
I follow that freedom which beckons and calls
to Colmcille, tall in his grove of oak,
raising his voice for the rhyming folk.

County by county you number them over;
Tyrone, Fermanagh . . . I stand by a lake,
and the bubbling curlew, the whistling plover
call over the whins in the chill daybreak
as the hills and the waters the first light take.

Let Down be famous for care-tilled earth,
for the little green hills and the harsh grey peaks,
the rocky bed of the Lagan's birth,
the white farm fat in the August weeks.
There's one more county my pride still seeks.

You give it the name and my quick thoughts run
through the narrow towns with their wheels of trade,
to Glenballyemon, Glenaan, Glendun,
from Trostan down to the braes of Layde,
for there is the place where the pact was made.

But you have as good a right as I
to praise the place where your face is known,
for over us all is the selfsame sky;

the limestone's locked in the strength of the bone,
and who shall mock at the steadfast stone?

So it's Ballinamallard, it's Crossmaglen,
it's Aughnacloy, it's Donaghadee,
it's Magherafelt breeds the best of men,
I'll not deny it. But look for me
on the moss between Orra and Slievenanee.

POSTSCRIPT, 1984

Those verses surfaced thirty years ago
when time seemed edging to a better time,
most public voices tamed, those loud untamed
as seasonal as tawdry pantomime,
and over my companionable land
placenames still lilted like a childhood rime.

The years deceived; our unforgiving hearts,
by myth and old antipathies betrayed,
flared into sudden acts of violence
in daily shocking bulletins relayed,
and through our dark dream-clotted consciousness
hosted like banners in some black parade.

Now with compulsive resonance they toll:
Banbridge, Ballykelly, Darkley, Crossmaglen,
summoning pity, anger and despair,
by grief of kin, by hate of murderous men
till the whole tarnished map is stained and torn,
not to be read as pastoral again.

BRENDAN KENNELLY

from CROMWELL

OUR PLACE

The murders are increasingly common
In our place which certain of the old songs
Celebrate as a changeless pastoral heaven.
Due, however, to some folks' sense of wrong
Nothing is right nowadays. I must confess
I've become a bit of a callous bastard
Myself. Sipping the latest atrocities
From our one good paper shows how little I care.

Consider, for example, this morning's gem:
Two youths, both about sixteen, and said
To be savagely bored and out of work
Battered an old man to death in his bed.
Making his sister lie in a style of some shame
They pinned her through the neck with a garden-fork.

MICHAEL LONGLEY

WOUNDS

Here are two pictures from my father's head –
I have kept them like secrets until now:
First, the Ulster Division at the Somme
Going over the top with 'Fuck the Pope!'
'No Surrender!': a boy about to die,
Screaming 'Give 'em one for the Shankill!'
'Wilder than Gurkhas' were my father's words
Of admiration and bewilderment.
Next comes the London-Scottish padre
Resettling kilts with his swagger-stick,

With a stylish backhand and a prayer.
Over a landscape of dead buttocks
My father followed him for fifty years.
At last, a belated casualty,
He said – lead traces flaring till they hurt –
'I am dying for King and Country, slowly.'
I touched his hand, his thin head I touched.

Now, with military honours of a kind,
With his badges, his medals like rainbows,
His spinning compass, I bury beside him
Three teenage soldiers, bellies full of
Bullets and Irish beer, their flies undone.
A packet of Woodbines I throw in,
A lucifer, the Sacred Heart of Jesus
Paralysed as heavy guns put out
The night-light in a nursery for ever;
Also a bus-conductor's uniform –
He collapsed beside his carpet-slippers
Without a murmur, shot through the head
By a shivering boy who wandered in
Before they could turn the television down
Or tidy away the supper dishes.
To the children, to a bewildered wife,
I think 'Sorry Missus' was what he said.

JAMES SIMMONS

CLAUDY

for Harry Barton, a song

The Sperrins surround it, the Faughan flows by,
at each end of Main Street the hills and the sky,
the small town of Claudy at ease in the sun
last July in the morning, a new day begun.

How peaceful and pretty if the moment could stop,
McIlhenny is straightening things in his shop,

and his wife is outside serving petrol, and then
a girl takes a cloth to a big window pane.

And McCloskey is taking the weight off his feet,
and McClelland and Miller are sweeping the street,
and, delivering milk at the Beaufort Hotel,
young Temple's enjoying his first job quite well.

And Mrs McLaughlin is scrubbing her floor,
and Artie Hone's crossing the street to a door,
and Mrs Brown, looking around for her cat,
goes off up an entry – what's strange about that?

Not much – but before she comes back to the road
that strange car parked outside her house will explode,
and all of the people I've mentioned outside
will be waiting to die or already have died.

An explosion too loud for your eardrums to bear,
and young children squealing like pigs in the square,
and all faces chalk-white and streaked with bright red,
and the glass and the dust and the terrible dead.

For an old lady's legs are ripped off, and the head
of a man's hanging open, and still he's not dead.
He is screaming for mercy, and his son stands and stares
and stares, and then suddenly, quick, disappears.

And Christ, little Katherine Aiken is dead,
and Mrs McLaughlin is pierced through the head.
Meanwhile to Dungiven the killers have gone,
and they're finding it hard to get through on the phone.

GERALD DAWE

THE CLOCK ON A WALL OF
FARRINGDON GARDENS, AUGUST 1971

I am the clock on a wall
of Farringdon Gardens. I
stopped dead at 7.30. They

tried to take me away
from the burning. I remember
the whooshing smoke.

But in the rush
I was left here
as if nothing had happened.

Part of my task is
not to get panicked.
I'm regular and reliable

and wake each morning
for work –
a bulwark of my society,

but when the fires
started and the windows
cracked like ice

I was snatched up
and out under this sky
to sit defenceless,

my springs and coils
and deep chimings stopped
at 7.30.

So if you come
across me in your reading –
a photo perhaps in some

glossy history –
remember the blackened walls
and roofless houses,

of what went on
before the three monkeys
and chipped mantelpieces,

in the backs of
sculleries and in front
bedrooms, before

the televisions
landed in tidily grown
gardens, think

just a little
of my time watching
these different people

who left their lives
in my hands
sitting on a wall of Farringdon Gardens.

JAMES SIMMONS

LAMENT FOR A DEAD POLICEMAN

His wife
My love and delight
the first day that we met
in King Street in Coleraine

I knew I'd never set
eyes on your like again.

You courted me a year
but did you ever doubt
that I'd have married you
before the week was out
if you had wanted to?

Though you dug with the wrong foot
for me you were all business
buying our hillside plot
on the Garvagh Line, for me,
raising the roof beam high
in a grove of oaks, for me,
the Sperrins a far smudge of blue.
My dad, the plumber, for me,
set gleaming basins and a bath
and a shower and fancy taps, for me,
working in spare hours
for free, like you, for me.

Old friends and institutions
made generous contributions.
My Uncle Tom, the joiner,
made cupboards, and a farmer
lent us his rotavator
to break the soil. A slater
worked evenings on the roof,
as if to offer proof
how much they all admired,
love, you who inspired
respect the way you served us
better than we deserved.

My memory lingers
on that spring day
you first approached me,
erect and smart
in the dark uniform

your family hated.
Who'd blame your pride,
the little strut in your step?
'Lord of the by-laws,'
I said. With one hand lifted
you slowed a speeding
lorry or moved on
a noisy drunk
or a bunch of rowdies.
Big head inclined,
you listened to old ladies
courteously. You laughed a lot
then, straightening us all out
in your dry Derry way.
You never seemed too hot
in your heavy overcoat,
or drenched in persistent rain,
belt and cap shining,
black truncheon and revolver.
Approach me again tonight,
lighten my dreams, lover.

Many who didn't like you,
impatient of the law,
held you in awe. Their shifty
eyes, their raised fists
fell, seeing your stature.
I thought while you were there
order and law would hold,
we might endure forever;
but, sweetheart of my soul,
one day of sheer bad luck
a little mixed-up thug,
with a gun in one hand
and a bun in the other, shot you.

My hero and my friend,
father from Londonderry,
mother from Maghera,
you never flattered

lawyer or magistrate,
JP or barrister,
however loud they could be
or condescending. You knew
the law as well or better,
in spirit and letter served it.
That was your source of power.
You never deviated
and were well loved and hated.

My dearest honey,
at our home tonight
what can I answer
Francis and wee Tom
when they ask for Daddy?
I wiped the blood
from our front door
with lukewarm water
and Fairy Liquid.
Your gore I swabbed,
darling, as you would
have done, my true one.

Sweet love, good father,
I thought so clever
you might dupe all danger,
I can hear their footsteps
still and the doorbell.
You lowered the paper
in our sunfilled kitchen
and caught your coat up
on your finger as usual
and drained your coffee
and sauntered the hall
idly to answer.
Like a stick in a biscuit tin
guns started.
My world caved in.

Your people want to wake you,
but that is not our way.
When you joined the police force
and not the IRA
didn't the whole bunch hate you?
Knowing what they condone,
they might as well have killed you.
Let them get off the phone
and give us peace to grieve you
that honour what you've been.
There will be tea or whiskey
for old friends who drop in.
Though God knows I want no one.
Nothing could lift this gloom
but you to wake and hold me,
my dear, in our own room
where I have put the children,
just to be less alone.
I will get in beside them
when everyone has gone.

His sister

Brother, I'm still ashamed.
Your whole life was lamed
from taking the hard bribe,
forsaking your own tribe
to live for an ideal
so simple and unreal,
the abstraction 'law and order',
when Ireland with a border
mocks a far older law
as all your kinfolk saw;
but you were super duper,
an Ulster Gary Cooper
for whom integrity,
elections, democracy,
were the first word and the last,
not the outrageous past,
the lies, the blatant slander,
prejudice, gerrymander.

You were the family's pride,
and we were mortified.
Tame Fenian, they would pat you.
Dear, they were laughing at you.

And still and all
we want to wake you.
I rang the bitch
you stooped to marry.
She was too busy
or too tired.
A private funeral
and no wake.
Have they no feelings?
Her husband dead
and her sleeping.

Most of the crowd
you once knew
are in the States
or on the broo;
but we'd see you right
for one good night,
a decent wake
for old times' sake.
We'd drink a last
toast to the best
outside right
ever from this estate.

His wife

Sister she may be –
I couldn't reply;
but I'm heart-sorry
it wasn't I
answered the doorbell
or ran before you
to face the gunbursts,
to gulder, to beg mercy
or gather the bullets

in my dress or my flesh,
to save you, any way.

But how could that be,
my law enforcer?
It was your place to face them,
mine is to mourn you.

Your racing pigeons
in the shed are fluttering.
Your two greyhounds
need exercise.
I will walk them myself
with the old leads
your hands wore shiny.

Strange sight, a woman
striding at twilight
behind dogs, mind empty.
The unnatural fruit
of murderous politics.
I am thinking of nothing
but your life-blood stiffening
your green shirt front.

Marrying you
altered my heart.
Another good man
maybe another day?
I keep that thought
away, unnatural.
What those wee skitters,
those sick teenagers
with gun power
and creepy ideas,
did is pure evil.
Even my children's
sweet bodies against me
make up for nothing.
I'll rear them well,

aching and empty.
It is weedgrown,
our old bower,
and our little stream
is almost dry. Oh, Tom!
Goodbye.

Stone dead upstairs as you are,
I still expect the patrol car
to call to pick you up. You seemed
so much at the centre. You scanned
the papers for signs, you tossed
in your sleep with worry. They will be lost
without you, decisive and so terse
and clear. Things are going to get worse,
although these last ten years
we have spent counting murders
of friends and colleagues,
old men and other Teagues
(we called them 'forty-niners'),
the retired or part-timers,
the easy touches, the ripe fruit,
though many times a new recruit,
a boy in a Land-Rover, was hurt
or blown to bits by a mine in a culvert,
remote-controlled. How much you hated
remote leaders who manipulated
the young impressionables, the unemployed.
And what was the phrase got you annoyed?
(You said, 'The smoothest drivel's the worst.')
Violence has reached an acceptable level.

The slickness of the media sickens me,
the tone of the questions of TV
reporters, their phoney sympathy,
fishing for widows' tears.

My face is trapped there in the news,
contorted, breaking with intimate grief
beside the grave, at every fireside.

Could they see I was proud too?
But they never want the whole story
or follow it through below the surface.
The viewing audience might get bored.

Your black cap sat on your coffin
on the British flag you served so well.
There were lines of bitter confused colleagues,
praised and abused with loaded voices.
There was an older man in tears:
'If they'd untie our bloody hands,
let us alone loose in the ghettos
and root the bastards out. We know them!'
I could hear Tom answering, 'Aye,
fair enough if we go by the book.
You can't enforce the law breaking it.
What's half broken is broke entirely.
Remember, that was the Bs' mistake.

'The distinctive feature
of Irish life, politically' –
he could spell it out rightly –
'isn't just bigotry, it's the easy
toleration of violence by any side,
moral confusion, tearful cruelty,
acceptance of crime becoming collusion.'

It is spring now.
Our garden is lovely:
daffodils, primroses,
simple and bright.
Listlessly weeding,
the sap-flow and singing
sharpens my longing.

I know no waiting
can change this aching.
My husband is dead,
my bed is empty,
my heart is sore.

I suppose you can hear
nothing. Every gesture
is waving goodbye
at thin air.

If I knew what to do
that hasn't been done
I would do it:
letters of protest,
a march of the women
to Stormont or Dublin.
I would spend time
and money, mortgage
the house again
and sell the car,
join with the Peace Women
or anyone to break through,
to find a policy
to draw diehards and wreckers
inside the law.
But who would I speak to?
Jim Prior or Gerry Adams,
Paisley or John Hume
or Molyneaux?
They are only repeating
themselves, point-scoring,
and I've nothing to say
except what you said:
'There's a law there
to enforce and to obey.
If you want to alter it
there is a lawful way.'

One more policeman dead
matters to very few. That's
a change from better days. The dangers
they go through daily, wives and children
terrified, justify high wages;
but worried him too. 'We're still
getting recruits, but who?' Tom said.

'What they say goes on in Castlereagh
might very well be true.' Maybe
he's better out of it, uncorrupted.

I've stopped crying. A bad-
tempered, good-looking woman
with dark eyes stares back
at me from the mirror.
Her husband, the policeman,
has gone into the night
for the last time,
able to help no one,
he lies stiff and useless,
off duty forever.

ROBERT JOHNSTONE

OCCASIONS OF LOVE

When I think to name
the occasions of love
I come to the death
of our neighbour's son.

Constable Mee, *mown down
in a hail of bullets/
shot from a passing car/
claimed by the IRA*

– the papers and my father
told their stories –
and if I were to film
the Great Ulster Movie

I would picture the gunman
stepping into a gunpowder mist,

backlit, feeling odd and tall
(like John Wayne, I'd hint),

striding across the wide pavement
to where the young lad lay,
a black bundle by our door
in his new, loose uniform,

and the gun would be cocked
and brought to his temple
and fired twice.
And fired twice.

But I would rather write
a novel about love:
Constable Mee on his home beat
nodding to his father's friends,

how we grow nostalgic
for an array of stores,
a society of Sabbath girls
in hats and pastel colours,

the common feeling of the folk,
how a body might join
one side or another
for a delicate reason.

It would have to end
with my return from England,
entering our house,
shutting out his final place,

his blood and brains
black and white
making a sign
on our front-door step.

PADRAIC FIACC

STATION/AN *ORDO*
Rank, that deep abyss between man and man.
                              from Nietzsche

While the women and children are
Shopping down the town
On a still-lingering-from
-childhood
Saturday afternoon,

The teener with the frizzy hair
Lets it grow
To look like a Hottentot,

Plays the guitar
For his kid sister, is
Her big pop star, shoots

Dead the boy-faced policeman
Guarding the chapel in a bad
District down the road,

When apprehended, says

'It was definitely not murder
Sir: Orders is Orders!'

CIARAN CARSON

BLOODY HAND

Your man, says the Man, *will walk into the bar like this* – here his fingers
Mimic a pair of legs, one stiff at the knee – *so you'll know exactly*

What to do. He sticks a finger to his head. Pretend it's child's play –
The hand might be a horse's mouth, a rabbit or a dog. Five handclaps.
Walls have ears: the shadows you throw are the shadows you try to
   throw off.

I snuffed out the candle between finger and thumb. Was it the left
   hand
Hacked off at the wrist and thrown to the shores of Ulster? Did Ulster
Exist? Or the Right Hand of God, saying *Stop* to this and *No* to that?
My thumb is the hammer of a gun. The thumb goes up. The thumb
   goes down.

GERALD DAWE

COUNT

My only problem is your death
when the radio was stuttering
over breakfast in this flat,
the predicted west gale welting
around our postage-stamp garden,
a fat crow crouched under the wall,
and the early morning warmth
dazed, an impractical consciousness
footering with cups, toast laid
in their apparent order,
when first I heard your name.

It sounded crazy, somehow or other
as incoherent as a dream:
your name, age, place of birth,
and then the on-the-spot commentary
reasoning details of why and how they
waited in a car for you coming out
of a huckster-shop with cigarettes
and pumped six bullets: five when you
sprawled on the street. It's hard to
make that count. The boy that did it

was a few years younger. Twenty years,
six bullets, nine in the morning.
I toy like a child with these numbers.

EAMON GRENNAN

SOUL MUSIC: THE DERRY AIR

A strong drink, hundred-year-old
schnapps, to be sipped at, invading
the secret places that lie in wait and
lonely between bone and muscle, or
counting (Morse code for insomniacs)
the seconds round the heart
when it stutters to itself. Or to be
taken in at the eyes in small doses,
phrase by somatic phrase, a line
of laundry after dawn, air clean as
vodka, snow all over, the laundry
lightly shaking itself
from frigid sleep. Shirts, flowered sheets,
pyjamas, empty trousers, empty
socks – risen as at a last day's dawn
to pure body, light as air. Whiteness
whiter than snow, blueness bluer than
new day brightening the sky-lid
behind trees stripped of their illusions
down to a webbed geometry
subtler than speech. A fierce blue eye
farther off than God, witnessing
house-boxes huddled together
for comfort, fronting blindly
the deserted streets down which in time
come farting lorries full of soldiers.
You are a fugitive *I*, a singing
nerve: you flit from garden to garden
in your fit of silence, bits of you

flaking off in steam and sizzling
like hot fat in the snow. Listen
to the pickers and stealers, the shots,
man-shouts, women wailing, the cry of kids
who clutch stuffed dolls or teddy bears
and shiver, gripping tight as a kite
whatever hand is offered. Here
is the light glinting on top-boots, on
the barrel of an M-16 that grins, holding
its breath, beyond argument. And here is
a small room where robust winter sunlight
rummages much of the day when the day
is cloudless, making some ordinary potted plants
flower to your surprise again, again,
and again: pink, anaemic red, wax-white
their resurrection petals. Like hearts
drawn by children, like oiled arrowheads,
their unquestioning green leaves seem
alive with expectation.

THOMAS MCCARTHY

COUNTING THE DEAD ON THE RADIO, 1972

I

All that winter we lined and limed the earth.
We read books too, and ordered even more –
History rested on the brown hall table
beside the bird-guides and seed catalogues.
We read books as hungrily as Edmund
Burke, with more affection than any dauphiness.
Chaos in hard covers broke in upon us
with beautifully assembled themes, perfect
indices. Their authors played games with
being Irish, my father said. He should know.
Elsewhere, there were troubles that
the keenest authors couldn't deal with.

The way books had juggled nostalgia and fear
left us useless in the face of threat.
Who has been making midnight phone calls?
Who has been canvassing in the name of the dead?
My father has left for the city, running scared:
he wants no part in this. He has left
his number but says we should only trust
the *News*. We'll read more books, my mother said.
Fatherless, the radio has plenty to say.

II

My brother had been hunting a rabbit at the water-
trough; we heard the muffled thuds and grunts
of its torture, its boy-inflicted wounds.
My mother brings the tea to the living-room,
drawing sons from their serious porcelain books
into low air-raids across lemon juice.
Southern ears clogged by too much of this,
we can barely comprehend what the radio says –
something has happened up in the North; it has ruined
the Taoiseach's weekend. Adolescent soldiers
have gone wild. Peace shouldn't be fatal like this.
Lemon rind sticks to my mother's throat.
She throws up in an effort to understand. I say
Mama, a whole regiment has been attacked
by a Catholic priest waving a blood-stained
handkerchief. That's what the radio says.
My brother, with rabbit blood on his arm, sips tea,
puts his adolescent ear to the ill-tuned radio
whose crackles could be gunfire or a mild electric storm.
A household filled with books, a brother used to death:
my mother coughs again. We retune the wireless set.

SEAMUS DEANE

AFTER DERRY, 30 JANUARY 1972

Lightnings slaughtered
The distance. In the harmless houses
Faces narrowed. The membrane
Of power darkened
Above the valley,
And in a flood of khaki
Burst. Indigoed
As rain they came
As the thunder radioed
For a further
Haemorrhage of flame.

The roads died, the clocks
Went out. The peace
Had been a delicately flawed
Honeymoon signalling
The fearful marriage
To come. Death had been
A form of doubt.
Now it was moving
Like a missionary
Through the collapsed cities
Converting all it came among.

And when the storm passed
We came out of the back rooms
Wishing we could say
Ruin itself would last.
But the dead would not
Listen. Nor could we speak
Of love. Brothers had been
Pitiless. What could ignite
This sodden night?
Let us bury the corpses.
Fast. Death is our future

And now is our past.
There are new children
In the gaunt houses.
Their eyes are fused.
Youth has gone out
Like a light. Only the insects
Grovel for life, their strange heads
Twitching. No one kills them
Anymore. This is the honeymoon
Of the cockroach, the small
Spiderless eternity of the fly.

SEAMUS HEANEY

CASUALTY

I

He would drink by himself
And raise a weathered thumb
Towards the high shelf,
Calling another rum
And blackcurrant, without
Having to raise his voice,
Or order a quick stout
By a lifting of the eyes
And a discreet dumb-show
Of pulling off the top;
At closing time would go
In waders and peaked cap
Into the showery dark,
A dole-kept breadwinner
But a natural for work.
I loved his whole manner,
Sure-footed but too sly,
His deadpan sidling tact,
His fisherman's quick eye
And turned observant back.

Incomprehensible
To him, my other life.
Sometimes, on his high stool,
Too busy with his knife
At a tobacco plug
And not meeting my eye,
In the pause after a slug
He mentioned poetry.
We would be on our own
And, always politic
And shy of condescension,
I would manage by some trick
To switch the talk to eels
Or lore of the horse and cart
Or the Provisionals.

But my tentative art
His turned back watches too:
He was blown to bits
Out drinking in a curfew
Others obeyed, three nights
After they shot dead
The thirteen men in Derry.
PARAS THIRTEEN, the walls said,
BOGSIDE NIL. That Wednesday
Everybody held
His breath and trembled.

II

It was a day of cold
Raw silence, wind-blown
Surplice and soutane:
Rained-on, flower-laden
Coffin after coffin
Seemed to float from the door
Of the packed cathedral
Like blossoms on slow water.
The common funeral
Unrolled its swaddling band,
Lapping, tightening

Till we were braced and bound
Like brothers in a ring.

But he would not be held
At home by his own crowd
Whatever threats were phoned,
Whatever black flags waved.
I see him as he turned
In that bombed offending place,
Remorse fused with terror
In his still knowable face,
His cornered outfaced stare
Blinding in the flash.

He had gone miles away
For he drank like a fish
Nightly, naturally
Swimming towards the lure
Of warm lit-up places,
The blurred mesh and murmur
Drifting among glasses
In the gregarious smoke.
How culpable was he
That last night when he broke
Our tribe's complicity?
'Now you're supposed to be
An educated man,'
I hear him say. 'Puzzle me
The right answer to that one.'

III

I missed his funeral,
Those quiet walkers
And sideways talkers
Shoaling out of his lane
To the respectable
Purring of the hearse . . .
They move in equal pace
With the habitual
Slow consolation

Of a dawdling engine,
The line lifted, hand
Over fist, cold sunshine
On the water, the land
Banked under fog: that morning
I was taken in his boat,
The screw purling, turning
Indolent fathoms white,
I tasted freedom with him.
To get out early, haul
Steadily off the bottom,
Dispraise the catch, and smile
As you find a rhythm
Working you, slow mile by mile,
Into your proper haunt
Somewhere, well out, beyond . . .

Dawn-sniffing revenant,
Plodder through midnight rain,
Question me again.

EAVAN BOLAND

CHILD OF OUR TIME
for Aengus

Yesterday I knew no lullaby
But you have taught me overnight to order
This song, which takes from your final cry
Its tune, from your unreasoned end its reason;
Its rhythm from the discord of your murder,
Its motive from the fact you cannot listen.

We who should have known how to instruct
With rhymes for your waking, rhythms for your sleep
Names for the animals you took to bed,
Tales to distract, legends to protect,

Later an idiom for you to keep
And living, learn, must learn from you, dead –

To make our broken images rebuild
Themselves around your limbs, your broken
Image, find for your sake whose life our idle
Talk has cost, a new language. Child
Of our time, our times have robbed your cradle.
Sleep in a world your final sleep has woken.

JOHN MONTAGUE

FALLS FUNERAL

Unmarked faces
fierce with grief

a line of children
led by a small coffin

the young
mourning the young

a sight beyond tears
beyond pious belief

David's brethren
in the Land of Goliath.

TOM PAULIN

UNDER THE EYES

Its retributions work like clockwork
Along murdering miles of terrace-houses

Where someone is saying, 'I am angry,
I am frightened, I am justified.
Every favour, I must repay with interest,
Any slight against myself, the least slip,
Must be balanced out by an exact revenge.'

The city is built on mud and wrath.
Its weather is predicted; its streetlamps
Light up in the glowering, crowded evenings.
Time-switches, ripped from them, are clamped
To sticks of sweet, sweating explosive.
All the machinery of a state
Is a set of scales that squeezes out blood.

Memory is just, too. A complete system
Nothing can surprise. The dead are recalled
From schoolroom afternoons, the hill quarries
Echoing blasts over the secured city;
Or, in a private house, a Judge
Shot in his hallway before his daughter
By a boy who shut his eyes as his hand tightened.

A rain of turds; a pair of eyes; the sky and tears.

MICHAEL LONGLEY

THE BUTCHERS

When he had made sure there were no survivors in his house
And that all the suitors were dead, heaped in blood and dust
Like fish that fishermen with fine-meshed nets have hauled
Up gasping for salt water, evaporating in the sunshine,
Odysseus, spattered with muck and like a lion dripping blood
From his chest and cheeks after devouring a farmer's bullock,
Ordered the disloyal housemaids to sponge down the armchairs
And tables, while Telemachos, the oxherd and the swineherd
Scraped the floor with shovels, and then between the portico

And the roundhouse stretched a hawser and hanged the women
So none touched the ground with her toes, like long-winged thrushes
Or doves trapped in a mist-net across the thicket where they roost,
Their heads bobbing in a row, their feet twitching but not for long,
And when they had dragged Melanthios's corpse into the haggard
And cut off his nose and ears and cock and balls, a dog's dinner,
Odysseus, seeing the need for whitewash and disinfectant,
Fumigated the house and the outhouses, so that Hermes
Like a clergyman might wave the supernatural baton
With which he resurrects or hypnotises those he chooses,
And waken and round up the suitors' souls, and the housemaids',
Like bats gibbering in the nooks of their mysterious cave
When out of the clusters that dangle from the rocky ceiling
One of them drops and squeaks, so their souls were bat-squeaks
As they flittered after Hermes, their deliverer, who led them
Along the clammy sheughs, then past the oceanic streams
And the white rock, the sun's gatepost in that dreamy region,
Until they came to a bog-meadow full of bog-asphodels
Where the residents are ghosts or images of the dead.

PAUL MULDOON

THE MORE A MAN HAS
THE MORE A MAN WANTS

At four in the morning he wakes
to the yawn of brakes,
the snore of a diesel engine.
Gone. All she left
is a froth of bra and panties.
The scum of the Seine
and the Farset.
Gallogly squats in his own pelt.
A sodium street light
has brought a new dimension
to their black taxi.
By the time they force an entry

he'll have skedaddled
among hen runs and pigeon lofts.

The charter flight from Florida
touched down at Aldergrove
minutes earlier,
at 3.54 a.m.
Its excess baggage takes the form
of Mangas Jones, Esquire,
who is, as it turns out, Apache.
He carries only hand luggage.
'Anything to declare?'
He opens the powder-blue attaché-
case. 'A pebble of quartz.'
'You're an Apache?' 'Mescalero.'
He follows the corridor's
arroyo till the signs read *Hertz*.

He is going to put his foot down
on a patch of waste ground
along the Stranmillis embankment
when he gets wind
of their impromptu fire.
The air above the once-sweet stream
is aquarium-
drained.
And six, maybe seven, skinheads
have formed a quorum
round a burnt-out heavy-duty tyre.
So intent on sniffing glue
they may not notice Gallogly,
or, if they do, are so far gone.

Three miles west as the crow flies
an all-night carry-out
provides the cover
for an illegal drinking club.
While the bar man unpacks a crate
of Coca-Cola,
one cool customer

takes on all comers in a video game.
He grasps what his two acolytes
have failed to seize.
Don't they know what kind of take-away
this is, the glipes?
Vietmanese. Viet-ma-friggin'-*knees*.
He drops his payload of napalm.

Gallogly is wearing a candy-stripe
king-size sheet,
a little something he picked up
off a clothes line.
He is driving a milk van
he borrowed from the Belfast Co-op
while the milkman's back
was turned.
He had given the milkman a playful
rabbit punch.
When he stepped on the gas
he flooded the street
with broken glass.
He is trying to keep a low profile.

The unmarked police car draws level
with his last address.
A sergeant and eight constables
pile out of a tender
and hammer up the stairs.
The street bristles with static.
Their sniffer dog, a Labrador bitch,
bursts into the attic
like David Balfour in *Kidnapped*.
A constable on his first dawn swoop
leans on a shovel.
He has turned over a
new leaf in her ladyship's herb patch.
They'll take it back for analysis.

All a bit much after the night shift
to meet a milkman

who's double-parked his van
closing your front door after him.
He's sporting your
Donegal tweed suit and your
Sunday shoes and politely raises your
hat as he goes by.
You stand there with your mouth open
as he climbs into the still-warm
driving seat of your Cortina
and screeches off towards the motorway,
leaving you uncertain
of your still-warm wife's damp tuft.

Someone on their way to early Mass
will find her hog-tied
to the chapel gates –
O Child of Prague –
big-eyed, anorexic.
The lesson for today
is pinned to her bomber jacket.
It seems to read *Keep off the Grass*.
Her lovely head has been chopped
and changed.
For Beatrice, whose fathers
knew Louis Quinze,
to have come to this, her perruque
of tar and feathers.

He is pushing the maroon Cortina
through the sedge
on the banks of the Callan.
It took him a mere forty minutes
to skite up the M1.
He followed the exit sign
for Loughgall and hared
among the top-heavy apple orchards.
This stretch of the Armagh/Tyrone
border was planted by Warwickshiremen
who planted in turn
their familiar quick-set damson hedges.

The Cortina goes to the bottom.
Gallogly swallows a plummy-plum-plum.

'I'll warrant them's the very pair
o' boys I seen abroad
in McParland's bottom, though where
in under God –
for thou art so possessed with murd'rous hate –
where they come from God only knows.'
'They were mad for a bite o' mate,
I s'pose.'
'I doubt so. I come across a brave dale
o' half-chawed damsels. Wanst wun disappeared
I follied the wun as yelly as Indy male.'
'Ye weren't afeared?'
'I follied him.' 'God save us.'
'An' he driv away in a van belongin' t'*Avis*.'

The grass sprightly as Astroturf
in the September frost
and a mist
here where the ground is low.
He seizes his own wrist
as if, as if
Blind Pew again seized Jim
at the sign of the 'Admiral Benbow'.
As if Jim Hawkins led Blind Pew
to Billy Bones
and they were all one and the same,
he stares in disbelief
at an Aspirin-white spot he pressed
into his own palm.

Gallogly's thorn-proof tweed jacket
is now several sizes too big.
He has flopped
down in a hay shed
to ram a wad of hay into the toe
of each of his ill-fitting
brogues, when he gets the drift

of ham and eggs.
Now he's led by his own wet nose
to the hacienda-style
farmhouse, a baggy-kneed animated
bear drawn out of the woods
by an apple pie
left to cool on a windowsill.

She was standing at the picture window
with a glass of water
and a Valium
when she caught your man
in the reflection of her face.
He came
shaping past the milking parlour
as if he owned the place.
Such is the integrity
of their quarrel
that she immediately took down
the legally held shotgun
and let him have both barrels.
She had wanted only to clear the air.

Half a mile away across the valley
her husband's UDR patrol
is mounting a check-point.
He pricks up his ears
at the crack
of her prematurely arthritic hip-
joint,
and commandeers one of the jeeps.
There now, only a powder burn
as if her mascara had run.
The bloody puddle
in the yard, and the shilly-shally
of blood like a command wire
petering out behind a milk churn.

A hole in the heart, an ovarian
cyst.

Coming up the Bann
in a bubble.
Disappearing up his own bum.
Or, running on the spot
with all the minor aplomb
of a trick-cyclist.
So thin, side-on, you could spit
through him.
His six foot of pump water
bent double
in agony or laughter.
Keeping down-wind of everything.

White Annetts. Gillyflowers. Angel Bites.
When he names the forgotten names
of apples
he has them all off pat.
His eye like the eye of a travelling rat
lights on the studied negligence
of these scraws of turf.
A tarpaulin. A waterlogged pit.
He will take stock of the Kalashnikov's
filed-down serial number,
seven sticks of unstable
commercial gelignite
that have already begun to weep.
Red Strokes. Sugar Sweet. Widows' Whelps.

Buy him a drink and he'll regale you
with how he came in for a cure
one morning after the night before
to the *Las Vegas* Lounge and Cabaret.
He was crossing the bar's
eternity of parquet floor
when his eagle eye
saw something move on the horizon.
If it wasn't an Indian.
A Sioux. An ugly Sioux.
He means, of course, an Oglala
Sioux busily tracing the family tree

of an Ulsterman who had some hand
in the massacre at Wounded Knee.

He will answer the hedge-sparrow's
Littlebitofbreadandnocheese
with a whole bunch
of freshly picked watercress,
a bulb of garlic,
sorrel,
with many-faceted blackberries.
Gallogly is out to lunch.
When his cock rattles its sabre
he takes it in his dab
hand, plants one chaste kiss
on its forelock,
and then, with a birl and a skirl,
tosses it off like a caber.

The UDR corporal had come off duty
to be with his wife
while the others set about
a follow-up search.
When he tramped out just before twelve
to exercise the greyhound
he was hit by a single high-velocity
shot.
You could, if you like, put your fist
in the exit wound
in his chest.
He slumps
in the spume of his own arterial blood
like an overturned paraffin lamp.

Gallogly lies down in the sheugh
to munch
through a Beauty of
Bath. He repeats himself, *Bath*,
under his garlic-breath.
Sheugh, he says. *Sheugh*.
He is finding that first 'sh'

increasingly difficult to manage.
Sh-leeps. A milkmaid sinks
her bare foot
to the ankle
in a simmering dung hill
and fills the slot
with beastlings for him to drink.

In Ovid's conspicuously tongue-in-cheek
account of an eyeball
to eyeball
between the goddess Leto
and a shower of Lycian reed cutters
who refuse her a cup of cloudy
water
from their churned-up lake,
Live then forever in that lake of yours,
she cries, and has them
bubble
and squeak
and plonk themselves down as bullfrogs
in their icy jissom.

A country man kneels on his cap
beside his neighbour's fresh
grave-mud
as Gallogly kneels to lap
the primrose-yellow
custard.
The knees of his hand-me-down duds
are gingerish.
A pernickety seven-
year-old girl-child
parades in her mother's trousseau
and mumbles a primrose
Kleenex tissue
to make sure her lipstick's even.

Gallogly has only to part the veil
of its stomach wall

to get right under the skin,
the spluttering heart
and collapsed lung,
of the horse in *Guernica*.
He flees the Museum of Modern Art
with its bit between his teeth.
When he began to cough
blood, Hamsun rode the Minneapolis/
New York night train
on top of the dining-car.
One long, inward howl.
A porter-drinker without a thrapple.

A weekend trip to the mountains
North of Boston
with Alice, Alice A.
and her paprika hair,
the ignition key
to her family's Winnebago camper,
her quim
biting the leg off her.
In the oyster bar
of Grand Central Station
she gobbles a dozen Chesapeakes –
'Oh, I'm not particular as to size' –
and, with a flourish of tabasco,
turns to gobble him.

A brewery lorry on a routine delivery
is taking a slow,
dangerous bend.
The driver's blethering
his code name
over the Citizens' Band
when someone ambles
in front of him. Go, Johnny, Go, Go, Go.
He's been dry-gulched
by a sixteen-year-old numb
with Mogadon,
whose face is masked by the seamless

black stocking filched
from his mum.

When who should walk in but Beatrice,
large as life, or larger,
sipping her one glass of lager
and singing her one song.
If he had it to do all over again
he would let her shave his head
in memory of '98
and her own, the French, Revolution.
The son of the King of the Moy
met this child on the Roxborough
estate. *Noblesse*, she said. *Noblesse
oblige*. And her tiny nipples
were bruise-bluish, wild raspberries.
The song she sang was 'The Croppy Boy'.

Her *grand'mère* was once asked to tea
by Gertrude Stein,
and her *grand'mère* and Gertrude
and Alice B., *chère* Alice B.
with her hook-nose,
the three of them sat in the nude
round the petits fours
and repeated *Eros is Eros is Eros*.
If he had it to do all over again
he would still be taken in
by her Alice B. Toklas
Nameless Cookies
and those new words she had him learn:
hash, hashish, *lo perfido assassin*.

Once the local councillor straps
himself into the safety belt
of his Citroën
and skids up the ramp
from the municipal car park
he upsets the delicate balance
of a mercury-tilt

boobytrap.
Once they collect his smithereens
he doesn't quite add up.
They're shy of a foot, and a calf
which stems
from his left shoe like a severely
pruned-back shrub.

Ten years before. The smooth-as-a-
front-lawn at Queen's
where she squats
before a psilocybin god.
The indomitable gentle-bush
that had Lanyon or Lynn
revise their elegant ground plan
for the university quad.
With calmness, with care,
with breast milk, with dew.
There's no cure now.
There's nothing left to do.
The mushrooms speak through her.
Hush-hush.

'Oh, I'm not particular as to size,'
Alice hastily replied
and broke off a bit of the edge
with each hand
and set to work very carefully,
nibbling
first at one
and then the other.
On the Staten Island Ferry
two men are dickering
over the price
of a shipment of Armalites,
as Henry Thoreau was wont to quibble
with Ralph Waldo Emerson.

That last night in the Algonquin
he met with a flurry

of sprites,
the assorted shades
of Wolfe Tone, Napper Tandy,
a sanguine
Michael Cusack
brandishing his blackthorn.
Then, Thomas Meagher
darts up from the Missouri
on a ray
of the morning star
to fiercely ask
what has become of Irish hurling.

Everyone has heard the story of
a strong and beautiful bug
which came out of the dry leaf
of an old table of apple-tree wood
that stood
in a farmer's kitchen in Massachusetts
and which was heard gnawing out
for several weeks –
When the phone trills
he is careful not to lose his page –
Who knows what beautiful and winged life
whose egg
has been buried for ages
may unexpectedly come forth? 'Tell-tale.'

Gallogly carries a hunting bow
equipped
with a bow sight
and a quiver
of hunting arrows
belonging to her brother.
Alice has gone a little way off
to do her job.
A timber wolf,
a caribou,
or merely a trick of the light?
As, listlessly,

he lobs
an arrow into the undergrowth.

Had you followed the river Callan's
Pelorus Jack
through the worst drought
in living memory
to the rains of early Autumn
when it scrubs its swollen,
scab-encrusted back
under a bridge, the bridge you look down from,
you would be unlikely to pay much heed
to yet another old banger
no one could be bothered to tax,
or a beat-up fridge
well-stocked with gelignite,
or some five hundred yards of Cortex.

He lopes after the dribs of blood
through the pine forest
till they stop dead
in the ruins of a longhouse
or hogan.
Somehow, he finds his way
back to their tent.
Not so much as a whiff of her musk.
The girl behind the Aer Lingus
check-in desk
at Logan
is wearing the same scent
and an embroidered capital letter *A*
on her breast.

Was she Aurora, or the goddess Flora,
Artemidora, or Venus bright,
or Helen fair beyond compare
that Priam stole from the Grecian sight?
Quite modestly she answered me
and she gave her head one fetch up
and she said I am gathering musheroons

135

to make my mammy ketchup.
The dunt and dunder
of a culvert-bomb
wakes him
as it might have woke Leander.
And she said I am gathering musheroons
to make my mammy ketchup O.

Predictable as the gift of the gab
or a drop of the craythur
he noses round the six foot deep
crater.
Oblivious to their Landrover's
olive-drab
and the Burgundy berets
of a snatch-squad of Paratroopers.
Gallogly, or Gollogly,
otherwise known as Golightly,
otherwise known as Ingoldsby,
otherwise known as English,
gives forth one low cry of anguish
and agrees to come quietly.

They have bundled him into the cell
for a strip-
search.
He perches
on the balls of his toes, my my,
with his legs spread
till both his instep arches
fall.
He holds himself at arm's
length from the brilliantly Snowcem-ed
wall, a game bird
hung by its pinion tips
till it drops, in the fullness of time,
from the mast its colours are nailed to.

They have left him to cool his heels
after the obligatory

bath,
the mug shots, fingerprints
et cetera.
He plumps the thin bolster
and hints
at the slop bucket.
Six o'clock.
From the A Wing of Armagh jail
he can make out
the Angelus bell
of St Patrick's cathedral
and a chorus of 'For God and Ulster'.

The brewery lorry's stood at a list
by the *Las Vegas*
throughout the afternoon,
its off-side rear tyres down.
As yet, no one has looked agog
at the smuts and rusts
of a girlie mag
in disarray on the passenger seat.
An almost invisible, taut
fishing line
runs from the Playmate's navel
to a pivotal
beer keg.
As yet, no one has risen to the bait.

I saw no mountains, no enormous spaces,
no magical growth and metamorphosis
of buildings, nothing remotely like
a drama or a parable
in which he dons these lime-green
dungarees,
green Wellingtons,
a green helmet of aspect terrible.
The other world to which mescalin
admitted me was not the world of visions;
it existed out there, in what I could see
with my eyes open.

137

He straps a chemical pack on his back
and goes in search of some Gawain.

Gallogly pads along the block
to raise his visor
at the first peep-hole.
He shamelessly
takes in her lean piglet's
back, the back
and boyish hams
of a girl at stool.
At last. A tiny goat's-pill.
A stub of crayon
with which she has squiggled
a shamrock, yes,
but a shamrock after the school
of Pollock, Jackson Pollock.

I stopped and stared at her face to face
and on the spot a name came to me,
a name with a smooth, nervous sound:
Ylayali.
When she was very close
I drew myself up straight
and said in an impressive voice,
'Miss, you are losing your book.'
And Beatrice, for it is she, she squints
through the spy-hole
to pass him an orange,
an Outspan orange some visitor has spiked
with a syringe-ful
of vodka.

The more a man has the more a man wants,
the same I don't think true.
For I never met a man with one black eye
who ever wanted two.
In the *Las Vegas* Lounge and Cabaret
the resident group –
pot bellies, Aran knits –

have you eating out of their hands.
Never throw a brick at a drowning man
when you're near to a grocer's store.
Just throw him a cake of Sunlight soap,
let him wash himself ashore.
You will act the galoot, and gallivant,
and call for another encore.

Gallogly, Gallogly, O Gallogly
juggles
his name like an orange
between his outsize baseball glove
paws,
and ogles
a moon that's just out of range
beyond the perimeter wall.
He works a gobbet of Brylcreem
into his quiff
and delves
through sand and gravel,
shrugging it off
his velveteen shoulders and arms.

> *Just*
> *throw*
> *him*
> *a*
> *cake*
> *of*
> *Sunlight*
> *soap,*
> *let*
> *him*
> *wash*
> *him-*
> *self*
> *ashore.*

Into a picture by Edward Hopper
of a gas station

in the mid-West
where Hopper takes as his theme
light, the spooky
glow of an illuminated sign
reading Esso or Mobil
or what-have-you –
into such a desolate oval
ride two youths on a motorbike.
A hand gun. Balaclavas.
The pump attendant's grown so used
to hold-ups he calls after them:
Beannacht Dé ar an obair.

The pump attendant's not to know
he's being watched by a gallowglass
hot-foot from a woodcut
by Derricke,
who skips across the forecourt
and kicks the black
plastic bucket
they left as a memento.
Nor is the gallowglass any the wiser.
The bucket's packed with fertilizer
and a heady brew
of sugar and Paraquat's
relentlessly gnawing its way through
the floppy knot of a Durex.

It was this self-same pump attendant
who dragged the head and torso
clear
and mouthed an Act of Contrition
in the frazzled ear
and overheard
those already-famous last words
Moose . . . Indian.
'Next of all wus the han'.' 'Be Japers.'
'The sodgers cordonned-off the area
wi' what-ye-may-call-it tape.'
'Lunimous.' 'They foun' this hairy

han' wi' a drowneded man's grip
on a lunimous stone no bigger than a . . .'

'Huh.'

PADRAIC FIACC

MORE TERRORISTS
for Lynch

The prayer book is putting on fat
With *in memoriam* cards.

The dead steal back
Like snails on the draining board

Caught after dark
Out of their shells.

Their very
Outnumbering, swarmy cunning
Betters

My 'cut head' and
Scares me as
Pascal was

At too many stars.

RITA ANN HIGGINS

H–BLOCK SHUTTLE
for L. McKeown

We see nothing
from the Inter-Kesh-Shuttle
the H-mobile,
only the people seated
on the other side
(and no one really knows
what side they are on).

Somewhere between Hs,
an overdue light bill,
thoughts of a holiday for two
(in anywhere but Gibraltar)
and the one who's doing life,

the H-mobile stops,
we wait for the doors to open
Tic toc, tic toc, tic toc.

Time for a head count.
He counts our heads
on his fingers
for a living,
while the people seated here
count the relatives
they have left
(some are running
out of uncles).

Some brazen it
with a false laugh
some stare ahead
forgetting to blink.

A woman whispers
'We're going to the showers,'

others throw Mass card glances
at their shoes
(with them he counts
the back of their heads).

'Hey mister,
what do you do
for a shilling
a queen's shilling?'

'I count heads
for a living
my clean living.'

'Do you speak
to the heads
that you count?'

'I'm not paid
to speak to the heads
who don't count
I'm paid to count
the heads who don't speak.'

'And why
do the heads
that you count
not speak?'

'Outside the dogs bark
to ensure
that the heads
who don't count
that I count
don't speak . . . '

'And what about
the no-windows scare?'

'No windows are there
to ensure
that the heads
who don't count
that I count
don't see.'

'And what is
it out there
that the heads
who you count
shouldn't see?'

'I count heads
on my fingers
for a living
for my clean living
for my queen's shilling.

'I get paid
to count heads
who don't count,
not to tell you

'what the heads
who don't count
that I count
shouldn't see.'

We see nothing
from the Inter-Kesh-Shuttle,
the H-mobile,
only the people seated
on the other side
(and no one really knows
what side they are on).

DEREK MAHON

AS IT SHOULD BE

We hunted the mad bastard
Through bog, moorland, rock, to the star-lit west
And gunned him down in a blind yard
Between ten sleeping lorries
And an electricity generator.

Let us hear no idle talk
Of the moon in the Yellow River.
The air blows softer since his departure.

Since his tide burial during school hours
Our kiddies have known no bad dreams.
Their cries echo lightly along the coast.

This is as it should be.
They will thank us for it when they grow up
To a world with method in it.

PAUL MULDOON

GATHERING MUSHROOMS

The rain comes flapping through the yard
like a tablecloth that she hand-embroidered.
My mother has left it on the line.
It is sodden with rain.
The mushroom shed is windowless, wide,
its high-stacked wooden trays
hosed down with formaldehyde.
And my father has opened the Gates of Troy
to that first load of horse manure.
Barley straw. Gypsum. Dried blood. Ammonia.

Wagon after wagon
blusters in, a self-renewing gold-black dragon
we push to the back of the mind.
We have taken our pitchforks to the wind.

All brought back to me that September evening
fifteen years on. The pair of us
tripping through Barnett's fair demesne
like girls in long dresses
after a hail-storm.
We might have been thinking of the fire-bomb
that sent Malone House sky-high
and its priceless collection of linen
sky-high.
We might have wept with Elizabeth McCrum.
We were thinking only of psilocybin.
You sang of the maid you met on the dewy grass –
And she stooped so low gave me to know
it was mushrooms she was gathering O.

He'll be wearing that same old donkey-jacket
and the sawn-off waders.
He carries a knife, two punnets, a bucket.
He reaches far into his own shadow.
We'll have taken him unawares
and stand behind him, slightly to one side.
He is one of those ancient warriors
before the rising tide.
He'll glance back from under his peaked cap
without breaking rhythm:
his coaxing a mushroom – a flat or a cup –
the nick against his right thumb;
the bucket then, the punnet to left or right,
and so on and so forth till kingdom come.

We followed the overgrown tow-path by the Lagan.
The sunset would deepen through cinnamon
to aubergine,
the wood-pigeon's concerto for oboe and strings,
allegro, blowing your mind.

And you were suddenly out of my ken, hurtling
towards the ever-receding ground,
into the maw
of a shimmering green-gold dragon.
You discovered yourself in some outbuilding
with your long-lost companion, me,
though my head had grown into the head of a horse
that shook its dirty-fair mane
and spoke this verse:

Come back to us. However cold and raw, your feet
were always meant
to negotiate terms with bare cement.
Beyond this concrete wall is a wall of concrete
and barbed wire. Your only hope
is to come back. If sing you must, let your song
tell of treading your own dung,
let straw and dung give a spring to your step.
If we never live to see the day we leap
into our true domain,
lie down with us now and wrap
yourself in the soiled grey blanket of Irish rain
that will, one day, bleach itself white.
Lie down with us and wait.

AISLING

I was making my way home late one night
this summer, when I staggered
into a snow drift.

Her eyes spoke of a sloe-year,
her mouth a year of haws.

Was she Aurora, or the goddess Flora,
Artemidora, or Venus bright,
or Anorexia, who left
a lemon stain on my flannel sheet?

It's all much of a muchness.

In Belfast's Royal Victoria Hospital
a kidney machine
supports the latest hunger-striker
to have called off his fast, a saline
drip into his bag of brine.

A lick and a promise. Cuckoo spittle.
I hand my sample to Doctor Maw.
She gives me back a confident *All Clear*.

RICHARD MURPHY

AMAZEMENT

These are the just
Who kill unjustly men they call unjust.

These are the pure in heart
Who see God smeared in excrement on walls.

These are the patriots
Who starve to give the ravening media food.

These are the martyrs
Who die for a future buried in the past.

These are the sacrifice
A word imprisoned and a word could save.

PAUL MULDOON

CHRISTO'S

Two workmen were carrying a sheet of asbestos
down the Main Street of Dingle;
it must have been nailed, at a slight angle,
to the same-sized gap between Brandon

and whichever's the next mountain.
Nine o'clock. We watched the village dogs
take turns to spritz the hotel's refuse-sacks.
I remembered Tralee's unbiodegradable flags

from the time of the hunger-strikes.
We drove all day past mounds of sugar-beet,
hay-stacks, silage-pits, building-sites,
a thatched cottage even –

all of them draped in black polythene
and weighted against the north-east wind
by concrete blocks, old tyres; bags of sand
at a makeshift army post

across the border. By the time we got to Belfast
the whole of Ireland would be under wraps
like, as I said, 'one of your man's landscapes'.
'Your man's? You don't mean Christo's?'

KERRY CARSON

MOURNE

Mourne country. Under
Chimney Rock,
they cut the granite
block by block.

Mourne country. When
a neighbour dies
he chops the mountains
down to size.

Mourne country. Half a
parish sent
its contours for a
monument.

Mourne country. On the
broken bones
we pile the hills for
symbol stones.

Mourne country. Daily,
chink by chink,
the tombs rise and the
mountains sink.

Mourne country. Will
we soldier on
till all our Commedaghs
are gone?

Mourne country. We
have graves to make.
How many Binnians
will it take?

JOHN F. DEANE

ON THE KILLING IN SOUTH ARMAGH

You have left something on the side of our road, in tall grass, among
vetch, wild strawberries and meadowsweet. Slumped like a refuse-
sack his body, his head has blossomed into a huge, a jungle flower;

you have tied his hands behind his back because hands too can speak, and pray. This is your wayside bundle, a bouquet to the love between his wife and him; you have made a lily of his flesh for his children to remember, a dark rose of his skull to offer to your wife among the pains of her childbearing, ditchwater of his blood as a gift at your daughter's wedding-feast.

MICHAEL LONGLEY

WREATHS

THE CIVIL SERVANT

He was preparing an Ulster fry for breakfast
When someone walked into the kitchen and shot him:
A bullet entered his mouth and pierced his skull,
The books he had read, the music he could play.

He lay in his dressing gown and pyjamas
While they dusted the dresser for fingerprints
And then shuffled backwards across the garden
With notebooks, cameras and measuring tapes.

They rolled him up like a red carpet and left
Only a bullet hole in the cutlery drawer:
Later his widow took a hammer and chisel
And removed the black keys from his piano.

THE GREENGROCER

He ran a good shop, and he died
Serving even the death-dealers
Who found him busy as usual
Behind the counter, organised
With holly wreaths for Christmas,
Fir trees on the pavement outside.

Astrologers or three wise men
Who may shortly be setting out

For a small house up the Shankill
Or the Falls, should pause on their way
To buy gifts at Jim Gibson's shop,
Dates and chestnuts and tangerines.

THE LINEN WORKERS

Christ's teeth ascended with him into heaven:
Through a cavity in one of his molars
The wind whistles: he is fastened for ever
By his exposed canines to a wintry sky.

I am blinded by the blaze of that smile
And by the memory of my father's false teeth
Brimming in their tumbler: they wore bubbles
And, outside of his body, a deadly grin.

When they massacred the ten linen workers
There fell on the road beside them spectacles,
Wallets, small change, and a set of dentures:
Blood, food particles, the bread, the wine.

Before I can bury my father once again
I must polish the spectacles, balance them
Upon his nose, fill his pockets with money
And into his dead mouth slip the set of teeth.

SEAMUS HEANEY

THE STRAND AT LOUGH BEG
in memory of Colum McCartney

All round this little island, on the strand
Far down below there, where the breakers strive,
Grow the tall rushes from the oozy sand.
               Dante, *Purgatorio*, I, 100–103

Leaving the white glow of filling stations
And a few lonely streetlamps among fields

You climbed the hills towards Newtownhamilton
Past the Fews Forest, out beneath the stars –
Along that road, a high, bare pilgrim's track
Where Sweeney fled before the bloodied heads,
Goat-beards and dogs' eyes in a demon pack
Blazing out of the ground, snapping and squealing.
What blazed ahead of you? A faked road block?
The red lamp swung, the sudden brakes and stalling
Engine, voices, heads hooded and the cold-nosed gun?
Or in your driving mirror, tailing headlights
That pulled out suddenly and flagged you down
Where you weren't known and far from what you knew:
The lowland clays and waters of Lough Beg,
Church Island's spire, its soft treeline of yew.

There you used hear guns fired behind the house
Long before rising time, when duck shooters
Haunted the marigolds and bulrushes,
But still were scared to find spent cartridges,
Acrid, brassy, genital, ejected,
On your way across the strand to fetch the cows.
For you and yours and yours and mine fought shy,
Spoke an old language of conspirators
And could not crack the whip or seize the day:
Big-voiced scullions, herders, feelers round
Haycocks and hindquarters, talkers in byres,
Slow arbitrators of the burial ground.

Across that strand of yours the cattle graze
Up to their bellies in an early mist
And now they turn their unbewildered gaze
To where we work our way through squeaking sedge
Drowning in dew. Like a dull blade with its edge
Honed bright, Lough Beg half shines under the haze.
I turn because the sweeping of your feet
Has stopped behind me, to find you on your knees
With blood and roadside muck in your hair and eyes,
Then kneel in front of you in brimming grass
And gather up cold handfuls of the dew
To wash you, cousin. I dab you clean with moss

Fine as the drizzle out of a low cloud.
I lift you under the arms and lay you flat.
With rushes that shoot green again, I plait
Green scapulars to wear over your shroud.

A POSTCARD FROM NORTH ANTRIM
in memory of Sean Armstrong

A lone figure is waving
From the thin line of a bridge
Of ropes and slats, slung
Dangerously out between
The cliff-top and the pillar rock.
A nineteenth-century wind.
Dulse-pickers. Sea campions.

A postcard for you, Sean,
And that's you, swinging alone,
Antic, half-afraid,
In your gallowglass's beard
And swallow-tail of serge:
The Carrick-a-Rede Rope Bridge
Ghost-written on sepia.

Or should it be your houseboat
Ethnically furnished,
Redolent of grass?
Should we discover you
Beside those warm-planked, democratic wharves
Among the twilights and guitars
Of Sausalito?

Drop-out on a come-back,
Prince of no-man's land
With your head in clouds or sand,
You were the clown
Social worker of the town

Until your candid forehead stopped
A pointblank teatime bullet.

Get up from your blood on the floor.
Here's another boat
In grass by the lough shore,
Turf smoke, a wired hen-run –
Your local, hoped for, unfound commune.
Now recite me *William Bloat*,
Sing of the *Calabar*

Or of Henry Joy McCracken
Who kissed his Mary Ann
On the gallows at Cornmarket.
Or Ballycastle Fair.
'Give us the raw bar!'
'Sing it by brute force
If you forget the air.'

Yet something in your voice
Stayed nearly shut.
Your voice was a harassed pulpit
Leading the melody
It kept at bay,
It was independent, rattling, non-transcendent
Ulster – old decency

And Old Bushmills,
Soda farls, strong tea,
New rope, rock salt, kale plants,
Potato-bread and Woodbine.
Wind through the concrete vents
Of a border check-point.
Cold zinc nailed for a peace line.

Fifteen years ago, come this October,
Crowded on your floor,
I got my arm round Marie's shoulder
For the first time.
'Oh, Sir Jasper, do not touch me!'

155

You roared across at me,
Chorus-leading, splashing out the wine.

from STATION ISLAND

VII

I had come to the edge of the water,
soothed by just looking, idling over it
as if it were a clear barometer

or a mirror, when his reflection
did not appear but I sensed a presence
entering into my concentration

on not being concentrated as he spoke
my name. And though I was reluctant
I turned to meet his face and the shock

is still in me at what I saw. His brow
was blown open above the eye and blood
had dried on his neck and cheek. 'Easy now,'

he said, 'it's only me. You've seen men as raw
after a football match . . . What time it was
when I was wakened up I still don't know

but I heard this knocking, knocking, and it
scared me, like the phone in the small hours,
so I had the sense not to put on the light

but looked out from behind the curtain.
I saw two customers on the doorstep
and an old landrover with the doors open

parked on the street so I let the curtain drop;
but they must have been waiting for it to move
for they shouted to come down into the shop.

She started to cry then and roll round the bed,
lamenting and lamenting to herself,
not even asking who it was. "Is your head

astray, or what's come over you?" I roared, more
to bring myself to my senses
than out of any real anger at her

for the knocking shook me, the way they kept it up,
and her whingeing and half-screeching made it worse.
All the time they were shouting, "Shop!

Shop!" so I pulled on my shoes and a sportscoat
and went back to the window and called out,
"What do you want? Could you quieten the racket

or I'll not come down at all." "There's a child not well.
Open up and see what you have got – pills
or a powder or something in a bottle,"

one of them said. He stepped back off the footpath
so I could see his face in the street lamp
and when the other moved I knew them both.

But bad and all as the knocking was, the quiet
hit me worse. She was quiet herself now,
lying dead still, whispering to watch out.

At the bedroom door I switched on the light.
"It's odd they didn't look for a chemist.
Who are they anyway at this time of the night?"

she asked me, with the eyes standing in her head.
"I know them to see," I said, but something
made me reach and squeeze her hand across the bed

before I went downstairs into the aisle
of the shop. I stood there, going weak
in the legs. I remember the stale smell

of cooked meat or something coming through
as I went to open up. From then on
you know as much about it as I do.'

'Did they say nothing?' 'Nothing. What would they say?'
'Were they in uniform? Not masked in any way?'
'They were barefaced as they would be in the day,

shites thinking they were the be-all and the end-all.'
'Not that it is any consolation,
but they were caught,' I told him, 'and got jail.'

Big-limbed, decent, open-faced, he stood
forgetful of everything now except
whatever was welling up in his spoiled head,

beginning to smile. 'You've put on weight
since you did your courting in that big Austin
you got the loan of on a Sunday night.'

Through life and death he had hardly aged.
There always was an athlete's cleanliness
shining off him and except for the ravaged

forehead and the blood, he was still that same
rangy midfielder in a blue jersey
and starched pants, the one stylist on the team,

the perfect, clean, unthinkable victim.
'Forgive the way I have lived indifferent –
forgive my timid circumspect involvement,'

I surprised myself by saying. 'Forgive
my eye,' he said, 'all that's above my head.'
And then a stun of pain seemed to go through him

and he trembled like a heatwave and faded.

CONOR CARSON

MARIE WILSON
Enniskillen, 8 November 1987

Under the statue
  of the Unknown Soldier
a man prepares
  a bomb. He is
an unknown soldier.

The patron saint of warriors
  is Michael.
Between the unknown soldiers
  is a wall.
It is the gable
  of St Michael's Hall.

This was Remembrance Sunday.
  Poppy Day.
They came to hear
  the bugles in the square.
They did not count
  the unknown soldiers there.

Today there were no sermons.
  Unknown soldiers
said later it had not
  gone off as planned.
Under the bricks
  she held her father's hand.

Today there was no Last Post.
  Her last words
were 'Daddy, I love you.'
  He said he would trust
God. But her poppy
  lay in the dust.

The protector of unknown soldiers
  is Michael.
The father is at the grave.
  A bell peals.
The name Michael
  means 'God heals'.

PETER MCDONALD

SUNDAY IN GREAT TEW
8th November 1987

1

It's time to get back to the car. Already, at half-past three,
the light's three-quarters gone, and back across the green
you can watch the shifting greys of a subtle fog by now
coming over to freeze the steps we leave, our ghosts' footprints,

to slight marks in November grass, and that's the last
of us this afternoon, this year, in this model village
a half-hour's drive from Oxford, where we come in summer
like the other tourists, to drink decent beer, sniff woodsmoke,

and admire thatched roofs on sturdy, stone-built houses,
as though the whole place were a replica of some England,
an idea on show, unchanging, glassy, not quite touchable.
But this is November, and Sunday. It is Sunday in Great Tew.

2

Every visit nowadays is an act of remembrance,
measuring changes in us against some other summer
when we sat here drinking, and swapped our random gossip
– friends, work and books, hard politics or love –

across a wooden table in an always busy pub
with proper beer on sale, not the watery Oxford slops,

160

and where, as their speciality, they sell hand-made pipes,
briars and clay-pipes, every one the genuine article,

(though these, admittedly, we never got around to buying);
one year we're talking about that headstrong, happy girl
you'd chased unluckily for months; another, and we're discussing
far-off acts of war, the real thing, here in the Falkland Arms.

3

The manor house, concealed behind thick trees and hedges,
might well be home now for some eccentric millionaire
who seldom shows his face; from the road going uphill
to the church, you can see through gaps down to the house itself,

heavy and strong, like the brash history it suggests,
having and holding so much; was it here since the Civil War,
when the bookish man who owned the place, Lord Falkland,
was a loyalist who found himself outmanoeuvred?

Once he played patron here to the poet Abraham Cowley
– outmanoeuvred himself, in his way, by Parliament's
staunch worker Milton, true to different lights, but blind,
po-faced, pig-headed and holy, almost an Ulsterman.

4

Names of the wars change, and of course the protagonists change:
the church contains its various slabs of memorial stone
with names of the dead men, where today a single wreath
of poppies does its duty, pays them its stiff homage

of glaring red flowers for death, rootless and papery,
bunched together in grief or pride, or with indifference,
on a Sunday like any other Sunday in November;
there's a smell of damp mixed with the smell of genteel ladies

and the cold slips forward from the walls and the dark floor
so that here, too, we must become aliens, shut out
from whatever we might be tempted to call our own, reminded
that the dead are close, that here the poppy is an English flower.

There are no words to find for the dead, and no gestures,
no sermons to be turned, no curses to lay now and for ever
on one house, or the other, or on both; there is no need
to rerun the scalding images they have left in our keeping,

or pitch hot misery into this cold comfort, as though
one ill-bred outburst here might make sense of it;
there is no need to watch television in the afternoon
to understand that nobody has ever died with a good reason,

and see the Irish slaughter one another like wogs;
there is no need, only now a blinding appetite,
this afternoon, tomorrow, the day after; so tonight in the Killyhevlin
Hotel the team from ITN will be ordering champagne.

6

One drink today, one pint of beer, and one short walk
in the sober afternoon around an English village,
a conversation jumping from one silence to another
in ripe Oxonian vowels, two figures on their own

in some pretend backwater with picture-postcard views,
slipping discreetly into a proper country churchyard
and quoting poetry, and laughing now that everything's
too late, imagining the right history for the place,

inglorious, largely mute: two generals discussing terms,
their fists set hard on the oak table that's between them,
where neither will say the word 'defeat', though both return
with different names for victory to their beaten people.

7

Even in the middle of winter, the sky is everywhere,
folded above us as we walk with hands sunk in our pockets,
our fingers worrying over cold coins and key-rings;
it covers us completely as a numbing anaesthetic

so that every time we might look up, the two of us,
the trees we can see with fog trailing in their branches,
the scarecrow standing up in its one blank field
(or what looks from here like a scarecrow), the row of old houses

snug and expensive and empty, even the pub behind us,
all become incidental, oblique marks set in the margin,
swept out to the edges of a single, clear perspective,
the one that matters most, or least, and never changes.

8

A flower of crumpled paper with its button of black plastic
has fallen from somebody's coat, and is lying here beside
a vacant phone-box opposite the village school
along with an empty packet of twenty Benson and Hedges

and what looks like a bus-ticket; such modest litter
might be the last thing you notice, and for all the cars parked
there's nobody here but us walking out in the open,
and even we are making our way back to a car,

opening, closing doors, clicking in seat-belts, switching on
dipped headlights and starting the engine; turning around
and taking a right at the deserted school,
on our way home, leaving absolutely nothing behind us.

JOHN F. DEANE

REMEMBRANCE DAY

Behind the statue of St Teresa of the Flowers
a brown package: the message, the ransom note.

Somewhere a room
where men in balaclavas play at dice;
'safe houses'.

Rose petals fall on us from the clouds.

A soldier broods over named and unnamed dead
of another war; the cenotaph; the empty tomb.

The gable end of a street
has swollen out like a balloon.

Our prayers are poppies pinned in our lapels;
our arms have been growing into wreaths;

'in the quiet of the night we go on crying, very hard'.

*

After the bombardment
apple-blossom fell, like snow, in Normandy;
retreating soldiers pushed through Caen towards Paris;

under rubble of her town the little saint
lay undisturbed; I choose, she had said, everything,
her arms folded, her eyes held down,

turning and turning in the chestnut-tree walk
of her convent grounds,
the sky above her full of leaves, like prayers.

Someone comes, with wheelbarrow and rake
and works among the shadows of the trees.

When they clothed her, snow fell on the gardens,
the chestnut-trees were apple orchards blossoming.

PADRAIC FIACC

INTIMATE LETTER 1973

Our Paris part of Belfast has
Decapitated lamp posts now. Our meeting
Place, the Book Shop, is a gaping
Black hole of charred timber.

Remember that night with you, in-
valided in the top room when
They were throwing petrol bombs through
The windows of Catholics, how
My migraine grew to such
A pitch, Brigid said 'Mommy,
I think Daddy is going to burst!'

We all run away from each other's
Particular hell. I didn't
Survive you and her thrown
To the floor when they blew up the Co-
Op at the bottom of the street or Brigid
Waking screaming after this
Or that explosion. Really,
I was the first one to go:

It was I who left you . . .

REQUIN

in memory of my young poet friend Gerry McLaughlin,
murdered 7 April 1975

How I admired your bravado –
Dandering down the road alone
In the dark, yelling 'I'll see
You again tomorrow', but
They pump six bullets into you.

Now you are lying in
A blood puddle, yelling

'There's no "goodbye",
No "safe home" in
This Coffin Country where
Your hands are clawed . . . '

How can I tell anyone
I'm born, born lying in
This ditch of a cold Belfast dawn
With the bullet-mangled body of
A dead boy, and can't
Can't get away? A young
Brit soldier wanders
Over to my old donkey honk
Of bitter *Miserere*, of
Dereliction on the street:

'What is it mate, what is it?

'What's Wrong?'

CIARAN CARSON

THE MOUTH

There was this head had this mouth he kept shooting off.
   Unfortunately.
It could have been worse for us than it was for him.
   Provisionally.
But since nothing in this world is certain and you don't know
   who hears what
We thought it was time he bit off more than he could chew.
   Literally.
By the time he is found there'll be nothing much left to tell
   who he was.

But of course some clever dick from the 'Forscenic Lab'
   reconstructs
Him, what he used to be – not from his actual teeth, not
   fingerprints,
But from the core – the toothmarks of the first and last bite
   he'd taken of
This sour apple. But then we would have told them anyway.
   Publicity.

ROBERT LOWELL

IDENTIFICATION IN BELFAST
IRA bombing

The British Army now carries two rifles,
one with rubber rabbit-pellets for children,
the other's of course for the Provisionals . . .
'When they first showed me the boy, I thought oh good,
it's not him because he is a blonde –
I imagine his hair was singed dark by the bomb.
He had nothing on him to identify him,
except this box of joke trick matches;
he liked to have them on him, even at mass.
The police were unhurried and wonderful,
they let me go on trying to strike a match . . .
I just wouldn't stop – you cling to anything –
I couldn't believe I couldn't light one match –
only joke-matches . . . Then I knew he was Richard.'

ROGER MCGOUGH

THE IDENTIFICATION

So you think it's Stephen?
Then I'd best make sure
Be on the safe side as it were.
Ah, there's been a mistake. The hair
you see, it's black, now Stephen's fair . . .
What's that? The explosion?
Of course, burnt black. Silly of me.
I should have known. Then let's get on.

The face, is that a face I ask?
That mask of charred wood
blistered, scarred could
that have been a child's face?
The sweater, where intact, looks
in fact all too familiar.
But one must be sure.

The scoutbelt. Yes that's his.
I recognize the studs he hammered in
not a week ago. At the age
when boys get clothes-conscious
now you know. It's almost
certainly Stephen. But one must
be sure. Remove all trace of doubt.
Pull out every splinter of hope.

Pockets. Empty the pockets.
Handkerchief? Could be any schoolboy's.
Dirty enough. Cigarettes?
Oh this can't be Stephen.
I don't allow him to smoke you see.
He wouldn't disobey me. Not his father.

But that's his penknife. That's his all right.
And that's his key on the keyring

Gran gave him just the other night.
So this must be him.

I think I know what happened
. . . . . . about the cigarettes
No doubt he was minding them
for one of the older boys.
Yes that's it.
That's him.
That's our Stephen.

CIARAN CARSON

CAMPAIGN

They had questioned him for hours. Who exactly was he? And when
He told them, they questioned him again. When they accepted who he
    was, as
Someone not involved, they pulled out his fingernails. Then
They took him to a waste-ground somewhere near the Horseshoe
    Bend, and told him
What he was. They shot him nine times.

A dark umbilicus of smoke was rising from a heap of burning tyres.
The bad smell he smelt was the smell of himself. Broken glass and
    knotted Durex.
The knuckles of a face in a nylon stocking. I used to see him in the
    Gladstone Bar,
Drawing pints for strangers, his almost-perfect fingers flecked with
    scum.

LAST ORDERS

Squeeze the buzzer on the steel mesh gate like a trigger, but
It's someone else who has you in their sights. Click. It opens. Like
    electronic

Russian roulette, since you never know for sure who's who, or what
You're walking into. I, for instance, could be anybody. Though I'm told
Taig's written on my face. See me, would *I* trust appearances?

Inside a sudden lull. The barman lolls his head at us. We order *Harp* –
Seems safe enough, everybody drinks it. As someone looks daggers at us
From the *Bushmills* mirror, a penny drops: how simple it would be for
    someone
Like ourselves to walk in and blow the whole place, and ourselves, to
    Kingdom Come.

SEAMUS DEANE

A BURIAL

The broken sods, a whipped flag,
The broad river beyond. Gunfire;
The young graves blotted all over.

Angels of morning light dance
On the silver needles of the estuary.
The helicopter prowls, a dragonfly
Popping its shuttered eyes.

Here we have a pause before rain,
And the clatter of clay
Feet on the porch of heaven.

In the stripped rain we wonder
What is going on here.
The cloudburst seems elegy enough.
Drooked shadows raise

White cellophaned flowers
In the darkened air.
Others kneel one-kneed

On a handkerchief. Cars
Glisten. Cameras at full exposure
Click. *Zeiss* and *Leica*
Whirr like crickets. Someone folds

A pistol in waterproof.
He is about to start his dry life,
This one, under the earth roof,

Tunnelling to his companions
In the honeycomb below
That weakens, with its intricacy,
The earth we hide in now.

JOHN F. DEANE

LE DORMEUR DU VAL: ANTRIM

Sunrise; a stream from some distant spring
stirs in undergrowth like a waking child; brown
bubbles with silver bubbles on their back bring
life to primroses, narcissi, vetch; a man
lies in a froth of sunshine, his face down
in the water, drinking; dew is a dust
of night light on his back and last year's dun
leaves are nestling him; he is still, as if he had just
slaked a long thirst. Nearby a wren
makes morning music; through a banquet hall
of sunshafts, reeds, the boles of trees, tense
urgency of traffic on a road. It is cold
in the wood but he is not shivering, his head
in the water and the mosses stained bright red.

FRANK ORMSBY

AFTERMATH

Chalk-marks that traced the body's line
Cannot be found, the bricks are plastered bare.
The wind has scoured the alley clean.
What comfort there?

Stains on the doorstep that were red
Grow light as stone, worn by the tread of men.
By foot on foot the ghost is laid.
What comfort then?

Limbs are forgetting limbs they shared
And hearts the hearts that answered them before –
In pulse as if they never cared.
No comfort more.

JOHN HEWITT

NEITHER AN ELEGY NOR A MANIFESTO
for the people of my province and the rest of Ireland

Bear in mind these dead:
I can find no plainer words.
I dare not risk using
that loaded word, Remember,
for your memory is a cruel web
threaded from thorn to thorn across
a hedge of dead bramble, heavy
with pathetic atomies.

I cannot urge or beg you
to pray for anyone or anything,
for prayer in this green island

is tarnished with stale breath,
worn smooth and characterless
as an old flagstone, trafficked
with journeys no longer credible
to lost destinations.

The careful words of my injunction
are unrhetorical, as neutral
and unaligned as any I know:
they propose no more than thoughtful response;
they do not pound with drum-beats
of patriotism, loyalty, martyrdom.

So I say only: Bear in mind
those men and lads killed in the streets;
but do not differentiate between
those deliberately gunned down
and those caught by unaddressed bullets:
such distinctions are not relevant.

Bear in mind the skipping child hit
by the anonymous ricochet;
the man shot at his own fireside
with his staring family round him;
the elderly woman
making tea for the firemen
when the wall collapsed;
and the garrulous neighbours at the bar
when the bomb exploded near them;
the gesticulating deaf-mute stilled
by the soldier's rifle in the town square;
and the policeman dismembered
by the booby-trap in the car.

I might have recited a pitiful litany
of the names of all the dead:
but these could effectively be presented
only in small batches,
like a lettered tablet in a village church,

valid while everyone knew everyone,
or longer, where a family name persists.

Accident, misfortune, disease, coincidence
of genetic factors or social circumstance,
may summon courage, resolution, sympathy,
to whatever level one is engaged.
Natural disasters of lava and hurricane,
famine or flood in far countries, will evoke
compassion for the thin-shanked survivors.

Patriotism has to do with keeping
the country in good heart, the community
ordered with justice and mercy;
these will enlist loyalty and courage often,
and sacrifice, sometimes even martyrdom.
Bear these eventualities in mind also;
they will concern you forever:
but, at this moment, bear in mind these dead.

WILLIAM PESKETT

THE INHERITORS
for Paul Muldoon

And the ones that got tough
ripped the soft parts
from the sea.
With a spine and a jaw
they pressed a clear advantage,
picking bones with ones
whose shadows met their own.
Gasping, they broke the surface.

The ones that had legs
came up where there was nothing.
Starting as one,

they split into bands
and savaged the green ground.
Ambivalent, they slid in the swamp
from home to home, cleverer,
keeping their options open.

The ones that could crawl
stood up and dried
the afterbirth from their backs.
Somehow they grew to break
the treaty of the land:
becoming gross they tore
the flesh of the sinless
and took three elements in their stride.

The ones that were feathered
came to know the slaughter
of the plain. Gliding from cliffs
they tumbled to the line of flight.
Innocent in the air, their shapes
against the sun began to drop –
below, their claws ripped fur
from nervous carcasses.

And the ones that gave suck
ran like warm blood
through high branches.
With a crib for their young
their lives might have been maternal
but for precedent. Not born
to run with the innocent,
inheritors, we kill.

MICHAEL LONGLEY

KINDERTOTENLIEDER

There can be no songs for dead children
Near the crazy circle of explosions,
The splintering tangent of the ricochet,

No songs for the children who have become
My unrestricted tenants, fingerprints
Everywhere, teethmarks on this and that.

4

'Making things happen . . . '

from 'Anseo'
PAUL MULDOON

SEÁN LUCY

MEN OF ACTION

Chinstrap has done his armoured duty
And the streets are cleared;
The savage population in its caves
Licks its wounds, sulks and jeers.

Flashface, son of oppression, will answer soon
With a keg of dread:
After the smokejump and the stark bang
From the shattered street scrape up the scattered dead.

PAUL MULDOON

THE WEEPIES

Most Saturday afternoons
At the local Hippodrome
Saw the Pathé-News rooster,
Then the recurring dream

Of a lonesome drifter
Through uninterrupted range.
Will Hunter, so gifted
He could peel an orange

In a single, fluent gesture,
Was the leader of our gang.
The curtain rose this afternoon
On a lion, not a gong.

When the crippled girl
Who wanted to be a dancer

179

Met the married man
Who was dying of cancer,

Our hankies unfurled
Like flags of surrender.
I believe something fell asunder
In even Will Hunter's hands.

PADRAIC FIACC

THE BRITISH CONNECTION
a litany of terror

In Belfast, Europe, your man
Met the Military come to raid
The house: 'Over my dead body
Sir,' he said, brandishing
A real-life sword from some
Old half-forgotten war . . .

And youths with real bows and arrows
And coppers and marbles good as bullets
And old time thrupenny bits and stones
Screws, bolts, nuts (Belfast confetti),

And kitchen knives, pokers, Guinness tins
And nail-bombs down by the Shore Road

And guns under the harbour wharf
And bullets in the docker's tea tin
And gelignite in the tool shed
And grenades in the scullery larder
And weedkiller and sugar
And acid in the French letter

And sodium chlorate and nitrates
In the suburban garage
In the boot of the car

And guns in the oven grill
And guns in the spinster's shift

And ammunition and more, more
Guns in the broken-down rusted
Merry-go-round in the scrapyard –

Almost as many hard-on
Guns as there are Union Jacks.

PAUL MULDOON

ANSEO

When the Master was calling the roll
At the primary school in Collegelands,
You were meant to call back *Anseo*
And raise your hand
As your name occurred.
Anseo, meaning here, here and now,
All present and correct,
Was the first word of Irish I spoke.
The last name on the ledger
Belonged to Joseph Mary Plunkett Ward
And was followed, as often as not,
By silence, knowing looks,
A nod and a wink, the Master's droll
'And where's our little Ward-of-court?'

I remember the first time he came back
The Master had sent him out
Along the hedges
To weigh up for himself and cut
A stick with which he would be beaten.
After a while, nothing was spoken;
He would arrive as a matter of course
With an ash-plant, a salley-rod.

Or, finally, the hazel-wand
He had whittled down to a whip-lash,
Its twist of red and yellow lacquers
Sanded and polished,
And altogether so delicately wrought
That he had engraved his initials on it.

I last met Joseph Mary Plunkett Ward
In a pub just over the Irish border.
He was living in the open,
In a secret camp
On the other side of the mountain.
He was fighting for Ireland,
Making things happen.
And he told me, Joe Ward,
Of how he had risen through the ranks
To Quartermaster, Commandant:
How every morning at parade
His volunteers would call back *Anseo*
And raise their hands
As their names occurred.

PATRICK DEELEY

1969

It was sunset and Claffey said:
'God spare ye the health!'
That's all he could muster
by way of soothing the burst

blisters on our palms as we
trudged out his clanking gate,
haydust's tickle at work
in our throats, and the winnings

of a hot-tempered day
settling in fields behind us.

182

Father shouldered the pitchforks.
Hairs finer than rakings wisped

my belly, my brother's chin.
We declined the handsel
of two passing orchards,
regarding ourselves as men.

A stranger, suited, self-assured,
struck up with us in the field
known as *Smoothing Iron*.
His smalltalk primed some purpose

we couldn't comprehend. Father
stiffened, suddenly wary of him.
'I was up North. On a job –
you know what I mean.'

Bramblebush dark, stone stile.
We were pushed on ahead.
Bits of their talk followed.
'Will you not do that for us?'

'Clear off to hell! You're talking
to the wrong man.' Father
came over the stile alone,
never afterwards mentioned

the incident. My brother and I
grew away to our own concerns.
Two decades have elapsed,
spillage of taunt and threat,

maiming and brokenness,
lives prematurely stopped.
I am no wiser about that man,
what he wanted, what he wants.

SEAMUS HEANEY

from VIKING DUBLIN: TRIAL PIECES

I am Hamlet the Dane,
skull-handler, parablist,
smeller of rot

in the state, infused
with its poisons,
pinioned by ghosts
and affections,

murders and pieties,
coming to consciousness
by jumping in graves,
dithering, blathering.

CIARAN CARSON

HAMLET

As usual, the clock in The Clock Bar was a good few minutes fast:
A fiction no one really bothered to maintain, unlike the story
The comrade on my left was telling, which no one knew for certain truth:
*Back in 1922, a sergeant, I forget his name, was shot outside the National
   Bank . . .*
Ah yes, what year was it that they knocked it down? Yet, its memory's
   as fresh
As the inky smell of new pound notes - which interferes with the beer-
   and-whiskey
Tang of now, like two dogs meeting in the revolutionary 69 of a long sniff,
Or cattle jostling shit-stained flanks in the Pound. For *pound*, as some wag
Interrupted, was an off-shoot of the Falls, from the Irish, *fál*, a hedge;
Hence, *any kind of enclosed thing*, its twigs and branches commemorated
By the soldiers' drab and olive camouflage, as they try to melt

Into a brick wall; red coats might be better, after all. *At any rate,*
This sergeant's number came up; not a winning one. The bullet had his name
   on it.
Though Sergeant X, as we'll call him, doesn't really feature in the story:
The nub of it is, *This tin can which was heard that night, trundling down*
From the bank, down Balaclava Street. Which thousands heard, and no one ever
Saw. Which was heard for years, any night that trouble might be
Round the corner . . . and when it skittered to a halt, you knew
That someone else had snuffed it: a name drifting like an afterthought,
A scribbled wisp of smoke you try and grasp, as it becomes diminuendo,
   then
Vanishes. For *fál,* is also *frontier, boundary,* as in *the undiscovered country*
From whose bourne no traveller returns, the illegible, thorny hedge of time
   itself –
Heartstopping moments, measured not by the pulse of a wristwatch, nor
The archaic anarchists' alarm-clock, but a mercury tilt device
Which 'only connects' on any given bump on the road. So, by this wingèd
   messenger
The promise 'to pay the bearer' is fulfilled:

As someone buys another round, an Allied Irish Bank ten-pound note
   drowns in
The slops of the counter; a Guinness stain blooms on the artist's impression
Of the sinking of *The Girona*; a tiny foam hisses round the salamander
   brooch
Dredged up to show how love and money endure, beyond death and the
   Armada,
Like the bomb-disposal expert in his suit of salamander-cloth.
Shielded against the blast of time by a strangely mediaeval visor,
He's been outmoded by this jerky robot whose various attachments include
A large hook for turning over corpses that may be booby-trapped;
But I still have this picture of his hands held up to avert the future
In a final act of *No surrender,* as, twisting through the murky fathoms
Of what might have been, he is washed ashore as pearl and coral.

This *strange eruption to our state* is seen in other versions of the Falls:
A no-go area, a ghetto, a demolition zone. For the ghost, as it turns out –
All this according to your man, and I can well believe it – this tin ghost,
Since the streets it haunted were abolished, was never heard again.
The sleeve of Raglan Street has been unravelled; the helmet of Balaclava

Is torn away from the mouth. The dim glow of Garnet has gone out,
And with it, all but the memory of where I lived. I, too, heard the ghost:
A roulette trickle, or the hesitant annunciation of a downpour, ricocheting
Off the window; a goods train shunting distantly into a siding,
Then groaning to a halt; the rainy cries of children after dusk.
For the voice from the grave reverberates in others' mouths, as the sails
Of the whitethorn hedge swell up in a little breeze, and tremble
Like the spiral blossom of Andromeda: so suddenly are shrouds and branches
Hung with street-lights, celebrating all that's lost, as fields are reclaimed
By the Starry Plough. So we name the constellations, to put a shape
On what was there; so, the storyteller picks his way between the isolated
   stars.

But, *Was it really like that?* And, *Is the story true?*
You might as well tear off the iron mask, and find that no one, after all,
Is there: nothing but a cry, a summons, clanking out from the smoke
Of demolition. Like some son looking for his father, or the father for his
   son,
We try to piece together the exploded fragments. Let these broken spars
Stand for the Armada and its proud full sails, for even if
The clock is put to rights, everyone will still believe it's fast:
The barman's shouts of *time* will be ignored in any case, since time
Is conversation; it is the hedge that flits incessantly into the present,
As words blossom from the speakers' mouths, and the flotilla returns to
   harbour,
Long after hours.

MICHAEL LONGLEY

FLEANCE

I entered with a torch before me
And cast my shadow on the backcloth
Momentarily: a handful of words,
One bullet with my initials on it –
And that got stuck in a property tree.

186

I would have caught it between my teeth
Or, a true professional, stood still
While the two poetic murderers
Pinned my silhouette to history
In a shower of accurate daggers.

But as any illusionist might
Unfasten the big sack of darkness,
The ropes and handcuffs, and emerge
Smoking a nonchalant cigarette,
I escaped – only to lose myself.

It took me a lifetime to explore
The dusty warren beneath the stage
With its trapdoor opening on to
All that had happened above my head
Like noises-off or distant weather.

In the empty auditorium I bowed
To one preoccupied caretaker
And, without removing my make-up,
Hurried back to the digs where Banquo
Sat up late with a hole in his head.

DEREK MAHON

THE SPRING VACATION
for Michael Longley

Walking among my own this windy morning
In a tide of sunlight between shower and shower,
I resume my old conspiracy with the wet
Stone and the unwieldy images of the squinting heart.
Once more, as before, I remember not to forget.

There is a perverse pride in being on the side
Of the fallen angels and refusing to get up.

We could *all* be saved by keeping an eye on the hill
At the top of every street, for there it is,
Eternally, if irrelevantly, visible –

But yield instead to the humorous formulae,
The hidden menace in the knowing nod.
Or we keep sullen silence in light and shade,
Rehearsing our astute salvations under
The cold gaze of a sanctimonious God.

One part of my mind must learn to know its place.
The things that happen in the kitchen houses
And echoing back-streets of this desperate city
Should engage more than my casual interest,
Exact more interest than my casual pity.

JOHN HEWITT

A BELFASTMAN ABROAD
ARGUES WITH HIMSELF

Admit the fact, you might have stood your ground
and kept one corner clear for decency,
making no claims, but like a friendly tree,
offering shade to those who'd gather round.
You should have spoken when that evil man
first raised his raucous shout, to all who lied
given the lie direct, that little clan
who later marched for justice, joined with pride.

Now from safe distance, you assert your right
to public rage. This town is, after all,
where I was born and lived for fifty years.
I knew its crooked masters well by sight,
endured its venom and survived its sneers –
I scratch these verses on its flame-scorched wall.

MICHAEL LONGLEY

LETTERS

returning over the nightmare ground
we found the place again . . .
                              Keith Douglas

TO THREE IRISH POETS

I

This, the twentieth day of March
In the first year of my middle age,
Sees me the father of a son:
Now let him in your minds sleep on
Lopsided, underprivileged
And, out of his tight burrow edged,

Your godchild while you think of him
Or, if you can't accept the term,
Don't count the damage but instead
Wet, on me, the baby's head:
About his ears our province reels
Pulsating like his fontanel,

And I, with you, when I baptise
Must calculate, must improvise
The holy water and the font,
Anything else that he may want,
And, 'priest of the muses', mock the
Malevolent *deus loci*.

II

Now that the distant islands rise
Out of the corners of my eyes
And the imagination fills
Bog-meadow and surrounding hills,
I find myself addressing you
As though I'd always wanted to:

In order to take you all in
I've had to get beneath your skin,
To colonise you like a land,
To study each distinctive hand
And, by squatter's rights, inhabit
The letters of its alphabet,

Although when I call him Daniel
(Mother and baby doing well),
Lost relations take their places,
Namesakes and receding faces:
Late travellers on the Underground
People my head like a ghost town.

III

Over the cobbles I recall
Cattle clattering to the North Wall
Till morning and the morning's rain
Rinsed out the zig-zags of the brain,
Conducting excrement and fear
Along that lethal thoroughfare:

Now every lost bedraggled field
Like a mythopoeic bog unfolds
Its gelignite and dumdums:
And should the whole idea become
A vegetable run to seed in
Even our suburban garden,

We understudy for the hare's
Disappearance around corners,
The approximate untold barks
Of the otters we call water-dogs –
A dim reflection of ourselves,
A muddy forepaw that dissolves.

IV

Blood on the kerbstones, and my mind
Dividing like a pavement,

Cracked by the weeds, by the green grass
That covers our necropolis,
The pity, terror . . . What comes next
Is a lacuna in the text,

Only blots of ink conceding
Death or blackout as a reading:
For this, his birthday, must confound
Baedekers of the nightmare ground –
And room for him beneath the hedge
With succour, school and heritage

Is made tonight when I append
Each of your names and name a friend:
For yours, then, and the child's sake
I who have heard the waters break
Claim this my country, though today
Timor mortis conturbat me.

TO JAMES SIMMONS

We were distracted by too many things . . .
the wine, the jokes, the music, fancy gowns.
We were no good as murderers, we were clowns.

– Who stated with the Irish queer
A preference for girls to beer –
Here's an attempt at telling all,
My confession unilateral:
Not that it matters for my part
Because I have your lines by heart,

Because the poetry you write
Is the flicker of a night-light
Picking out where it is able
Objects on the dressing table,
Glancing through the great indoors
Where love and death debate the chores,

And where, beneath a breast, you see
The blue veins in filigree,
The dust in a glass of water,
In a discarded french letter
The millions acting our their last
Collaborations with the past.

Yes, to entertain your buddies
With such transcendental studies
Rather than harmonise with hams
In yards of penitential psalms
I count among your better turns:
Play your guitar while Derry burns,

Pipe us aboard the sinking ship
Two by two . . . But before the trip
A pause, please, while the hundredth line
Squanders itself in facile rhyme –
A spry exposé of our game
But paradigmatic all the same

Like talking on as the twelfth chime
Ends nineteen hundred and ninety-nine,
The millennium and number:
For never milestones, but the camber
Dictates this journey till we tire
(So much for perning in a gyre!):

True to no 'kindred points', astride
No iridescent arc besides,
Each gives the other's lines a twist
Over supper, dinner, breakfast
To make a sort of Moebius Band,
Eternal but quotidian . . .

So, post me some octosyllabics
As redolent of death and sex
Or keep this for the rainy days
When, mindful of the final phase,

We diagnose it a relapse,
A metric following the steps

Of an ageing ballroom dancer
(Words a bow-tie round a cancer):
Or a reasonable way to move –
A Moonlight Saunter out to prove
That poetry, a tongue at play
With lip and tooth, is here to stay.

To exercise in metaphor
Our knockings at the basement door,
A ramrod mounted to invade
The vulva, Hades' palisade,
The Gates of Horn and Ivory
Or the Walls of Londonderry.

TO DEREK MAHON

And did we come into our own
When, minus muse and lexicon,
We traced in August sixty-nine
Our imaginary Peace Line
Around the burnt-out houses of
The Catholics we'd scarcely loved,
Two Sisyphuses come to budge
The sticks and stones of an old grudge,

Two poetic conservatives
In the city of guns and long knives,
Our ears receiving then and there
The stereophonic nightmare
Of the Shankill and the Falls,
Our matches struck on crumbling walls
To light us as we moved at last
Through the back alleys of Belfast?

Why it mattered to have you here
You who journeyed to Inisheer
With me, years back, one Easter when

With MacIntyre and the lone Dane
Our footsteps lifted up the larks,
Echoing off those western rocks
And down that darkening arcade
Hung with the failures of our trade,

Will understand. We were tongue-tied
Companions of the island's dead
In the graveyard among the dunes,
Eavesdroppers on conversations
With a Jesus who spoke Irish –
We were strangers in that parish,
Black tea with bacon and cabbage
For our sacraments and pottage,

Dank blankets making up our Lent
Till, islanders ourselves, we bent
Our knees and cut the watery sod
From the lazy-bed where slept a God
We couldn't count among our friends,
Although we'd taken in our hands
Splinters of driftwood nailed and stuck
On the rim of the Atlantic.

That was Good Friday years ago –
How persistent the undertow
Slapped by currachs ferrying stones,
Moonlight glossing the confusions
Of its each bilingual wave – yes,
We would have lingered there for less . . .
Six islanders for a ten-bob note
Rowed us out to the anchored boat.

TO SEAMUS HEANEY

From Carrigskeewaun in Killadoon
I write, although I'll see you soon,
Hoping this fortnight detonates
Your year in the United States,
Offering you by way of welcome

To the sick counties we call home
The mystical point at which I tire
Of Calor gas and a turf fire.

Till we talk again in Belfast
Pleasanter far to leave the past
Across three acres and two brooks
On holiday in a post box
Which dripping fuchsia bells surround,
Its back to the prevailing wind,
And where sanderlings from Iceland
Court the breakers, take my stand,

Disinfecting with a purer air
That small subconscious cottage where
The Irish poet slams his door
On slow-worm, toad and adder:
Beneath these racing skies it is
A tempting stance indeed – *ipsis*
Hibernicis hiberniores –
Except that we know the old stories,

The midden of cracked hurley sticks
Tied to recall the crucifix,
Of broken bones and lost scruples,
The blackened hearth, the blazing gable's
Telltale cinder where we may
Scorch our shins until that day
We sleepwalk through a No Man's Land
Lipreading to an Orange band.

Continually, therefore, we rehearse
Goodbyes to all our characters
And, since both would have it both ways,
On the oily roll of calmer seas
Launch coffin-ship and life-boat,
Body with soul thus kept afloat,
Mind open like a half-door
To the speckled hill, the plovers' shore.

So let it be the lapwing's cry
That lodges in the throat as I
Raise its alarum from the mud,
Seeking for your sake to conclude
Ulster Poet our Union Title
And prolong this sad recital
By leaving careful footprints round
A wind-encircled burial mound.

TONY HARRISON

THE ACT

for Michael Longley and James Simmons

Newcastle Airport and scarcely 7 a.m.
yet they foot the white line out towards the plane
still reeling (or as if) from last night's FED
or macho marathons in someone's bed.
They scorn the breakfast croissants and drink beer
and who am I to censure or condemn?
I know oblivion's a balm for man's poor brain
and once roistered in male packs as bad as them.
These brews stoke their bravado, numb their fear
but anaesthetise all joy along with pain.

To show they had a weekend cunt or two
they walked as if they'd shagged the whole world stiff.
The squaddies' favourite and much-bandied words
for describing what they'd done on leave to birds
as if it were pub-brawl or DIY
seem to be, I quote, 'bang', 'bash', or 'screw',
if they did anything (a biggish if!)
more than the banter boomed now at the crew
as our plane levels off in a blue sky
along with half-scared cracks on catching syph.

They've lit Full Strengths on DA 141
despite NO SMOKING signs and cabin crew's
polite requests; they want to disobey
because they bow to orders every day.
The soldiers travel pretty light and free
as if they left Newcastle for the sun,
in winter with bare arms that show tattoos.
The stewardesses clearly hate this run,
the squaddies' continuous crude repartee
and constant button pushing for more booze.

I've heard the same crude words and smutty cracks
and seen the same lads on excursion trains
going back via ferry from Stranraer
queuing at breakfast at the BR bar,
cleaning it out of Tartan and Brown Ale.
With numbered kitbags piled on luggage racks
just after breakfast bombed out of their brains,
they balance their empty cans in wobbly stacks.
An old woman, with indulgence for things male,
smiles at them and says, 'They're nobbut wains!'

Kids, mostly cocky Geordies and rough Jocks
with voices coming straight out of their boots,
the voices heard in newsreels about coal
or dockers newly dumped onto the dole
after which the army's the next stop.
One who's breakfasted on Brown Ale cocks
a nail-bitten, nicotined right thumb, and shoots
with loud saliva salvos a red fox
parting the clean green blades of some new crop
planted by farm families with old roots.

A card! The stewardesses almost throw it
into our laps not wanting to come near
to groping soldiers. We write each fact
we're required to enter by 'The Act':
profession; place of birth; purpose of visit.
The rowdy squaddy, though he doesn't know it
(and if he did he'd brand the freak as 'queer'),

is sitting next to one who enters 'poet'
where he puts 'Forces'. But what is it?
My purpose? His? *What* are we doing here?

Being a photographer seems bad enough.
God knows the catcalls that a poet would get!
Newcastle-bound for leave the soldiers rag
the press photographer about his bag
and call him Gert or Daisy, and all laugh.
They shout at him in accents they'd dub 'pouf'
Yoo hoo, hinny! Like your handbag pet!
Though what he's snapped has made him just as tough
and his handbag hardware could well photograph
these laughing features when they're cold and set.

I don't like the thought of these lads manning blocks
but saw them as you drove me to my flight,
now khakied up, not kaylied but alert,
their minds on something else than Scotch or skirt,
their elbows bending now to cradle guns.
The road's through deep green fields and wheeling flocks
of lapwings soaring, not the sort of sight
the sentry looks for in his narrow box.
'Cursed by dullards whom no cannon stuns'
I quote. They won't read what we three write.

They occupy NO SMOKING seats and smoke,
commandos free a few days from command
which cries for licence and I watch them cram
anything boozeable, Brown Ale to Babycham,
into their hardened innards, and they drain
whisky/lemonade, Bacardi/Coke,
double after double, one in either hand,
boys' drinks spirit-spiked for the real *bloke!*
Neither passengers nor cabin crew complain
as the squaddies keep on smoking as we land.

And as the morning Belfast plane descends
on Newcastle and one soldier looks,
with tears, on what he greets as 'Geordie grass'

and rakes the airport terrace for 'wor lass'
and another hollers to his noisy mates
he's going to have before their short leave ends
'firkins of fucking FED, fantastic fucks!'
I wish for you, my Ulster poet friends,
pleasures with no rough strife, no iron gates,
and letter boxes wide enough for books.

MICHAEL LONGLEY

ALTERA CITHERA

A change of tune, then,
On another zither,
A new aesthetic, or
The same old songs
That are out of key,
Unwashed by epic oceans
And dipped by love
In lyric waters only?

> Given under our hand
> (With a ballpoint pen)
> After the Latin of Gaius
> Sextus Propertius,
> An old friend, the shadow
> Of his former self
> Who – and this I append
> Without his permission –

Loaded the dice before
He put them in his sling
And aimed at history,
Bringing to the ground
Like lovers Caesar,
Soldiers, politicians
And all the dreary
Epics of the muscle-bound.

199

DEREK MAHON

THE LAST OF THE FIRE KINGS

I want to be
Like the man who descends
At two milk churns

With a bulging
String bag and vanishes
Where the lane turns,

Or the man
Who drops at night
From a moving train

And strikes out over the fields
Where fireflies glow
Not knowing a word of the language.

Either way, I am
Through with history –
Who lives by the sword

Dies by the sword.
Last of the fire kings, I shall
Break with tradition and

Die by my own hand
Rather than perpetuate
The barbarous cycle.

Five years I have reigned
During which time
I have lain awake each night

And prowled by day
In the sacred grove
For fear of the usurper,

Perfecting my cold dream
Of a place out of time,
A palace of porcelain

Where the frugivorous
Inheritors recline
In their rich fabrics
Far from the sea.

But the fire-loving
People, rightly perhaps,
Will not countenance this,

Demanding that I inhabit,
Like them, a world of
Sirens, bin-lids
And bricked-up windows –

Not to release them
From the ancient curse
But to die their creature and be thankful.

JOHN HEWITT

THE DILEMMA

Born in this island, maimed by history
and creed-infected, by my father taught
the stubborn habit of unfettered thought
I dreamed, like him, all people should be free.
So, while my logic steered me well outside
that ailing church which claims dominion
over the questing spirit, I denied
all credence to the state by rebels won
from a torn nation, rigged to guard their gain,
though they assert their love of liberty,

which craft has narrowed to a fear of Rome.
So, since this ruptured country is my home,
it long has been my bitter luck to be
caught in the crossfire of their false campaign.

PAUL MULDOON

THE BOUNDARY COMMISSION

You remember that village where the border ran
Down the middle of the street,
With the butcher and baker in different states?
Today he remarked how a shower of rain

Had stopped so cleanly across Golightly's lane
It might have been a wall of glass
That had toppled over. He stood there, for ages,
To wonder which side, if any, he should be on.

PAUL DURCAN

IN MEMORY: THE MIAMI SHOWBAND:
MASSACRED 31 JULY 1975

Beautiful are the feet of them that preach the gospel of peace,
Of them that bring glad tidings of good things

In a public house, darkly-lit, a patriotic (sic)
Versifier whines into my face: 'You must take one side
Or the other, or you're but a fucking romantic.'
His eyes glitter hate and ambition, porter and whiskey,
And I realize that he is blind to the braille connection
Between a music and a music-maker.
'You must take one side or the other
Or you're but a fucking romantic':

The whine is icy
And his eyes hang loose like sheets from poles
On a bare wet hillside in winter
And his mouth gapes like a cave in ice;
It is a whine in the crotch of whose fear
Is fondled a dream-gun blood-smeared;
It is in war – not poetry or music –
That men find their niche, their glory hole;
Like most of his fellows
He will abide no contradiction in the mind:
He whines: 'If there is birth, there cannot be death'
And – jabbing a hysterical forefinger into my nose and eyes –
'If there is death, there cannot be birth'.
Peace to the souls of those who unlike my confrère
Were true to their trade
Despite death-dealing blackmail by fanatics and racists:
You made music, and that was all: You were realists
And beautiful were your feet.

SEAMUS HEANEY

PUNISHMENT

I can feel the tug
of the halter at the nape
of her neck, the wind
on her naked front.

It blows her nipples
to amber beads,
it shakes the frail rigging
of her ribs.

I can see her drowned
body in the bog,
the weighing stone,
the floating rods and boughs.

Under which at first
she was a barked sapling
that is dug up
oak-bone, brain-firkin:

her shaved head
like a stubble of black corn,
her blindfold a soiled bandage,
her noose a ring

to store
the memories of love.
Little adulteress,
before they punished you

you were flaxen-haired,
undernourished, and your
tar-black face was beautiful.
My poor scapegoat,

I almost love you
but would have cast, I know,
the stones of silence.
I am the artful voyeur

of your brain's exposed
and darkened combs,
your muscles' webbing
and all your numbered bones:

I who have stood dumb
when your betraying sisters,
cauled in tar,
wept by the railings,

who would connive
in civilized outrage
yet understand the exact
and tribal, intimate revenge.

IN MEMORIAM FRANCIS LEDWIDGE

killed in France 31 July 1917

The bronze soldier hitches a bronze cape
That crumples stiffly in imagined wind
No matter how the real winds buff and sweep
His sudden hunkering run, forever craned

Over Flanders. Helmet and haversack,
The gun's firm slope from butt to bayonet,
The loyal, fallen names on the embossed plaque –
It all meant little to the worried pet

I was in nineteen forty-six or seven,
Gripping my Aunt Mary by the hand
Along the Portstewart prom, then round the crescent
To thread the Castle Walk out to the strand.

The pilot from Coleraine sailed to the coal-boat.
Courting couples rose out of the scooped dunes.
A farmer stripped to his studs and shiny waistcoat
Rolled the trousers down on his timid shins.

At night when coloured bulbs strung out the sea-front
Country voices rose from a cliff-top shelter
With news of a great litter – 'We'll pet the runt!' –
And barbed wire that had torn a Friesian's elder.

Francis Ledwidge, you courted at the seaside
Beyond Drogheda one Sunday afternoon.
Literary, sweet-talking, countrified,
You pedalled out the leafy road from Slane

Where you belonged, among the dolorous
And lovely: the May altar of wild flowers,
Easter water sprinkled in outhouses,
Mass-rocks and hill-top raths and raftered byres.

I think of you in your Tommy's uniform,
A haunted Catholic face, pallid and brave,

205

Ghosting the trenches with a bloom of hawthorn
Or silence cored from a Boyne passage-grave.

It's summer, nineteen-fifteen. I see the girl
My aunt was then, herding on the long acre.
Behind a low bush in the Dardanelles
You suck stones to make your dry mouth water.

It's nineteen-seventeen. She still herds cows
But a big strafe puts the candles out in Ypres:
'My soul is by the Boyne, cutting new meadows . . .
My country wears her confirmation dress.'

'To be called a British soldier while my country
Has no place among nations . . . ' You were rent
By shrapnel six weeks later. 'I am sorry
That party politics should divide our tents.'

In you, our dead enigma, all the strains
Criss-cross in useless equilibrium
And as the wind tunes through this vigilant bronze
I hear again the sure confusing drum

You followed from Boyne water to the Balkans
But miss the twilit note your flute should sound.
You were not keyed or pitched like these true-blue ones
Though all of you consort now underground.

FRANK ORMSBY

THE WAR PHOTOGRAPHERS

Working with one eye closed or heads buried
under their drapes, they focus to preserve
the drowned shell-hole, the salient's rubble of dead,
the bleached bones of sepoys torn from the earth.

Their stills haunt us: a stretcher piled with skulls
at Cold Harbour, graves in a barren wood
that in one hour's carnage lost its name
to history and the world's memory of death.

The worst has happened, they confirm the worst:
but show us too the makeshift hospital,
the sad errand of the hospital van
among the ruins. Also enough of sky
to suggest the infinity of angles,

that behind sandbags, under the hostile towers
someone is finding time for a wry note
on bowel movements, an entry that affirms
the loved salience of what is always there:
flower of Auschwitz, bird of the Western Front.

MICHAEL LONGLEY

THE WAR POETS

Unmarked were the bodies of the soldier-poets
For shrapnel opened up again the fontanel
Like a hailstone melting towards deep water
At the bottom of a well, or a mosquito
Balancing its tiny shadow above the lip.

It was rushes of air that took the breath away
As though curtains were drawn suddenly aside
And darkness streamed into the dormitory
Where everybody talked about the war ending
And always it would be the last week of the war.

CIARAN CARSON

BELFAST CONFETTI

Suddenly as the riot squad moved in, it was raining exclamation marks,
Nuts, bolts, nails, car-keys. A fount of broken type. And the explosion
Itself – an asterisk on the map. This hyphenated line, a burst of rapid fire . . .
I was trying to complete a sentence in my head, but it kept stuttering,
All the alleyways and side-streets blocked with stops and colons.

I know this labyrinth so well – Balaclava, Raglan, Inkerman, Odessa
    Street –
Why can't I escape? Every move is punctuated. Crimea Street. Dead
    end again.
A Saracen, Kremlin-2 mesh. Makrolon face-shields. Walkie-talkies.
    What is
My name? Where am I coming from? Where am I going? A fusillade of
    question-marks.

GEORGE BUCHANAN

REVOLUTIONARY REVOLUTION

Insidious in ways no gunfire touches, revolution
must have revolution in it too,
not be the same old murder.

The cry for a tender
style has never been so truly from the heart,
so treated as nothing much.

A SPEAKER IN THE SQUARE

We hear her in the square. At two o'clock
fawn moths in thousands enter shops and cars.

There's a rush to shut the windows. Then
she steps to the platform without the brazen bearing
of usual parliament men. She can't do
miracles and sway the crowd; make listeners
advocates. She is heard
less for what she says than for her tossing
hair. Her love is to ideas,
the devastating love. Richness of feeling
is the prosperity she advocates.
'We won't permit a frozen future
or a manipulated one. Rebel.
Not by knifing constables, filling
the square with shots. No military coup.
Only a rise in temperature.
Freedom isn't freedom if people are cold.
Truth isn't truth if told by citizens
who don't care. We need an illumination
from glances. Human sunlight . . .'

Newspapers say it's true: WAR IS OFF.
For how long? History hasn't yet related.
Can the Prime Minister stay in office if
no war is threatened? He faces novel problems
when the electors aren't too deeply worried.
Without a mandate to be frivolous
he feels he must resign.

Author of elegant iambics, she
comes in a wintry moment, melts the ice
in a masculine country famous for reserve,
is carried to power by a flock of writers.
The Poetic State is founded.

SEAMUS HEANEY

SANDSTONE KEEPSAKE

It is a kind of chalky russet
solidified gourd, sedimentary
and so reliably dense and bricky
I often clasp it and throw it from hand to hand.

It was ruddier, with an underwater
hint of contusion, when I lifted it,
wading a shingle beach on Inishowen.
Across the estuary light after light

came on silently round the perimeter
of the camp. A stone from Phlegethon,
bloodied on the bed of hell's hot river?
Evening frost and the salt water

made my hand smoke, as if I'd plucked the heart
that damned Guy de Montfort to the boiling flood –
but not really, though I remembered
his victim's heart in its casket, long venerated.

Anyhow, there I was with the wet red stone
in my hand, staring across at the watch-towers
from my free state of image and allusion,
swooped on, then dropped by trained binoculars:

a silhouette not worth bothering about,
out for the evening in scarf and waders
and not about to set times wrong or right,
stooping along, one of the venerators.

TOM PAULIN

WHERE ART IS A MIDWIFE

In the third decade of March,
A Tuesday in the town of Z—

The censors are on day-release.
They must learn about literature.

There are things called ironies,
Also symbols, which carry meaning.

The types of ambiguity
Are as numerous as the enemies

Of the state. Formal and bourgeois,
Sonnets sing of the old order,

Its lost gardens where white ladies
Are served wine in the subtle shade.

This poem about a bear
Is not a poem about a bear.

It might be termed a satire
On a loyal friend. Do I need

To spell it out? Is it possible
That none of you can understand?

W. R. RODGERS

HOME THOUGHTS FROM ABROAD

Hearing, this June day, the thin thunder
Of far-off invective and old denunciation

Lambasting and lambegging the homeland,
I think of that brave man Paisley, eyeless
In Gaza, with a daisy-chain of millstones
Round his neck; groping, like blind Samson,
For the soapy pillars and greased poles of lightning
To pull them down in rains and borborygmic roars
Of rhetoric. (There but for the grace of God
Goes God.) I like his people and I like his guts
But I dislike his gods who always end
In gun-play. Some day, of course, he'll be one
With the old giants of Ireland – such as
Denis of the Drought, or Iron-Buttocks –
Who had at last to be reduced to size,
Quietly shrunken into 'wee people'
And put out to grass on the hills for good,
Minimized like cars or skirts or mums;
Photostated to fit a literate age
And filed safely away on the dark shelves
Of memory; preserved in ink, oak-gall,
Alcohol, aspic, piety, wit. A pity,
Perhaps, if it is drama one wants. But,
Look at it this way: in this day and age
We can't really have giants lumbering
All over the place, cluttering it up,
With hair like ropes, flutes like telegraph poles,
And feet like tramcars, intent only on dogging
The fled horse of history and the Boyne.
So today across the Irish Sea I wave
And wish him well from the bottom of my heart
Where truth lies bleeding, its ear-drums burst
By the blatter of his hand-me-down talk.
In fond memory of his last stand
I dedicate this contraceptive pill
Of poetry to his unborn followers,
And I place
This bunch of beget-me-nots on his grave.

PAUL MULDOON

from 7 MIDDAGH STREET

And were Yeats living at this hour
it should be in some ruined tower

not malachited Ballylee
where he paid out to those below

one gilt-edged scroll from his pencil
as though he were part-Rapunzel

and partly Delphic oracle.
As for his crass, rhetorical

posturing, 'Did that play of mine
send out certain men (*certain* men?)

the English shot . . . ?'
the answer is 'Certainly not'.

If Yeats had saved his pencil-lead
would certain men have stayed in bed?

For history's a twisted root
with art its small, translucent fruit

and never the other way round.
The roots by which we were once bound

are severed here, in any case,
and we are all now dispossessed;

prince, poet, construction worker,
salesman, soda fountain jerker –

all equally isolated.
Each loads flour, sugar and salted

beef into a covered wagon
and strikes out for his Oregon,

each straining for the ghostly axe
of a huge, blond-haired lumberjack.

. . . .

LOUIS

. . . When Hart Crane fell
from the *Orizaba*
it was into the *trou normand* of the well

at Carrickfergus castle.
All very Ovidian,
as the ghostly
Healfdene

once remarked of both sorts of kipper
we were forced to eat
at supper

every night in Reykjavik;
one tasted of toe-nails, one of the thick
skin on the soles of the feet.

★

He now affects an ulster lined with coypu
and sashays like an albino rabbit
down the same Fifth Avenue
where Avida Dollars
once squired an ocelot
on a solid
gold chain snaffled from Bonwit Teller's.
It seems that Scott Fitzgerald wrote *Ivanhoe*
or the *Rubáiyát*
and Chester Kallman = Agape.

★

Wystan likes to tell how he lost his faith
in human nature

in a movie-theatre
at 85th

and York, where the neighbourhood Huns
had taken a break from baking buns

to egg
on Hitler to his *Sieg*

im Poland; the heavy bear that went to bed
with Delmore Schwartz was bad

and the rye in Yorkville's *Schwartzbrot*
shot through with ergot.

Since when he's set himself up as a stylite
waiting for hostilities

to cease, a Dutch master
intent only on painting an oyster

or lemon
(all those afternoons in the Ashmolean)

or the slur of light in a red goblet
while Montagues and Capulets

run riot, as they did five years ago
in the Short Strand and Sandy Row.

Then my father preached 'Forget the past'
and episcopized

into the wind
and again refused to sign the Covenant;

though the seam of gold a Unitedman strikes
in Wicklow in 1796

which Parnell will later pan and assay
to make a ring for Kitty O'Shea

was well and truly played
out, no bishop could ever quite contemplate

a life merely nasty, British and short.
Delmore was ushered

from that same movie-theatre
with 'Everything you do matters';

the displacement of soap-suds in a basin
may have some repercussion

for a distant ship:
only last night I tried to butt the uneven

pages of a *Belfast News-Letter* from 1937
into some sort of shape . . .

★

> *Imagine a great white highway*
> *a quarter of a mile broad*
> *extending the length of Ireland*
> *from the Giant's Causeway*
> *to Mizen Head*
> *and you can grasp the magnitude*
> *of our annual output of linen.*

★

Among the blue flowers of the flax a linnet
sang out 'Lundy'

at the implications of that bleach-
green. 'It was merely a figure of speech.'

'Call it what you like.
The grey skies of an Irish Republic

'are as nothing compared to this blue dome.'
He tailed off over the flax-dam

to return with a charm of goldfinches
who assailed me with their 'Not an inch'

and their 'No', and yet again, 'No'.
As they asperged me with kerosene

I recognized the voice of Sir Edward Carson;
'Bid me strike a match and blow.'

★

In dreams begin responsibilities;
it was on account of just such an allegory
that Lorca
was riddled with bullets

and lay mouth-down
in the fickle shadow of his own blood.
As the drunken soldiers of the *Gypsy Ballads*
started back for town

they heard him calling through the mist,
'When I die leave the balcony shutters open.'
For poetry *can* make things happen –
not only can, but *must* –

and the very painting of that oyster
is in itself a political gesture.

As O'Daly well knows. It was in the olive-grove
where Lorca's buried

that he envisaged *Two Pieces of Bread*
Expressing the Idea of Love

with its miniature duellists and chess-pawn
expressing also his idea of Spain.
(If only he were here
today to make his meaning absolutely clear.)

So that, for me, brandy and smoked
quail and a crumpled baguette
conjure O'Daly, then themselves, then Beckett's
'¡Uptherepublic!',

then Beatrice and Benedick
in the back seat of Eleanor's mother's Pontiac.

★

After drinking all night in a Sands Street shebeen
where a sailor played a melodeon
made from a merman's spine
I left by the back door of Muldoon's

(it might have been the Rotterdam)
on a Monday morning, falling in with
the thousands of shipyardmen who tramped
towards the front gates of Harland and Wolff.

The one-eyed foreman had strayed out of Homer;
'MacNeice? That's a Fenian name.'
As if to say, 'None of your sort, none of you

will as much as go for a rubber hammer
never mind chalk a rivet, never mind caulk a seam
on the quinquereme of Nineveh.'

CIARAN CARSON

THE IRISH FOR NO

Was it a vision, or a waking dream? I heard her voice before I saw
What looked like the balcony scene in *Romeo and Juliet*, except Romeo
Seemed to have shinned up a pipe and was inside arguing with her. The casements
Were wide open and I could see some Japanese-style wall-hangings, the dangling
Quotation marks of a yin-yang mobile. *It's got nothing*, she was snarling, *nothing*
To do with politics, and, before the bamboo curtain came down,
That goes for you too!

It was time to turn into the dog's-leg short-cut from Chlorine Gardens
Into Cloreen Park, where you might see an *Ulster Says No* scrawled on the side
Of the power-block – which immediately reminds me of the Eglantine Inn
Just on the corner: on the missing *h* of Cloreen, you might say. We were debating,
Bacchus and the pards and me, how to render *The Ulster Bank – the Bank*
That Likes to Say Yes into Irish, and whether eglantine was alien to Ireland.
I cannot see what flowers are at my feet, when *yes* is the verb repeated,
Not exactly yes, but phatic nods and whispers. *The Bank That Answers All*
Your Questions, maybe? That Greek portico of Mourne granite, dazzling
With promises and feldspar, mirrors you in the Delphic black of its windows.

And the bruised pansies of the funeral parlour are dying in reversed gold letters,
The long sigh of the afternoon is not yet complete on the promontory where the victim,
A corporal in the UDR from Lisbellaw, was last seen having driven over half
Of Ulster, a legally-held gun was found and the incidence of stress came up
On the headland which shadows Larne Harbour and the black pitch of warehouses.

There is a melancholy blast of diesel, a puff of smoke which might be
    black or white.
So the harbour slips away to perilous seas as things remain unsolved; we
    listen
To the *ex cathedra* of the fog-horn, and *drink and leave the world unseen* –

What's all this to the Belfast business-man who drilled
Thirteen holes in his head with a Black & Decker? It was just a normal
    morning
When they came. The tennis-court shone with dew or frost, a little
    before dawn.
The border, it seemed, was not yet crossed: the Milky Way trailed
    snowy brambles,
The stars clustered thick as blackberries. They opened the door into the
    dark:
The murmurous haunt of flies on summer eves. Empty jam-jars.
Mish-mash. Hotch-potch. And now you rub your eyes and get acquainted
    with the light
A dust of something reminiscent drowses over the garage smell of creosote,
The concrete: blue clouds in porcelain, a paint-brush steeped in a
    chipped cup;
Staples hyphenate a wet cardboard box as the upturned can of oil still spills
And the unfed cat toys with the yin-yang of a tennis-ball, debating
    whether *yes* is *no.*

TOM PAULIN

A NATION, YET AGAIN
after Pushkin

That kitsch lumber-room is stacked
with a parnassian dialect:
'love, hope, and quiet reputation
kissed us for a short season
and the gamey letters that we swopped,
in clipped verse, soon had to stop.'
No one, then, praised either side,

though some dipped down among the shades
to find Aeneas and to file
a delicate, a tough, new style
that draws the language to the light
and purifies its tribal rites.
I'm tense now: talk of sharing power,
prophecies of civil war,
new reasons for a secular
mode of voicing the word *nation*
set us on edge, this generation,
and force the poet to play traitor
or act the half-sure legislator.
No matter; there's a classic form
that's in the blood, that makes me warm
to better, raise, build up, refine
whatever gabbles without discipline:
see, it takes me now, these hands stir
to bind the northern to the southern stars.

YEVGENY YEVTUSHENKO

PUSHKIN IN BELFAST

I am a man, and thereby I am tragic.
I am a man, and I am accustomed to death.
In death as such is not the essence of tragedy.
Suicides look forward to dying.
But to grow accustomed to killing –
God forbid! Nothing is more terrible than habit.

He who exults at another's tragedy
will be punished for his arrogance.
But who are you? The shadow of all who exist.
Without the tragedies of others you cannot be.
Be careful with another's tragedy,
Do not inflame their suffering through tactlessness.

Tactless I was, it seems, in Belfast,
mistakenly I took my camera,
substituting it, tourist-style, for sight,
and now for this, swearing an English oath,
a pimply little soldier waved
his sub-machine-gun at me.

I could understand him. Who wants
to figure in an unflattering photo!
Poor boy . . . It was not his fault . . . Caught
in an ancient conflict of Christians
he awaited with trembling back in spotted
combat jacket a bullet from a window.

Well, what could he foresee or see!
The windowpanes around were mirror-like,
as if they were death's sunglasses,
and from behind them, unseen but seeing,
the dim whites of rifles' eyes
sought out all those who profess a different faith.

However this age of progress may be extolled,
terror is to be found not just in Belfast.
The fear of losing one's job – is not this terror?
And how many have noiselessly been broken
by the terror of earning a living, of life,
a terror bloodless only for so long?

So why should one take offence in Belfast
amid terror in its pure form?
If one is alive, it is a sin to take offence.
Along a university corridor
I walked, seeking the answer to so much,
and suddenly heard something bigger than a bomb.

Through a door: 'Frost and sun – a marvellous day',
and then: 'You are still dozing, my charming friend . . . '
A lecture on Pushkin was going on amid
all the street shootings, and the letter bombs,

and the smell of dynamite on the breeze,
and fear of what may be to come.

Before the next bomb is thrown:
'It's time, my friend – the heart seeks peace . . . '
But where is peace? In scaffolding like this?
It's not some vulgar little detective story
the Irish boy is reading haltingly:
' . . . and blood-stained youths beheld'.

Through the keyhole I could see a young Irish girl
taking it all down scrupulously in her notebook.
She found the names quite difficult,
such as, well, let's say: 'Küchelbecker',
but, holding her pen back for a moment,
she was too shy to ask how it is spelled.

The lecturer was speaking about the Decembrists,
smoothing the sideburns on the ridges of his
handsome, embattled à la Gladstone, face.
He had touched, exciting his hearers' attention,
on D'Anthès and Natalia Nikolaevna,
but suddenly glanced sighing at his watch.

I walked with the crowd of Belfast students,
whispering: ' . . . and on the ruins of autocracy . . . '
The terror around was as customary as life.
The girl students twittered . . . Who shall blame them
for not knowing that in the next lecture
Pushkin will be killed?

(translated by Marcus Wheeler)

TOM PAULIN

A WRITTEN ANSWER

This poem by Rupert Brookeborough
is all about fishing and the stout B-men

(they live for always in our hearts,
their only crime was being loyal),
there is a lough in it and stacks of rivers,
also a brave wee hymn to the sten-gun.
The poet describes Gough of the Curragh
and by his use of many metric arts
he designs a fictionary universe
which has its own laws and isn't quite
the same as this place that we call real.
His use of metonymy is pretty desperate
and the green symbolism's a contradiction,
but I like his image of the elm and chestnut,
for to me this author is a fly man
and the critics yonder say his work is all right.

SEAMUS HEANEY

EXPOSURE

It is December in Wicklow:
Alders dripping, birches
Inheriting the last light,
The ash tree cold to look at.

A comet that was lost
Should be visible at sunset,
Those million tons of light
Like a glimmer of haws and rose-hips,

And I sometimes see a falling star.
If I could come on meteorite!
Instead I walk through damp leaves,
Husks, the spent flukes of autumn,

Imagining a hero
On some muddy compound,

His gift like a slingstone
Whirled for the desperate.

How did I end up like this?
I often think of my friends'
Beautiful prismatic counselling
And the anvil brains of some who hate me

As I sit weighing and weighing
My responsible *tristia*.
For what? For the ear? For the people?
For what is said behind-backs?

Rain comes down through the alders,
Its low conducive voices
Mutter about let-downs and erosions
And yet each drop recalls

The diamond absolutes.
I am neither internee nor informer;
An inner émigré, grown long-haired
And thoughtful; a wood-kerne

Escaped from the massacre,
Taking protective colouring
From bole and bark, feeling
Every wind that blows;

Who, blowing up these sparks
For their meagre heat, have missed
The once-in-a-lifetime portent,
The comet's pulsing rose.

FROM THE FRONTIER OF WRITING

The tightness and the nilness round that space
when the car stops in the road, the troops inspect
its make and number and, as one bends his face

towards your window, you catch sight of more
on a hill beyond, eyeing with intent
down cradled guns that hold you under cover

and everything is pure interrogation
until a rifle motions and you move
with guarded unconcerned acceleration –

a little emptier, a little spent
as always by that quiver in the self,
subjugated, yes, and obedient.

So you drive on to the frontier of writing
where it happens again. The guns on tripods;
the sergeant with his on-off mike repeating

data about you, waiting for the squawk
of clearance; the marksman training down
out of the sun upon you like a hawk.

And suddenly you're through, arraigned yet freed,
as if you'd passed from behind a waterfall
on the black current of a tarmac road

past armour-plated vehicles, out between
the posted soldiers flowing and receding
like tree shadows into the polished windscreen.

from STATION ISLAND

VIII

Black water. White waves. Furrows snowcapped.
A magpie flew from the basilica
and staggered in the granite airy space
I was staring into, on my knees
at the hard mouth of St Brigid's Bed.
I came to and there at the bed's stone hub
was my archaeologist, very like himself,

with his scribe's face smiling its straight-lipped smile,
starting at the sight of me with the same old
pretence of amazement, so that the wing
of woodkerne's hair fanned down over his brow.
And then as if a shower were blackening
already blackened stubble, the dark weather
of his unspoken pain came over him.
A pilgrim bent and whispering on his rounds
inside the bed passed between us slowly.

'Those dreamy stars that pulsed across the screen
beside you in the ward – your heartbeats, Tom, I mean –
scared me the way they stripped things naked.
My banter failed too early in that visit.
I could not take my eyes off the machine.
I had to head back straight away to Dublin,
guilty and empty, feeling I had said nothing
and that, as usual, I had somehow broken
covenants, and failed an obligation.
I half knew we would never meet again . . .
Did our long gaze and last handshake contain
nothing to appease that recognition?'

'Nothing at all. But familiar stone
had me half numbed to face the thing alone.
I loved my still-faced archaeology.
The small crab-apple physiognomies
on high crosses, carved heads in abbeys . . .
Why else dig in for years in that hard place
in a muck of bigotry under the walls
picking through shards and Williamite cannon balls?
But all that we just turned to banter too.
I felt that I should have seen far more of you
and maybe would have – but dead at thirty-two!
Ah poet, lucky poet, tell me why
what seemed deserved and promised passed me by?'

I could not speak. I saw a hoard of black
basalt axe heads, smooth as a beetle's back,
a cairn of stone force that might detonate,

the eggs of danger. And then I saw a face
he had once given me, a plaster cast
of an abbess, done by the Gowran master,
mild-mouthed and cowled, a character of grace.
'Your gift will be a candle in our house.'
But he had gone when I looked to meet his eyes
and hunkering instead there in his place
was a bleeding, pale-faced boy, plastered in mud.
'The red-hot pokers blazed a lovely red
in Jerpoint the Sunday I was murdered,'
he said quietly. 'Now do you remember?
You were there with poets when you got the word
and stayed there with them, while your own flesh and blood
was carted to Bellaghy from the Fews.
They showed more agitation at the news
than you did.'
                    'But they were getting crisis
first-hand, Colum, they had happened in on
live sectarian assassination.
I was dumb, encountering what was destined.'
And so I pleaded with my second cousin.
'I kept seeing a grey stretch of Lough Beg
and the strand empty at daybreak.
I felt like the bottom of a dried-up lake.'

'You saw that, and you wrote that – not the fact.
You confused evasion and artistic tact.
The Protestant who shot me through the head
I accuse directly, but indirectly, you
who now atone perhaps upon this bed
for the way you whitewashed ugliness and drew
the lovely blinds of the *Purgatorio*
and saccharined my death with morning dew.'

Then I seemed to waken out of sleep
among more pilgrims whom I did not know
drifting to the hostel for the night.

DEREK MAHON

RAGE FOR ORDER

Somewhere beyond the scorched gable end and the burnt-out buses
  there is a poet indulging
    his wretched rage for order –
or not as the case may be; for his
    is a dying art,
  an eddy of semantic scruples
    in an unstructurable sea.

    He is far from his people,
and the fitful glare of his high window is as
    nothing to our scattered glass.

His posture is grandiloquent and deprecating, like this,
    his diet ashes,
his talk of justice and his mother
    the rhetorical device
  of an etiolated emperor –
Nero if you prefer, no mother there.

  ' . . . and this in the face of love,
  death, and the wages of the poor . . . '

If he is silent, it is the silence of enforced humility;
  if anxious to be heard, it is the anxiety
    of a last word
when the drums start; for his is a dying art.

Now watch me as I make history. Watch as I tear down
  to build up with a desperate love,
    knowing it cannot be
  long now till I have need of his
    desperate ironies.

YEVGENY YEVTUSHENKO

ULSTER SAFARI

1

The fate of lions, like the fate of men, is thorny.
On a false couch of Irish grass,
like the mildest of present-day terrorists,
lie – stretched out – lions.
Indifferently the lions munch their breakfasts,
and each one is like a dumb sand-dune.
The lions await the call of Africa,
that should summon them home.

Brother lion, behind your wire fence,
you have not ceased to be real,
but each claw of yours, probing the iron,
has long understood that you are under arrest.

Sister lioness, you are by nature easy-going,
the tourists do not for long upset you;
but how will you teach your cubs, born unfree,
to hunt freely?
But she gets up – offended seemingly . . .
A shudder of wariness furrows her tail,
and suddenly she leaps at the car,
extending her body, grown steely in flight.
Did I see you tremble, madam chauffeur?
Are you afraid?
And you, with your blue eyes, are only twenty-three,
and your forefathers were Irish robbers.
If you've agreed to drive, then drive!
You too are inside this cage,
the difference only being that you're behind the wheel.
How strong is the window glass?
Suppose the clutch jams . . . You and I are
alone with a lioness.
And suddenly onto the glass her ginger paw

230

drops languidly, obliquely,
and the lioness presses against the glass as if crying
and even – or so it seemed to me - whispering.
Of course it was not crying or whispering –
only this hunted woman's visage,
only the terrified bitterness learned by a beast
and a cry, transformed by nature – into a roar.
How much there is that I should like to impart
in our one treasured moment
to you alone, sister lioness,
for you are a woman and will not give me away.

2

I too have a growing cub –
how shall I keep an eye on him?
What will they put into his little head?
What will I put there?
Here I am far from my Russia –
my snowy Africa,
but again I am tormented by thoughts of my son,
of the future of all children.
Here, both famed and reviled,
maddened by the gunfire cracks and flashes,
I feel confined by barbed fame,
like a lion in a mousetrap.
And some incite me to yap,
to prove my right to roar,
but that's all the same
as to make a lion in Ireland
yap at Africa.
I am begged by photographers,
adhesive little ladies,
as if I were a rare Siberian lion,
to show my teeth just for a smile,
but not to roar at them – dear no!
Fame –
for lions' teeth means unemployment.
Trust my words as you would a lion's roar:
a poet is a hunter who is hunted,
and you lions know that too.

Sister lioness, I have been to Londonderry,
where they would shoot up even lions' tails,
where in the night the hands
froze on the steering-wheel
from the uncertainty and emptiness.
And our headlights tore off the boyish face,
with peasant's freckles and rain-bespattered,
of a soldier in camouflage jacket
who jumped out, levelling his gun at us.
'Switch off your lights!' he shouted. 'Quick!'
He grabbed our papers, shaken by fear.
'Sorry. I thought you might be terrorists.
They blind us with their headlights.
So you're from Russia?'
　'Ah-ha, from Russia.'
'Why are you here?'
　'I was invited to read my poems.'
'Poems? In Derry? Boy! and were they pleased to see you?
This is a place for gravediggers, not poets.'
'Where are the hotels here?'
　'What hotels?
All the hotels have long since gone sky-high.'
'Well, is there a café then?'
'They've been blown up, too.
True, there's a Chinese restaurant,
but the food – O God!
Some sort of frogs or worms or snakes.
Can you use chopsticks?'
　'Yes, I can.'
And then I heard him whisper sadly:
'These Russkies are a pack of loonies,
that's for sure.'

4

And in the little China Garden restaurant
we perched somewhere to one side
as if we were pilgrims
who had organised themselves a feast
　in time of plague.

And we were tormented
not by octopus, scorpion or trepang –
but only by the way in which the curtain
in a window smashed by an explosion
was tossed about by the wind.
Sitting at the shaky little table,
around which the war went on invisibly,
I, half-tipsy, felt myself
now a Catholic, now a Protestant.
My destiny of fame
here seemed quite valueless.
'I am of the Orthodox!' –
I wanted to shout for the first time in my life.
But we did not linger
and – albeit shakily –
we headed off
in the direction from which,
or so it seemed,
shots could be heard in the distance.
O night streets of Londonderry,
    like repositories of darkness,
where in every tree
there is human fear of humans,
where casements are bricked up
    against bullets in the night,
and all these bricks have been filched
from the ruins of other houses.
Everything has been blown up:
the council chamber, and the courthouse,
and honour, and the flag, and the cross,
and the transparent lie according to which
freedom and progress exist.
We walked through the wreckage.
In the night wilderness
an old man with his little dog,
which lifted its leg over the remains of a 'pig',
even had an air of novelty.
And ticking bombs
were not averse to going off somewhere close.
It was a quiet St Bartholomew's night.

5

And the old man with his little dog came up to us,
treading as if in Dante's Inferno,
and told us an Irish ballad,
which I will retell for you.
'There was this Great Dane belonging to a Protestant
which only dimly sensed
   the meaning of God,
while the Catholic's balding mongrel
was not a Catholic, poor dog.
The Great Dane did not boast of its breeding,
nor was the mongrel shy about her lack of it,
and both dogs,
   breaking off the lead,
rushed up to each other,
   as if to freedom,
and from afar eyed one another –
the Romeo and Juliet of Londonderry.
The Catholic man was murdered on a waste lot,
walking his dog one evening.
And the dog howled even at daybreak
if only to attract some idler's notice with her howls,
but her dead master's hand,
now stiffened up,
   would not release the lead.
And in the morning the Protestant took his dog out
after buffing up its gilt collar-studs,
and the dog,
   kindly and simple at heart,
broke from the lead at the mongrel's howl,
and, forgetting it was a Protestant,
licked her face
and set up a joint howl with her.'
The old man ended his tale with a sigh:
'Dogs are purer atheists than us.
God is many-faceted,
   and, if that's right,
He takes after dogs, not men.'

6

So that's what an Ulster safari is about!
Sister lioness,
you will do better to live
in your game reserve
than on an island
    tossing in blood.
So that's what civilisation is about,
when, after months not stirring abroad,
Irish children are ready to seek escape,
clinging
    to your emaciated paps.
This is an accursed atomic Middle Age,
when it is harder for men than for lions to live,
when crosses are marked not in chalk,
    but in blood:
'He is of the wrong faith –
    we must stitch him up.'

I am neither a Protestant nor a Catholic,
but I am scared of a future void,
when all doors will be blown up on which
there has not been time to place a cross.
And what of indifference?
    It drinks and it chews . . .
Will we really live to see an age
when suddenly self-destroying man
will have become a rare species?

And the old man whispers –
    the Londonderry wood demon
with his little dog still in the land of the living:
'Where are we going
    and what do we believe in
amid so many senseless losses?
When man becomes a beast,
then a beast seems human.'
And, only from politeness clenching their jaws,
if pieces of sausage are thrown to them,

the lions
   turn away their noses
from evil-smelling humanity.
                    (*translated by Marcus Wheeler*)

PETER MCDONALD

COUNT DRACULA ENTERTAINS I

Unfortunately, it was never simple,
though for years now you've been dreaming
of wonderful solutions. Did I scare you?
I have this habit of coming through
just at the wrong time, like other things,
hunger, love, sleep for example.

Forgive the accent: you will understand
what it's like to be a foreigner abroad
or, for that matter, an alien at home,
where you curse it all, to the last bomb
waiting its moment on some empty road
that stretches out into the back of beyond

– which is my country too, of course,
completely surrounded by one blank sea
we call oblivion, despair.
Maybe one day you could spend some time there:
it's just the place to write your poetry,
to go to the bad, and then to worse.

Our comforts, I'm afraid, will be few
and simple, but you'll still have your visions
– a tree of light, then nothing but light –
and I'll still have my victims every night,
for ours would be the finest of collusions:
the best dreams are of dreams coming true.

SEAMUS HEANEY

HERCULES AND ANTAEUS

Sky-born and royal,
snake-choker, dung-heaver,
his mind big with golden apples,
his future hung with trophies,

Hercules has the measure
of resistance and black powers
feeding off the territory.
Antaeus, the mould-hugger,

is weaned at last:
a fall was a renewal
but now he is raised up –
the challenger's intelligence

is a spur of light,
a blue prong graiping him
out of his element
into a dream of loss

and origins – the cradling dark,
the river-veins, the secret gullies
of his strength,
the hatching grounds

of cave and souterrain,
he has bequeathed it all
to elegists. Balor will die
and Byrthnoth and Sitting Bull.

Hercules lifts his arms
in a remorseless V,
his triumph unassailed
by the powers he has shaken

and lifts and banks Antaeus
high as a profiled ridge,
a sleeping giant,
pap for the dispossessed.

TOM PAULIN

THE OTHER VOICE

Anglican firelight.
Jugged hare in a stone house.
The gowned schoolmaster

Has a saintly politeness.
'It is possible to wonder,'
I hear him say.

The wind soughs in the demesne.
Exiles light a candle
To the gods of place.

In the winter darkness
Of this mild village
There is the mossy fragrance

Of damp branches under leaves,
The sour yeast of fungus.
At the lighted doorway

I forget to shake hands.
'We must meet again,' he calls,
And I pretend to pretend.

★

I make that crossing again
And catch the salt freshness
Of early light on Queen's Island.

I lay claim to those marshes,
The Lagan, the shipyards,
The Ormeau Road in winter.

That back room off Donegall Pass,
Remember, where the cell met?
That cupboard of books, tracts and poems?

Plekhanov flares like a firework,
Trotsky crosses Siberia
Turning the pages of Homer,

Raskolnikov wears a long coat
And the end justifies the means.
'Soon the rosewood *meubles*

'Will shake in the drawing-rooms
On the Malone Road.
After the long marches

'There will be shares for us all
In the means of production.
Songs of a new society

'Will grow like flowers
From the barrel of a gun.
It's easy. It's easy.

'*Love is all you need.*'
The record sticks and the party
Spins on forever.

★

We wished it could happen.
Less often now, I wish it still.
For it seems like a barren

Simplicity with no ghosts.
And those dreams of gardens
Called me from the way, saying:

'Here are the small mercies,
A glass of wine, the pungent shade,
And a cagey friendship.

'Grace is a volume of Horace,
Bishops and pigeons
Cooing in a woggles shire.

'Life, my dear, is a fixed order
And your verse should flow
With a touching sweetness.

'Better a civil twilight
Than the level emptiness
Of pulp culture.'

★

In the visions of the night
When deep sleep falls on men,
The flickering pictures

Pass before our eyes.
The fear of necessity
In an absolute narrative.

History is happening:
Tanks and caterpillars,
A moth lying in the dust.

'Once, in Odessa, I watched
The governor cursing.
His back was turned in the hot square.

'A regiment with bark sandals,
A sprig of green in their caps.
Their tragedy scorched my mind.

'Those bark sandals, those green sprigs!
But the process of history
Must scorn an emotion.

'I am history now.
I carry time in my mind.
As sharp as an axe.'

★

The actors shake their fists.
I hear the same opinions
In a muddy light.

I see a regiment of clones
Waving their arms and shouting:
A glossy brutalism dances

To a parody of song.
Identikit opinions
In the camps of the punks.

The theatre is in the streets,
The streets are in the theatre,
The poet is torn to pieces.

★

What does a poem serve?
Only the pure circle of itself.
Now, between two coasts,

The servants of the state
Doze to the drum of engines.
Hammered stars, a dark dream,

The hard night in a dead bowl.
Where a free light wakes
To its spacious language

Choice is still possible.
I dream of a subtle voice,
Stare in a mirror and pray

To a shadow wandering
Beyond the cold shores
And tides of the Baltic.

★

In Buddhist Moscow,
In lamp-eyed St Petersburg,
Mandelstam is walking

Through the terrible night.
His lips are moving
In a lyric ripple.

The syllables chirp
Like a dolphin, lost
In the grey depths of the state.

'As I walk through the dark
I will tell you this:
That morning, in the buttery

'Of the Kremlin, I left
Because I could never stay
In the same room as Trotsky.

'Do you understand me?
Those ideals will fit you
Like a feral uniform.

'Hear how the wolves howl,
Functions of nature
On the frozen plains.

'All the dry glitters
In your cento of memories
Will never catch

'The living truth on the wing.
The bird has flown its nest
And the snow weighs

'On the gothic branches,
Lavish and cruel, like power.
What cadences, what rich voices

'Have you hardened against?
What images have you broken?
In the great dome of art

'(It was this we longed for
In our Petropolis)
I am free of history.

'Beyond dust and rhetoric,
In the meadows of the spirit
I kiss the Word.'

SEAMUS DEANE

OSIP MANDELSTAM

'The people need poetry.' That voice
That was last heard asking for warm
Clothes and money, also knew the hunger
We all have for the gold light
The goldfinch carries into the air
Like a tang of crushed almonds.

Nine months before heart-failure
Silenced his silk-sharp whistle
That haunted the steppes as though
A small shrapnel of birds scattered,
Bukharin, his protector, was shot
Along with Yagoda, Rykov, others.

The kerosene flash of his music
Leaps from the black earth,
From the whitening dead of the War
Who burn in its flammable spirit.
The fire-crop smokes in the Kremlin's
Eyes and the scorched marl

Cinders. Son of Petropolis, tell us,
Tell us how to turn into the flash,
To lie in the lice-red shirt
On the bank of the Styx and wait
For the gossamer of Paradise
To spider in our dirt-filled eyes.

SEAMUS HEANEY

CHEKHOV ON SAKHALIN
for Derek Mahon

So, he would pay his 'debt to medicine'.
But first he drank cognac by the ocean
With his back to all he travelled north to face.
His head was swimming free as the troikas

Of Tyumin, he looked down from the rail
Of his thirty years and saw a mile
Into himself as if he were clear water:
Lake Baikhal from the deckrail of the steamer.

That far north, Siberia was south.
Should it have been an ulcer in the mouth,
The cognac that the Moscow literati
Packed off with him to a penal colony –

Him, born, you may say, under the counter?
At least that meant he knew its worth. No cantor
In full throat by the iconostasis
Got holier joy than he got from that glass

That shone and warmed like diamonds warming
On some pert young cleavage in a salon,
Inviolable and affronting.
He felt the glass go cold in the midnight sun.

When he staggered up and smashed it on the stones
It rang as clearly as the convicts' chains
That haunted him. In the months to come
It rang on like the burden of his freedom

To try for the right tone – not tract, not thesis –
And walk away from floggings. He who thought to squeeze
His slave's blood out and waken the free man
Shadowed a convict guide through Sakhalin.

DEREK MAHON

THE SNOW PARTY
for Louis Asekoff

Bashō, coming
To the city of Nagoya,
Is asked to a snow party.

There is a tinkling of china
And tea into china;
There are introductions.

Then everyone
Crowds to the window
To watch the falling snow.

Snow is falling on Nagoya
And farther south
On the tiles of Kyōto.

Eastward, beyond Irago,
It is falling
Like leaves on the cold sea.

Elsewhere they are burning
Witches and heretics
In the boiling squares,

Thousands have died since dawn
In the service
Of barbarous kings;

But there is silence
In the houses of Nagoya
And the hills of Ise.

GEORGE BUCHANAN

LYLE DONAGHY, POET, 1902–1949

The product of peoples on two sides of a narrow sea,
he was raised with his head full of half-naked Greeks.
His rainy countryside didn't, scholastically, exist.
Under a tree he heard drums with their heavy beat
recommend a dislike which he didn't share.

He watched from a window the rain splashing
and after the rain the treedrip on the river.
His poem, a slow adding of words,

grew with a lack of urgency as trees grow.
The mind exudes stuff, not in sentences
baked to a style, but softly. Sir,
I don't address you in precious stones.

He heard clergy shouting from pulpits against
the sins of the body. Schooled in the prime
material of flowering girls and trees
he loved – poet-wise – poet-foolish –
with ex-puritan extravagance.

Turning a boulder in the grass, laughing
at the insects, he was filled with Whitman energy
as a train puffed by on the narrow-gauge.

Where do we go to find the evenings
which late sunshine on saplings used to make?
He piled stones savagely for a house for himself
in a valley, cautious about the trees,
not sinking to their calm, wanting to utter
a cry clear of the lake, an abstract
artifice beyond the natural liberties:
undid the academic ropes, waited for the surge.

ROY MCFADDEN

REUNION
I. M. Michael McLaverty

Within a fractured province; less:
Inside a town obscene with barricades
And rifles at the ready, bless,
God or Anon, before the picture fades

A congregation of four friends
Gathered to acclaim in separate ways

A long-loved book's rebirth, old hands
Renewing friendship with a wry surprise.

Before they crumble bread or spill
Wine's secret into glass, let glass reflect
Four faces singly stemmed, until
They share the wine's slow statement, and extract

From dregs and crumbs a sacrament
For two believing, two agnostic minds,
Each singular ingredient
Familial under the author's hosting hands:

As, after thirty years, the voice
Of that small masterpiece binds them together,
A four-leafed clover, to rejoice
That common ground survives disastrous weather.

DEREK MAHON

IN CARROWDORE CHURCHYARD
at the grave of Louis MacNeice

Your ashes will not stir, even on this high ground,
However the wind tugs, the headstones shake.
This plot is consecrated, for your sake,
To what lies in the future tense. You lie
Past tension now, and spring is coming round
Igniting flowers on the peninsula.

Your ashes will not fly, however the rough winds burst
Through the wild brambles and the reticent trees.
All we may ask of you we have. The rest
Is not for publication, will not be heard.
Maguire, I believe, suggested a blackbird
And over your grave a phrase from Euripides.

Which suits you down to the ground, like this churchyard
With its play of shadow, its humane perspective.
Locked in the winter's fist, these hills are hard
As nails, yet soft and feminine in their turn
When fingers open and the hedges burn.
This, you implied, is how we ought to live –

The ironical, loving crush of roses against snow,
Each fragile, solving ambiguity. So
From the pneumonia of the ditch, from the ague
Of the blind poet and the bombed-out town you bring
The all-clear to the empty holes of spring;
Rinsing the choked mud, keeping the colours new.

PAUL MULDOON

LUNCH WITH PANCHO VILLA

I

'Is it really a revolution, though?'
I reached across the wicker table
With another $10,000 question.
My celebrated pamphleteer,
Co-author of such volumes
As *Blood on the Rose,*
The Dream and the Drums,
And *How It Happened Here,*
Would pour some untroubled Muscatel
And settle back in his cane chair.

'Look, son. Just look around you.
People are getting themselves killed
Left, right and centre
While you do what? Write rondeaux?
There's more to living in this country
Than stars and horses, pigs and trees,

Not that you'd guess it from your poems.
Do you never listen to the news?
You want to get down to something true,
Something a little nearer home.'

I called again later that afternoon,
A quiet suburban street.
'You want to stand back a little
When the world's at your feet.'
I'd have liked to have heard some more
Of his famous revolution.
I rang the bell, and knocked hard
On what I remembered as his front door,
That opened then, as such doors do,
Directly on to a back yard.

II

Not any back yard, I'm bound to say,
And not a thousand miles away
From here. No one's taken in, I'm sure,
By such a mild invention.
But where (I wonder myself) do I stand,
In relation to a table and chair,
The quince-tree I forgot to mention,
That suburban street, the door, the yard –
All made up as I went along
As things that people live among.

And such a person as lived there!
My celebrated pamphleteer!
Of course, I gave it all away
With those preposterous titles.
The Bloody Rose? *The Dream and the Drums*?
The three-day-wonder of the flowering plum!
Or was I desperately wishing
To have been their other co-author,
Or, at least, to own a first edition
Of *The Boot Boys and Other Battles*?

'When are you going to tell the truth?'
For there's no such book, so far as I know,
As *How it Happened Here*,
Though there may be. There may.
What should I say to this callow youth
Who learned to write last winter –
One of those correspondence courses –
And who's coming to lunch today?
He'll be rambling on, no doubt,
About pigs and trees, stars and horses.

FRANK ORMSBY

APPLES, NORMANDY, 1944

Was it D+10 or D+12 we caught
the war artist sketching apples?

'I'm sick of tanks,' he said. 'I'm sick of ruins.
I'm sick of dead soldiers and soldiers on the move
and soldiers resting.
And to tell you the truth, I'm sick drawing refugees.
I want to draw apples.'

For all we know he's still sitting under a tree
somewhere between the Seine and Omaha,
or, russet with pleasure, striding past old dugouts
towards the next windfall –
sketch-books accumulating as he becomes
the Audubon of French apples,

or works on the single apple
– perfect, planetary – of his imagination.

SEAMUS HEANEY

THE HARVEST BOW

As you plaited the harvest bow
You implicated the mellowed silence in you
In wheat that does not rust
But brightens as it tightens twist by twist
Into a knowable corona,
A throwaway love-knot of straw.

Hands that aged round ashplants and cane sticks
And lapped the spurs on a lifetime of game cocks
Harked to their gift and worked with fine intent
Until your fingers moved somnambulant:
I tell and finger it like braille,
Gleaning the unsaid off the palpable.

And if I spy into its golden loops
I see us walk between the railway slopes
Into an evening of long grass and midges,
Blue smoke straight up, old beds and ploughs in hedges,
An auction notice on an outhouse wall –
You with a harvest bow in your lapel,

Me with the fishing rod, already homesick
For the big lift of these evenings, as your stick
Whacking the tips off weeds and bushes
Beats out of time, and beats, but flushes
Nothing: that original townland
Still tongue-tied in the straw tied by your hand.

The end of art is peace
Could be the motto of this frail device
That I have pinned up on our deal dresser –
Like a drawn snare
Slipped lately by the spirit of the corn
Yet burnished by its passage, and still warm.

5

'To the other shore . . . '

from 'States'
TOM PAULIN

PHILIP LARKIN

THE IMPORTANCE OF ELSEWHERE

Lonely in Ireland, since it was not home,
Strangeness made sense. The salt rebuff of speech,
Insisting so on difference, made me welcome:
Once that was recognised, we were in touch.

Their draughty streets, end-on to hills, the faint
Archaic smell of dockland, like a stable,
The herring-hawker's cry, dwindling, went
To prove me separate, not unworkable.

Living in England has no such excuse:
These are my customs and establishments
It would be much more serious to refuse.
Here no elsewhere underwrites my existence.

FLEUR ADCOCK

PLEASE IDENTIFY YOURSELF

British, more or less; Anglican, of a kind.
In Cookstown I dodge the less urgent question
when a friendly Ulsterbus driver raises it;
'You're not a Moneymore girl yourself?' he asks,
deadpan. I make a cowardly retrogression,
slip ten years back. 'No, I'm from New Zealand.'
'Are you now? Well, that's a coincidence:
the priest at Moneymore's a New Zealander.'
And there's the second question, unspoken.
Unanswered.
        I go to Moneymore
anonymously, and stare at all three churches.

In Belfast, though, where sides have to be taken,
I stop compromising – not that you'd guess,
seeing me hatless there among the hatted,
neutral voyeur among the shining faces
in the glossy Martyrs' Memorial Free Church.
The man himself is cheerleader in the pulpit
for crusader choruses: we're laved in blood,
marshalled in ranks. I chant the nursery tunes
and mentally cross myself. You can't stir me
with evangelistic hymns, Dr Paisley:
I know them. Nor with your computer-planned
sermon – Babylon, Revelation, whispers
of popery, slams at the IRA, more blood.
I scrawl incredulous notes under my hymnbook
and burn with Catholicism.
                                    Later
hacking along the Lower Falls Road
against a gale, in my clerical black coat,
I meet a bright gust of tinselly children
in beads and lipstick and their mothers' dresses
for Hallowe'en; who chatter and surround me.
Overreacting once again (a custom
of the country, not mine alone) I give them
all my loose change for their rattling tin
and my blessing – little enough. But now
to my tough Presbyterian ancestors,
Brooks and Hamilton, lying in the graves
I couldn't find at Moneymore and Cookstown
among so many unlabelled bones, I say:
I embrace you also, my dears.

NORMAN DUGDALE

SOME NOTES FOR IMPARTIAL OBSERVERS

Flown over, it is a conurbation
Much like any other: docks, sheds, sidings;

Traffic coiling through its gut; high-rise blocks,
Half-built estates spattering the country round.

Lived in, it is a minefield triggered
By invisible trip-wires. Wayleaves by day
Give access to some common zones, where the inhabitants
Frat cautiously, ears cocked for trouble.

By night, it drops all civic pretension
To assume a true plurality. Each warring village
Stands to, mobilised against the stranger,
Its strong points pubs, back alleyways its fields of fire,

Binlids radar. Take comfort, though. The hatreds
Generated here are locally consumed. Thus,
Regulated by the surgeon's knife, the rituals
Of decent burial, the economy

Registers near-perfect balance. You may expect, then,
A polite, if bored reception: to find your glittering
Goodwill irrelevant as a moon-shot,
Your advanced views (so thoughtfully designed) mere junk.

TOM PAULIN

STATES

That stretch of water, it's always
There for you to cross over
To the other shore, observing
The lights of cities on blackness.

Your army jacket at the rail
Leaks its kapok into a wind
That slices gulls over a dark zero
Waste a cormorant skims through.

Any state, built on such a nature,
Is a metal convenience, its paint
Cheapened by the price of lives
Spent in a public service.

The men who peer out for dawning
Gantries below a basalt beak
Think their vigils will make something
Clearer, as the cities close

With each other, their security
Threatened but bodied in steel
Polities that clock us safely
Over this dark; freighting us.

PURITY

Perhaps a maritime pastoral
Is the form best suited
To a northern capital
With its docks and gantries,
An oil refinery on the salt marsh.

Far from the playful celebration
Of good manners on a green field
There is always that dream
Of duck-down and eider,
The lichened island whose sour light
Lets us be ourselves.

Those luminous privacies
On a bleached coast
Are fierce and authentic,
And some of us believe in them.
They are the polities of love.

But in the brilliant distance
I see a crowded troopship

Moving down the blue lough
On a summer's morning,
Its anal colours
Almost fresh in the sun.
Those black boots are shining.
There is only a pink blur
Of identical features.

SEAMUS HEANEY

THE TOOME ROAD

One morning early I met armoured cars
In convoy, warbling along on powerful tyres,
All camouflaged with broken alder branches,
And headphoned soldiers standing up in turrets.
How long were they approaching down my roads
As if they owned them? The whole country was sleeping.
I had rights-of-way, fields, cattle in my keeping,
Tractors hitched to buckrakes in open sheds,
Silos, chill gates, wet slates, the greens and reds
Of outhouse roofs. Whom should I run to tell
Among all of those with their back doors on the latch
For the bringer of bad news, that small-hours visitant
Who, by being expected, might be kept distant?
Sowers of seed, erectors of headstones . . .
O charioteers, above your dormant guns,
It stands here still, stands vibrant as you pass,
The invisible, untoppled omphalos.

TOM PAULIN

FOOT PATROL, FERMANAGH

A pierrepoint stretch, mid-afternoon;
the last two go facing back
down the walled street below the chestnuts
this still claggy Sabbath.
They hold their rifles lightly, like dipped rods,
and in a blurt of sunshine
the aluminium paint on the customs shed
has a dead shine like a text
brushed onto basalt.
It's not that anything will happen next
in this hour that is as constant
as sin, and as original,
though why is it they remind me
of a prisoner led singing down a corridor
to a floor that isn't a floor any longer?

PADRAIC FIACC

ENEMY ENCOUNTER
for Lilac

Dumping (left over from the autumn)
Dead leaves, near a culvert
I come on
      a British Army Soldier
With a rifle and a radio
Perched hiding. He has red hair.

He is young enough to be my weenie
-bopper daughter's boy-friend.
He is like a lonely little winter robin.

We are that close to each other, I
Can nearly hear his heart beating.

I say something bland to make him grin,
But his glass eyes look past my side
-whiskers down
                     the Shore Road street.
I am an Irish man
                     and he is afraid
That I have come to kill him.

JOHN MONTAGUE

FOREIGN FIELD
for Edna Longley

Paddy's whole place was a clearing house:
A public phone in the hallway,
Folk huddled around a tiled fireplace.

But we were given tea in the front parlour,
Chill as the grave, a good place to talk,
Among brass trinkets, Long Kesh harps.

A patrol catwalks through the garden.
'You can see how we are being protected,'
Paddy jokes, with a well-rehearsed laugh.

A single shot. 'Jesus, that was close!'
The whole patrol crouches to the grass,
Though one slumps. 'Your man's hurt.

'You don't take cover with your rifle
Between your legs, like starting to dive.
Let's way out and see if he's alive.'

All the soldier barked was 'Freeze!'
But Paddy led us to where he lay,
A chubby lad, only about eighteen,

That hangdog look, hair close-cropped,
Surplus of a crowding England, now
Dying in a puddle of wet and blood.

And still the soldier: 'Don't move!'
Paddy ran back in to fetch some linen.
'Don't touch him!' He kneels down

To cover his skull gently, a broken egg.
'When a man's got, he's a non-combatant,'
Paddy apologises, shepherding us inside.

An hour later, an army ambulance raced up,
An army doctor leaps down. Out playing
Again, the children chant: 'Die, you bastard!'

Next morning, they checked out the area.
Someone had pruned an old tree in a garden,
Opening a new line of fire, instead.

CIARAN CARSON

ARMY

The duck patrol is waddling down the odd-numbers side of Raglan Street,
The bass-ackwards private at the rear trying not to think of a third eye
Being drilled in the back of his head. Fifty-five. They stop. The head
Peers round, then leaps the gap of Balaclava Street. He waves the body over
One by one. Forty-nine. Cape Street. A gable wall. Garnet Street. A gable
  wall.

Frere Street. Forty-seven. Forty-five-and-a-half. Milan Street. A grocer's
    shop.
They stop. They check their guns. Thirteen. Milton Street. An iron lamp-
    post.
Number one. Ormond Street. *Two ducks in front of a duck and two ducks*
Behind a duck, how many ducks? Five? *No. Three.* This is not the end.

NIGHT PATROL

Jerking his head spasmodically as he is penetrated by invisible gunfire,
The private wakes to a frieze of pull-outs from *Contact* and *Men Only.*
Sellotape and Blu-Tack. The antiquated plumbing is stuttering that he
Is not in Balkan Street or Hooker Street, but in a bunk bed
In the Grand Central Hotel: a room that is a room knocked into other
    rooms.

But the whole Victorian creamy façade has been tossed off
To show the inner-city tubing: cables, sewers, a snarl of Portakabins,
Soft-porn shops and carry-outs. A Telstar Taxis depot that is a hole
In a breeze-block wall, a wire grille and a voice-box uttering
    gobbledygook.

PADRAIC FIACC

from TEARS/A *LACRIMOSA*
for Geraldine

I UNISEX

After the bombing the British soldier
Looks up into the barbed-wire Irish
Twilight. His unflinching, open eyes
Deaden, yet involuntarily flood
With the colour of tea –
Drenches his combat jacket sleeve.

Now he is hugging,
Now he is giving
His male love
To a screaming fellow being he does
Not know if it is a man or a woman.

ROBERT JOHNSTONE

AS IF IT NEVER HAPPENED

This could be the ninth time.
I turn the lock imagining
a booby trap.

You feel nothing. When it explodes,
time stops, I switch
to another identical life.

In one world, relatives,
lovers mourn. But already
I am in the next and the door opens easily

as it always does and I sit at the wheel
and switch on, feeling only a quick pulse
and the strangeness of it all.

My self disintegrating.
My self partly integrating
with the air.

CIARAN CARSON

THE BOMB DISPOSAL

Is it just like picking a lock
With the slow deliberation of a funeral,
Hesitating through a darkened nave
Until you find the answer?

Listening to the malevolent tick
Of its heart, can you read
The message of the threaded veins
Like print, its body's chart?

The city is a map of the city,
Its forbidden areas changing daily.
I find myself in a crowded taxi
Making deviations from the known route,

Ending in a cul-de-sac
Where everyone breaks out suddenly
In whispers, noting the boarded windows,
The drawn blinds.

TOM PAULIN

A RUM COVE, A STOUT COVE

On the Barrack Islands far out
in the South Atlantic
the great-great-grandson (Sol Grout)
of Nelson's last bosun
is packing crawfish into a thick
barnacled keepbox marked *Briton
Kanning Factors Illimitated.*
It's his swart locks and cochin cheeks

that glim in the top left-hand corner
of 'Bold Bessie', the prime banner
that longs to LOL 301.
Like Gib, like the god called M'Lud,
and those tars behind locked doors
whistling *Britannia Rules*
in their slow skrimshandering
with worn and corded tools,
he's firm, Sol Grout, to the core,
the genius of these used islands
where no maritime elegists sing
of Resolution or Independence
with their harbourmaster's stores,
clagged mountains of ashy shale
and a small bird that no one has named –
a flightless timorous landrail
whose cry is rusted, hard, like chains.

MANICHEAN GEOGRAPHY I

Consider a coral or guano atoll
Where a breezy Union Jack
Flaps above the police station.

There is a rusting mission hut
Built out of flattened tin cans
(Bully beef, beans and tomato pilchards)

Where the Reverend Bungo Buller
And his prophet, Joe Gimlet,
Preach the gospel of cargoes.

They worship a white god
Of dentures and worn toothbrushes
Who will come to earth, Halleluia,

In a reconditioned Flying Fortress
Humping bales of fresh calico
And a crate of Black and Deckers.

Seeding like brisk parachutes,
The ancestral spirits will fall
From the pod of an airship,

And the chosen people will serve
Themselves with orange jube-jubes
In a brand-new discount warehouse.

AND WHERE DO YOU STAND
ON THE NATIONAL QUESTION?

Told him the shortest way to Tara was via Holyhead.

Stephen Dedalus

Apple-blossom, a great spread of it
above our heads.
This blue morning a new visitor
is laidback on a deckchair;
he's civil and clever,
a flinty mandarin
being entertained, like an oxymoron,
in this walled garden.
Ecco two glasses of young wine
. . . *et on mange des asperges.*
I imagine him
as the state's intelligence,
a lean man in a linen suit
who has come to question me
for picking up a pen
and taking myself a shade seriously.
'Paisley's plain tongue, his cult
of Bunyan and blood
in blind dumps like Doagh and Boardmills –
that's the enemy.'
I've an answer ready in the sun
but my eye tines the grass
for a tiny mound of soil:
the mole works underground,

a blind glove
that gropes the earth and cannot love.
'Your Lagan Jacobins, they've gone
with the *Northern Star*. I've heard
Hewitt and Heaney trace us back
to the Antrim weavers –
I can't come from *that*.'
'Why not, though? Isn't there
this local stir in us all? –
flick of the thumb, a word's relish,
the clitoral tick of an accent,
wee lick of spit or lovejuice?
I'd call that a brave kindness.'
Then a journey blows back at me –
rust-orange and green,
the Enterprise scudding north
past the brown burn of whin and bracken
till it halts and waits for clearance
under the gourly vigilance
of a corrie in bandit country –
'That's where the god, Autochthon,
is crossed by the hangman's rope.'
He counters with a short fiction
called *Molyneaux's Last Hope*.
'These islands are stepping-stones
to a metropolitan home,
an archipelago that's strung
between America and Europe.'
'So you're a band of Orange dandies?
Oscar in Père Lachaise with a sash on?'
'Well, not exactly . . . that's unfair –
like my saying it's a green mess you're after.'
'I want a form that's classic and secular,
the risen *République*,
a new song for a new constitution –
wouldn't you rather have that
than stay loose, baggy and British?
You don't *have* to fall back
on Burke and the Cruiser,
on a batty style

and slack o'whoozy emotion.'
We hit a pause like a ramp,
shrug and mark time
before we guess the design
of life after Prior:
the last civil servant
is dropping over from Whitehall.
Call him Sir Peregrine Falkland;
he's a bit thick – not a high-flyer –
but he'll do the trick.

PETER MCDONALD

TOTALLED

The costumes are a kind of late-colonial,
all primary colours and designer labels;
the hair's worn long and blow-dried, accents
are half-way between here and America;
a badge on his lapel says the producer
won't take no for an answer, and maybe
it's true he has a way with the impossible:
resprayed old cars, given a last polish,
catapult into walls and shop-windows,
into each other, they're always totalled,
and right on cue the flames come bursting
just to make everything final;
the sound's dubbed later, of fists connecting,
gunshots, brakes, happy or sad music.

Two men are waiting in a skyline office,
each one silently adding up the other
and playing the razor-cool executive.
The first smoothes a map, points to one corner,
and thinks out all the disadvantages –
it's too late, and impossible anyway,
to make much of that sector. He's starting

to speak now, with a shrug in his voice
and his eyes fixed on the middle distance,
part of him slipping out to some margin
as a young achiever jokes in a monotone
of how already he's allowed for losses
and nowadays, in any case, that country
is washed-up, written-off, a place for dead people.

NORMAN DUGDALE

PROVINCIA DESERTA

Well, here it is: not Botany Bay
But a penal settlement all the same,
The sentence life without remission – saving,
Of course, Sir, such as yourself, gentlemen newly come
To live here at the Governor's Lodge. Two years from now
You will be safely home again and dining out
On your bizarre experiences, which cannot fail
To please your hostess and amuse the company.

Let me then briefly sketch our way of life. First,
Custom binds us, hardly ever law. Mating,
Which takes the mind off other things,
We openly encourage, especially
For procreation: but only, note, within each tribe.
(Exogamy means instant ostracism.)
Condemned at birth, children are consigned
By parents to our priests for prompt initiation
In rituals of wrath, the wine of vengeance.
All punishment is random and condign, each
Adult male doubling as both predator
And victim – a symbiosis which ensures
All suffer in the end alike. Please don't be
Alarmed, though. Well-trained squads clean up the carnage
And maintain tolerably hygienic conditions
For temporary survivors.

You find this strange,
No doubt; and stranger still our fierce
Cleaving to the only thing
We share and murder for. It is a land,
You see, of quite surpassing beauty,
Of stream and mountain, lake and wood
With many haunting presences

Which will shadow you always, beckoning
Still, however far your country.

ANDREW WATERMAN

FROM THE OTHER COUNTRY

But you do not consider how long I have lived in this country.
Its skies move through my skull, and the changing light
over the water; like whales the humped mountains
surface in my dreams, and never were trees
thwart like these in flight from the salt harsh gales.

The customs of the people, it is true,
are not mine; in farms and one-street towns
they enact strict rituals of thrift, worship, pleasure.
Lights burn late where slow accounts are reckoned,
the drunk crashes prone in dying embers,

and beneath tribal tokens, ancient recitations.
Often indeed through main street and glen
drums throb savage annunciation, the door
opens to a rain of bullets, car-lights pick out
the corpse in a ditch. 'It's a madness going on,'

they say. Did you think madness so dull?
Look: how finite among the weltering green
these settlements, no margins to nourish the odd.

Knowing their place, they grow, pray, wed, kill, die.
Even their knowing smiles have a terrible innocence

which you do not understand. Nor, though you hear,
how their soft gutturals and singing intonation
infect my accent. I am welcomed
in bars and corner-shops, with 'It's a soft night.'
And yes, I have loved their girls.

See, where fine white clouds drift high above the meadow
the small farm daydreams all doors open:
they are all gone round the bend of the field, out of change.
Behind the clock on the mantel dust thickens on letters
strangely-deciphered, from children 'across the water'.

From where, too, on my screen come shimmering
images of the old labyrinthine cities,
sanities. Which I can revisit, resume
undetected; noticing how they find
bestial or glamorous our banalities,

and do not see the detail beneath stark outlines.
I am no longer sure that I wish to return,
even though it is winter here now, the sky and land
seeping greyly together. Unsettled, defined
by difference, I find I can live with this,

am strangely involved in, call it, a climate.
Yes, as the mad wind rises, sets the sea
resonating, whips waves white, and plucks
tiles from thin roofs, above which gulls
weave lamentation's dissonant vocables.

NORMAN DUGDALE

NIGHT-FERRY

Winking headlands dowsed by dawn
Smudge to shore on either bow. The Lough
Wrinkles, swells, a slow fat slug
Mounting Belfast's languid loin

Slobbing rocks from which gulls rise
To drift astern. Like rusty tramps
Mills and wharves slide broadside on,
Dribbling slops from their stained sides.

Confetti strews the puddled quay
Where wedding-parties roared farewell
The night before or sobbed through veils
To watch the stern-lights fade. Beyond

Wall-slogans run like wet mascara
Down gable-ends. The terraces
Wear jilted looks, deserted
In the morning, swollen-eyed,

But last night's rain has rinsed the streets
Of last night's vomit, last night's blood.
'Where to, sir?' asks the taximan. 'Home,'
I say. 'Where's that?' 'Home's here,' I say, 'for good.'

SMALL HOURS

Coming back from that long journey
Is always the same – always night, clouds
Scudding across the moon, rain-squalls
Bouncing off the tarmac, a big wind

273

Out of the heave and slop
Of the weltering Atlantic
Shoving the car crabwise
As you cross the dark plateau. Then

Suddenly the cratered city
Opens below, glittering there
Like a gigantic jewelled drinking-bowl,
And you slither down to find

Its doors slammed shut, blinds drawn
Against the stranger, its streets deserted
Though traffic-lights blink madly at road-ends.
And always you feel you are being watched

From alleyways and corners, stalked
As you halt or hesitate
Within the maze. Next day
You recognise the place as home,

Crumpled, mud-stained and familiar
As some old suit, camouflage
Which only half conceals from mind and eye
The sub-culture of murder and atrocity

Flourishing below. And you pick your way again
Warily with thousands more through one
Of history's less successful side-shows:
Best left, the archaeologists will say,

Its docklands derelict, its last tides ebbed,
As salt-marsh to the sea-birds, or to silence.

ITHACA

Beyond the black, rumbustious straits
Blurred harbour-lights heave into view.
I lurch onto the deck. A raw

Nor'easter rams the splintered landing-stage
Where figures flit in shadow, crouch
To grab our hawsers, winch us home.

Home? Is this then truly Ithaca
Again? The idiom ashore
Tastes salt-familiar yet strange, cuts
Like whipcord. Cloud-scurry and that one bleak star
Above the cliff-line massing north
Confirm a low meridian. What gifts

Have I or any brought this stony land,
Save empty hands, a few tall tales? They say
The roads this night are red with fire and blood.
But who are the usurpers? Who divides
Our patrimony? And when the dawn-mist lifts,
Which beggar shall be recognised as king?

ROY MCFADDEN

KEW GARDENS

Queuing in Kew Gardens
For tea and sandwiches –
The English order freedom
Where we take liberties –
We trespassed upon sunlight
And unfunereal flowers,
And no one thought to ask us
To prove our names were ours.
Unthreatened glass in windows
Reflected as we crossed,
And the present had a future
Not completely in the past;
Where children ran and shouted
Against a bantering breeze,

Without a glint of murder
In an innocence of trees.

Enduring English tea as
A chaser to the bread,
I swapped with a German widow
Our blitz for her air-raid;
And said sunshine seemed guilty
Like streetlamps in the war
In Dublin, while in Belfast
The dark went on as far
As the hills and the last siren
Straightening to All-Clear,
The kettle and the tea-cups
And the sip-away from fear.

Edwardian sunlight failing,
Like imperial grace,
On an afternoon of tea-cups,
I chose to reminisce
On mutual bombs and sirens,
Families under the stairs,
Rats blazing from the manholes,
Our Spitfires, their Messers;
On bankruptcy of empire,
Fraudulent nationhood:
Then framed an awkward handshake
For words I'd left unsaid.

For I hadn't marred our wartime
Brisk reminiscences
With a provincial quarrel
Remote beyond the trees;
Or complicated teatime
With cocktail theory
That Belfast was in ruins
Chasing identity.
The killer wears a mask, and
The victim gives his name
To just another headstone;

The clichés stay the same.
And the waitress hurried on to
Tidy another place;
And children ran and shouted
Against a bantering breeze.

PAUL WILKINS

A GRAVEYARD IN ULSTER

Aloft in a clump of trees, a crow scrapes
a cry across its throat. Passing on a bus
you can almost guess how desolate a place

this graveyard might once have been
before the wakening town stretched this far
to grip the tangled sheets of its fathers' dreams.

You can nearly hear your steps sound
in this windy Antrim tabernacle, imagine
a cortege dragging through the mud;

as the soil swamps a neighbour's corpse
the flat-capped mourners lighting pipes
stare out to sea, where a storm starts.

Common names fill the plots. The nailing
down of a coffin-lid hammers in memories
you never had. History is a road uncurling,

the shovelling of earth. Now bungalows
and the Golf Club edge closer
like smart kids to an alcoholic uncle.

The tiny church is as derelict
as a disused farmhouse on fruitless land,
the roof down, moss and sheep-shit

everywhere, weeds and overthrown walls.
An Englishman's dream of Ireland
in which the rain and sea, but not the numbers of the dead,
perpetually swell.

VICTOR PRICE

ENGLAND

Born to the harsh certainties
Of Ulster, where a spade's
A bloody shovel and you need to know
What foot to put to it, I came
About the middle of my life
To this mild park-land where
A settled culture had made men fat
While we were shivering behind hurdles. Here
The very trees have more solidity
Than our monuments; a house
Is not a raw cube dropped
Into a gash in a green wilderness,
But a time-weathered artefact
That's worked gently under the land's skin
And grown a part of it. Here
The loyalty I offered with a shrug
Has turned to love – oh not the kind
That drives clawed fingers into my chest
Each time I see those battered streets;
Something more equable than that,
Less strong in gusts but steadier all round.
I must have weathered, like the stones and trees.

WILLIAM PESKETT

FROM BELFAST TO SUFFOLK

First the pleasures fire the heart –
sutures of oak and elm
divide acres of polyploid grasses
into skull plates
to civilise every corner of the country.
Driving from the Low House
we might pass a dozen churches,
towers that indicate
walking distance across the fields
set alight with beacons.

More honest than the view from innocence
where plumes of smoke along the skyline
describe another operation,
here, the factory workers of the earth
are burning stubble,
purifying the season.
Later, driving tractors in the dark
the sharp spot-light turns
a glistening edge of soil
in long tracks across the land.

The night-police don't scare me here.
Like the man who, in the end,
neglects his mother for his wife
a faithfulness supersedes
the pleasures of the moon.
This demilitarised home
protects me like the other –
its signpost names pronounceable,
its fields the map
in my head.

CRAIG RAINE

FLYING TO BELFAST, 1977

It was possible to laugh
as the engines whistled to the boil,

and wonder what the clouds looked like –
shovelled snow, Apple Charlotte,

Tufty Tails . . . I enjoyed
the Irish Sea, the ships were faults

in a dark expanse of linen.
And then Belfast below, a radio

with its back ripped off,
among the agricultural abstract

of the fields. Intricate,
neat and orderly. The windows

gleamed like drops of solder –
everything was wired up.

I thought of wedding presents,
white tea things

grouped on a dresser,
as we entered the cloud

and were nowhere –
a bride in a veil, laughing

at the sense of event, only
half afraid of an empty house

with its curtains boiling
from the bedroom window.

ANDREW MOTION

LEAVING BELFAST
for Craig Raine

Driving at dusk on the steep road
north to the airport, *Look back*,
you say, *The finest view of Belfast*,
and point, proud of your choice to stay.

How clear the rows of streetlamps show
which way we came. I trace them slope
by slope through marshlands slipping down
to lanes, and find the roofs again,

their stern geographies of punishment
and love where silence deepens under rain.
Each sudden gust of light explains itself
as flames, but neither they, nor even

bombs redoubled on the hills tonight
can quite include me in their fear.
What does remains invisible, is lost
in curt societies whose deaths become

revenge by morning, and whose homes
are nothing more than all they pity most.
I watch the moon above them, filling rooms
with shadow politics, though whether

voices there pronounce me an intruder,
traitor, or a friend, I leave them now
as much a stranger as I came, and turn
to listen in the twilight for their griefs,

but hear instead the promise of conclusion
echoing towards me through these miles
of stubborn gorse, until it disappears
at last in darkness, out beyond the coast.

JOHN HEWITT

AN IRISHMAN IN COVENTRY

A full year since, I took this eager city,
the tolerance that laced its blatant roar,
its famous steeples and its web of girders,
as image of the state hope argued for,
and scarcely flung a bitter thought behind me
on all that flaws the glory and the grace
which ribbons through the sick, guilt-clotted legend
of my creed-haunted, Godforsaken race.
My rhetoric swung round from steel's high promise
to the precision of the well-gauged tool,
tracing the logic in the vast glass headlands,
the clockwork horse, the comprehensive school.

Then, sudden, by occasion's chance concerted,
in enclave of my nation, but apart,
the jigging dances and the lilting fiddle
stirred the old rage and pity in my heart.
The faces and the voices blurring round me,
the strong hands long familiar with the spade,
the whiskey-tinctured breath, the pious buttons,
called up a people endlessly betrayed
by our own weakness, by the wrongs we suffered
in that long twilight over bog and glen,
by force, by famine and by glittering fables
which gave us martyrs when we needed men,
by faith which had no charity to offer,
by poisoned memory, and by ready wit,
with poverty corroded into malice,
to hit and run and howl when it is hit.

This is our fate: eight hundred years' disaster,
crazily tangled as the Book of Kells;
the dream's distortion and the land's division,
the midnight raiders and the prison cells.
Yet like Lir's children banished to the waters
our hearts still listen for the landward bells.

6

'And hope and history rhyme . . . '

from 'Chorus' in *The Cure at Troy*
SEAMUS HEANEY

LOUIS MACNEICE

VALEDICTION

Their verdure dare not show . . . their verdure dare not show . . .
Cant and randy – the seals' heads bobbing in the tide-flow
Between the islands, sleek and black and irrelevant
They cannot depose logically what they want:
Died by gunshot under borrowed pennons,
Sniped from the wet gorse and taken by the limp fins
And slung like a dead seal in a boghole, beaten up
By peasants with long lips and the whisky-drinker's cough.
Park your car in the city of Dublin, see Sackville Street
Without the sandbags in the old photos, meet
The statues of the patriots, history never dies,
At any rate in Ireland, arson and murder are legacies
Like old rings hollow-eyed without their stones
Dumb talismans.
See Belfast, devout and profane and hard,
Built on reclaimed mud, hammers playing in the shipyard,
Time punched with holes like a steel sheet, time
Hardening the faces, veneering with a grey and speckled rime
The faces under the shawls and caps:
This was my mother-city, these my paps.
Country of callous lava cooled to stone,
Of minute sodden haycocks, of ship-sirens' moan,
Of falling intonations – I would call you to book
I would say to you, Look;
I would say, This is what you have given me
Indifference and sentimentality
A metallic giggle, a fumbling hand,
A heart that leaps to a fife band:
Set these against your water-shafted air
Of amethyst and moonstone, the horses' feet like bells of hair
Shambling beneath the orange cart, the beer-brown spring
Guzzling between the heather, the green gush of Irish spring.
Cursèd be he that curses his mother. I cannot be
Anyone else than what this land engendered me:
In the back of my mind are snips of white, the sails

Of the Lough's fishing-boats, the bellropes lash their tails
When I would peal my thoughts, the bells pull free –
Memory in apostasy.
I would tot up my factors
But who can stand in the way of his soul's steam-tractors?
I can say Ireland is hooey, Ireland is
A gallery of fake tapestries,
But I cannot deny my past to which my self is wed,
The woven figure cannot undo its thread.
On a cardboard lid I saw when I was four
Was the trade-mark of a hound and a round tower,
And that was Irish glamour, and in the cemetery
Sham Celtic crosses claimed our individuality,
And my father talked about the West where years back
He played hurley on the sands with a stick of wrack.
Park your car in Killarney, buy a souvenir
Of green marble or black bog-oak, run up to Clare,
Climb the cliff in the postcard, visit Galway city,
Romanticize on our Spanish blood, leave ten per cent of pity
Under your plate for the emigrant,
Take credit for our sanctity, our heroism and our sterile want
Columba Kevin and briny Brandan the accepted names,
Wolfe Tone and Grattan and Michael Collins the accepted
    names,
Admire the suavity with which the architect
Is rebuilding the burnt mansion, recollect
The palmy days of the Horse Show, swank your fill,
But take the Holyhead boat before you pay the bill;
Before you face the consequence
Of inbred soul and climatic maleficence
And pay for the trick beauty of a prism
In drug-dull fatalism.
I will exorcise my blood
And not to have my baby-clothes my shroud
I will acquire an attitude not yours
And become as one of your holiday visitors,
And however often I may come
Farewell, my country, and in perpetuum;
Whatever desire I catch when your wind scours my face
I will take home and put in a glass case

And merely look on
At each new fantasy of badge and gun.
Frost will not touch the hedge of fuchsias,
The land will remain as it was,
But no abiding content can grow out of these minds
Fuddled with blood, always caught by blinds;
The eels go up the Shannon over the great dam;
You cannot change a response by giving it a new name.
Fountain of green and blue curling in the wind
I must go east and stay, not looking behind,
Not knowing on which day the mist is blanket-thick
Nor when sun quilts the valley and quick
Winging shadows of white clouds pass
Over the long hills like a fiddle's phrase.
If I were a dog of sunlight I would bound
From Phoenix Park to Achill Sound,
Picking up the scent of a hundred fugitives
That have broken the mesh of ordinary lives,
But being ordinary too I must in course discuss
What we mean to Ireland or Ireland to us;
I have to observe milestone and curio
The beaten buried gold of an old king's bravado,
Falsetto antiquities, I have to gesture,
Take part in, or renounce, each imposture;
Therefore I resign, good-bye the chequered and the quiet hills
The gaudily-striped Atlantic, the linen-mills
That swallow the shawled file, the black moor where half
A turf-stack stands like a ruined cenotaph;
Good-bye your hens running in and out of the white house
Your absent-minded goats along the road, your black cows
Your greyhounds and your hunters beautifully bred
Your drums and your dolled-up Virgins and your ignorant dead.

PADRAIC FIACC

SAINT COLEMAN'S SONG FOR FLIGHT/
AN *ITE MISSA EST*
for Nancy and Brigid – flown

Run like rats from the plague in you.
Before death it is no virtue to be dead.
The crannog in the water, anywhere at all sure!
It is no virtue and it is not nature
To wait to writhe into the ground.

Not one in the Bible could see these dead
Packed on top of the other like dung
Not the two Josephs in Egypt
But would not run!

And Christ's blessing follow
(Is it not a blessing to escape storm?)

Pray to old Joseph – not a witless man –
Who had the brains not to want to die

But when his time came only and at home in bed,
The door shut on the world, that wolf outside
Munching the leper's head.

GERALD DAWE

NAMES

They call this 'Black North',
black from the heart out.
It doesn't matter about
particularities when mouths
mumble the handy sayings
and day-in minds tighten.

I've been here having thought
nowhere else was possible,
a condition of destiny or what
the old generations only fumbled
with: conceit, success, a fair
share of decent hardship,
forced into fierce recognition –
the cardhouse toppled.

In this extreme, perched
on the edge of the Atlantic,
you feel to look down
and gather around the details,
thinking to store them away,
bundle and pack in the exile's way –
the faithful journey
of turning your back
like the host of others,
the scholars and saints.
Line up and through the turn-
stile, click the ticket
and wait till you're clear of it.
You need never recall the other names.

PATRICK WILLIAMS

TRAILS

Ten years old with my father
I scoured the rough of the Royal County Down,
I mooched behind a tee as the nobles came
Chatting lightly, four skinny kids
Stumbling after under the weight of the clubs.
I saw my father offer what we'd found
And saw his hand close on the few shillings,
His free hand mock a quick salute:
'Right you are, sir! It's grand weather!'

He'd laugh that night with his peers in the Donard Bar.
Once, shocked, I heard a young man tell him
'Clear off. You're no better than a thief.
Get off the course now or I'll report you.'
I saw my father turn white and turn
As that man teed-up, tensed, swung
Cleanly, smashed the ball out of sight . . .
And my father walked to me with a funny grin.
He said, 'I think we'll head on home now, son.'
And home from scrubbing floors for a lady
My mother dropped breathless into a chair
And lit a cigarette. 'Look in the bag.'
Where under the bread and the spuds and the *Irish News*
Was Rider Haggard or Kipling, once Blake,
Thieved from shelves where she disturbed the dust.
We were afraid some Prod would report her
For earning while my father was unemployed.
Soon I thought our own kind no better,
If anything their weakness sickened more,
Consummate in their role of white negroes.
The sad, lovely songs of wounded Ireland,
Stories of the Tans blown sky-high,
The laughter round the fire turned sour for me.
I left the place where love lay bleeding
But every city where a plane touched down,
Beyond the barrier on every platform,
I limped into one I'd run there from.
Nowhere seemed where I could belong,
I tried to settle but was driven on
When I found that place crowded with the damned.
Where I was was hardly less confusion,
The world a grain of sand whirled where Love
Would never lean to see me move.
Lost on sore trails I turned for home
And here began a reconciliation
With my father's ghost drinking Guinness,
With my mother, rather out of breath.
Secretly I undertook a journey
And understood what I had always known,
Not Teague or Prod or England, Ireland – men

And women trained in ignorance, afraid.
I found myself not lost, not lost completely,
But prisoned where the lock, the key, was me.
At last I turned to you, not knowing you,
I turned to you at last, not trusting you,
Only knowing I would rather die
Free, by you, than die alone in jail.
My trails to us have only just begun
And questions ask one question answers fail,
But if the search is all there is, at least
In you it has a base, almost a home.

DEREK MAHON

AFTERLIVES
for James Simmons

1

I wake in a dark flat
To the soft roar of the world.
Pigeons neck on the white
Roofs as I draw the curtains
And look out over London
Rain-fresh in the morning light.

This is our element, the bright
Reason on which we rely
For the long-term solutions.
The orators yap, and guns
Go off in a back-street;
But the faith does not die

That in our time these things
Will amaze the literate children
In their non-sectarian schools
And the dark places be

Ablaze with love and poetry
When the power of good prevails.

What middle-class cunts we are
To imagine for one second
That our privileged ideals
Are divine wisdom, and the dim
Forms that kneel at noon
In the city not ourselves.

2

I am going home by sea
For the first time in years.
Somebody thumbs a guitar
On the dark deck, while a gull
Dreams at the masthead,
The moon-splashed waves exult.

At dawn the ship trembles; turns
In a wide arc to back
Shuddering up the grey lough
Past lightship and buoy,
Slipway and dry dock
Where a naked bulb burns;

And I step ashore in a fine rain
To a city so changed
By five years of war
I scarcely recognize
The places I grew up in,
The faces that try to explain.

But the hills are still the same
Grey-blue above Belfast.
Perhaps if I'd stayed behind
And lived it bomb by bomb
I might have grown up at last
And learnt what is meant by home.

ALAN ALEXANDER

FOR MY BROTHER IN BELFAST

Call me not hard of heart or say
My love is sounding brass because
I have lived so long in the sun,
Many times I have thought of Ulster
And in the swilling of a glass
Tramped a favourite road with the wind
In my teeth or stumbled somewhere
Upon your high laughter when we
Were both reckless after a dance,
The rain and the girls forgotten;
It is not simple, this living away
From the monotones of streets
Where hypocrisy has exploded;
Call me not hard of heart,
You are in the thick of it, while I
Pick up the paper thrown against my door
And think of you and suffer, as before.

TOM PAULIN

SURVEILLANCES

In the winter dusk
You see the prison camp
With its blank watchtowers;
It is as inevitable
As the movement of equipment
Or the car that carries you
Towards a violent district.

In the violet light
You watch a helicopter

293

Circling above the packed houses,
A long beam of light
Probing streets and waste ground.
All this might be happening
Underwater.

And if you would swop its functions
For a culture of bungalows
And light verse,
You know this is one
Of the places you belong in,
And that its public uniform
Has claimed your service.

AN ULSTER UNIONIST WALKS
THE STREETS OF LONDON

All that Friday
there was no flag –
no Union Jack,
no tricolour –
on the governor's mansion.
I waited outside the gate-lodge,
waited like a dog
in my own province
till a policeman brought me
a signed paper.
Was I meant to beg
and be grateful?
I sat on the breakfast-shuttle and I called –
I called out loud –
to the three Hebrew children
for I know at this time
there is neither prince, prophet, nor leader –
there is no power
we can call our own.
I grabbed a fast black –
ack, I caught a taxi –
to Kentish Town,

then walked the streets
like a half-foreigner
among the London Irish.
What does it feel like?
I wanted ask them –
what does it feel like
to be a child of that nation?
But I went underground
to the Strangers' House –
We vouch, they swore,
We deem, they cried,
till I said, 'Out . . .
I may go out that door
and walk the streets
searching my own people.'

HOWARD WRIGHT

YAHOO

My grandfather, white-haired even then,
related the story of Robert Lundy
opening Derry's oakwood gates.
'Londonderry' – he corrected himself.

Though everyone who was anyone was there,
and the bonfire reached a pinnacle
outside Ellis's Mock-Tudor pub
I wanted home, out of this old movie,

for suddenly above the crowd
danced a scarecrow, dressed in
black tie and tails, and white gloves,
a powdered wig flaking his top hat,

all carried on the shoulders of a local thug
small and hateful, a two-headed throwback

pushing children over palettes,
bald tyres and dead cats dowsed in petrol.

'Won't they burn him soon?'
'Soon,' my grandfather replied, above my head
and holding my little hand tighter
not prepared to give anything away.

'And will they close the gates?'
'Now there's a question, son –
we'll have to wait and see.' He bent down
and grinned: 'Let's wait and see.'

JOHN HEWITT

THE SEARCH
for Shirley and Darryl

We left the western island to live among strangers
in a city older by centuries
than the market town which we had come from
where the slow river spills out between green hills
and gulls perch on the bannered poles.

It is a hard responsibility to be a stranger;
to hear your speech sounding at odds with your neighbours';
holding your tongue from quick comparisons;
remembering that you are a guest in the house.

Often you will regret the voyage,
wakening in the dark night to recall that other place
or glimpsing the moon rising and recollecting
that it is also rising over named hills,
shining on known waters.

But sometimes the thought
that you have not come away from, but returned,

to this older place whose landmarks are yours also,
occurs when you look down a long street remarking
the architectural styles or move through a landscape
with wheat ripening in large fields.

Yet you may not rest here, having come back,
for this is not your abiding place, either.

The authorities declare that in former days
the western island was uninhabited,
just as where you reside now was once tundra,
and what you seek may be no more than
a broken circle of stones on a rough hillside, somewhere.

ROBINSON JEFFERS

THE BROADSTONE
near Finvoy, County Antrim

We climbed by the old quarries to the wide highland of heath,
On the slope of a swale a giant dolmen,
Three heavy basalt pillars upholding the enormous slab,
Towers and abides as if time were nothing.
The hard stones are hardly dusted with lichen in nobody knows
What ages of autumns in this high solitude
Since a recordless tribe of an unknown race lifted them up
To be the availing hero's memorial,
And temple of his power. They gathered their slighter
    dead from the biting
Winds of time in his lee, the wide moor
About him is swollen with barrows and breaks upon many stones,
Lean gray guardians of old urned ashes,
In waves on waves of purple heather and blithe spray of its bells.
Here lies the hero, more than half God,
And nobody knows his name nor his race, in the bee-bright
    necropolis,
With the stone circle and his tribe around him.

Sometimes perhaps (but who'd confess it?) in soft adolescence
We used to wonder at the world, and have wished
To hear some final harmony resolve the discords of life?
– Here they are all perfectly resolved.

FRANK ORMSBY

HOME

Once, in the Giant's Ring, I closed my eyes
and thought of Ireland,
the air-wide, skin-tight, multiple meaning of here.

When I opened them I was little the wiser,
in that, perhaps, one
with the first settlers in the Lagan Valley
and the Vietnamese boat-people of Portadown.

CIARAN CARSON

NIGHT OUT

Every Thursday night when we press the brass button on the galvanized
    wire mesh gate
A figure appears momentarily at the end of the strip-lit concrete passageway,
Then disappears. The gate squeaks open, slams shut almost instantly
    behind us.
Then through the semi-opaque heavy-duty polythene swing doors they
    might have taken
From a hospital. At the bar, we get the once-over once again.

Seven whiskeys later, the band is launching into *Four Green Fields*.
From somewhere out beyond the breeze-block walls we get a broken
    rhythm

Of machine-gun fire. A ragged chorus. So the sentence of the night
Is punctuated through and through by rounds of drink, of bullets, of
    applause.

HAIRLINE CRACK

It could have been or might have been. Everything Provisional and Sticky,
Daily splits and splinters at the drop of a hat or a principle –
The right hand wouldn't even know it was the right hand; some would
    claim it
As the left. If only this, if only that, if only pigs could fly.
Someone decides, hawk or dove. Ambushes are sprung. Velvet fist.
    Iron glove.

It was on the stroke of midnight by the luminous dial of the clock
When this woman, caught in crossfire, stooped for the dashboard
    cigarette lighter.
In that instant, a bullet neatly parted her permanent wave. So now
She tells the story, how a cigarette made all the odds. Between life. And
    death.

COCKTAILS

Bombing at about ninety miles an hour with the exhaust skittering
The skid-marked pitted tarmac of Kennedy Way, they hit the ramp and
    sailed
Clean over the red-and-white guillotine of the check-point and landed
On the M1 flyover, then disappeared before the Brits knew what hit
    them. So
The story went: we were in the Whip and Saddle bar of the Europa.

There was talk of someone who was shot nine times and lived, and
    someone else
Had the inside info on the Romper Room. We were trying to remember
    the facts

Behind the Black & Decker case, when someone ordered another drink
  and we entered
The realm of Jabberwocks and Angels' Wings, Widows' Kisses, Corpse
Revivers.

ANDREW WATERMAN

SUMMER TRUCE

The weather holds. From Strangford Lough to Swilly
soft arms of coast cradle still water.
Sunning before our shore's-edge cottage we
'enjoy it while it lasts', watch floated fronds
of seaweed among the rocks slightly
lifting with a glitter like broken glass.

And the radio talks into blue day –
to campions, sea-pinks, primroses run wild
over springy turf – of another sectarian killing,
a club blown up, several injured.
The tiny insistent voice is a black mote
in the mind, troubling the horizon

within which our concerns are local as
the cliff-path hesitating its few miles
to Portrush. We have our jokes, lovemaking,
morning-squabbles; John and Mary are at
each other's throats in phone-kiosks, kitchens;
another friend founders in private madness;

and 'Fuck off to Limavady' as the man said
last night to his girl, means over the edge
of the little world. But later ourselves beyond
Limavady, we find in Derry
the truce keeps up, with festive bunting and
the soldiers relaxed and eating ice-cream.

We drink Campari in sweet evening air
where mountains pour down to the lough-side;
seething at Reggie you shred a pound note with your teeth.
– And this morning sit writing it up in your journal
here on the city wall, where ten days back
that policeman was shot from no personal anger.

All peace is imperfect. At last Belfast: the pub
where we talk poetry is pocked from old bombings –
nothing's worth fixing these days. In the gents'
a washbasin grimed and fractured, filled with glass,
taps issuing only a parched gush of air.
Outside, still sunshine. Everyone waits for the break.

PAUL MULDOON

TRUCE

It begins with one or two soldiers
And one or two following
With hampers over their shoulders.
They might be off wildfowling

As they would another Christmas Day,
So gingerly they pick their steps.
No one seems sure of what to do.
All stop when one stops.

A fire gets lit. Some spread
Their greatcoats on the frozen ground.
Polish vodka, fruit and bread
Are broken out and passed round.

The air of an old German song,
The rules of Patience, are the secrets

They'll share before long.
They draw on their last cigarettes

As Friday-night lovers, when it's over,
Might get up from their mattresses
To congratulate each other
And exchange names and addresses.

DEREK MAHON

DERRY MORNING

The mist clears and the cavities
Glow black in the rubbled city's
Broken mouth. An early crone,
Muse of a fitful revolution
Wasted by the fray, she sees
Her *aisling* falter in the breeze,
Her oak-grove vision hesitate
By empty wharf and city gate.

Here it began, and here at least
It fades into the finite past
Or seems to: clattering shadows whop
Mechanically over pub and shop.
A strangely pastoral silence rules
The shining roofs and murmuring schools;
For this is how the centuries work –
Two steps forward, one step back.

Hard to believe this tranquil place,
Its desolation almost peace,
Was recently a boom-town wild
With expectation, each unscheduled
Incident a measurable
Tremor on the Richter Scale

Of world events, each vibrant scene
Translated to the drizzling screen.

What of the change envisioned here,
The quantum leap from fear to fire?
Smoke from a thousand chimneys strains
One way beneath the returning rains
That shroud the bomb-sites, while the fog
Of time receives the ideologue.
A Russian freighter bound for home
Mourns to the city in its gloom.

JAMES SIMMONS

AN IRISH EPIPHANY

Always after the martyrdom
the chip vans arrive.
In the free republic merchants
and visitors will thrive.

SEAMUS DEANE

GUERILLAS

When the Portuguese came in
From manoeuvres in the North
Atlantic, they brought a scent
Of oranges and dark tobacco
To our Arctic streets. Norwegians,
However, were tall and cold,
Drinkers of cheap wine
That blued their eyes more
Than was good for anyone

Who bothered them. Some women
Became sailors' dolls and others
Disapproved. We smelt corruption
In the hot grease of liquor
And foreign language that spat
Around us in *The Moonlight Club*.
Some pleasure writhed there
And some fear. A fight occurred
And then there came the Military
Police who hammered silence out
With night sticks, wall to wall.
And then we'd steal the drinks
Left on the tables they had pushed
Aside to clear the floor.
The whiskey was watered, we could tell.
A medical treacle had been served
As rum. But that was business.
Pollution entered everything and made it
Fierce. Real life was so impure
We savoured its poisons as forbidden
Fruit and, desolate with knowledge,
Grew beyond redemption. Teachers
Washed their hands of us.
Innocent of any specific crime,
We were beaten for a general guilt,
Regular as clockwork. We watched
And questioned nothing. There would be a time
When the foreign sailors would be gone.
Business would still be business.
Whiskey would still be watered,
Some girls would still be dolls;
The Arctic would have inched nearer,
Pollution have gone deeper
And life, entirely domestic, would carry on.

TOM PAULIN

A SEPTEMBER RISING

I nearly saw them this morning.
There was rust in the beech leaves,
The branches were twisted and nude, grey
In the glistening from a blue that stretched
The subtlest, the finest of frosts.

They were there in that air,
Faintly cheeping, chittering a white
Web in the blue. Changing and staying still.
Squaddies and navvies perhaps, but
Mainly the spirit grocers.

Beyond politeness, justified;
Beyond salt bacon and rickety bells
Jangled on light doors by their betters.
The invisible purveyors of provisions,
Glad now in their fine element.

They could chicker above the trees
In the blue air, they could be
Queerly happy and seethe like sprats,
Like fresh silver in the deepest drawer.
Everywhere their names are fading,

They are taken down, stranded
Among speed, on forgotten shelves
In the back offices of new democracies;
But they live, they live again
Above brick cities which are soldiers' villages.

SEAMUS HEANEY

TRIPTYCH

I

AFTER A KILLING

There they were, as if our memory hatched them,
As if the unquiet founders walked again:
Two young men with rifles on the hill,
Profane and bracing as their instruments.

Who's sorry for our trouble?
Who dreamt that we might dwell among ourselves
In rain and scoured light and wind-dried stones?
Basalt, blood, water, headstones, leeches.

In that neuter original loneliness
From Brandon to Dunseverick
I think of small-eyed survivor flowers,
The pined-for, unmolested orchid.

I see a stone house by a pier.
Elbow room. Broad window light.
The heart lifts. You walk twenty yards
To the boats and buy mackerel.

And today a girl walks in home to us
Carrying a basket full of new potatoes,
Three tight green cabbages, and carrots
With the tops and mould still fresh on them.

II

SIBYL

My tongue moved, a swung relaxing hinge.
I said to her, 'What will become of us?'
And as forgotten water in a well might shake
At an explosion under morning

Or a crack run up a gable,
She began to speak.
'I think our very form is bound to change.
Dogs in a siege. Saurian relapses. Pismires.

'Unless forgiveness finds its nerve and voice,
Unless the helmeted and bleeding tree
Can green and open buds like infants' fists
And the fouled magma incubate

'Bright nymphs . . . My people think money
And talk weather. Oil-rigs lull their future
On single acquisitive stems. Silence
Has shoaled into the trawlers' echo-sounders.

'The ground we kept our ear to for so long
Is flayed or calloused, and its entrails
Tented by an impious augury.
Our island is full of comfortless noises.'

III

AT THE WATER'S EDGE

On Devenish I heard a snipe
And the keeper's recital of elegies
Under the tower. Carved monastic heads
Were crumbling like bread on water.

On Boa the god-eyed, sex-mouthed stone
Socketed between graves, two-faced, trepanned,
Answered my silence with silence.
A stoup for rain water. Anathema.

From a cold hearthstone on Horse Island
I watched the sky beyond the open chimney
And listened to the thick rotations
Of an army helicopter patrolling.

A hammer and a cracked jug full of cobwebs
Lay on the windowsill. Everything in me

Wanted to bow down, to offer up,
To go barefoot, foetal and penitential,

And pray at the water's edge.
How we crept before we walked! I remembered
The helicopter shadowing our march at Newry,
The scared, irrevocable steps.

ARTHUR MCVEIGH

THOUGHT ON THE DERRY RIOTS

As I was walking round the streets of Derry
I saw old Hobbits
Looking very pleased.
He was wearing a policeman's hat
And about six watches
On his arm.
On his bicycle was
Half a landrover,
And in his hand
A bottle of wine.
I got to thinking there was a riot
And it looked as if old Hobbits had won.

SAM BURNSIDE

IN AND OUT OF DERRY

The Donegal mountains, sitting out there
Blue, blunt heaps of lignite, sad hinterland
To a burning city; and the heavy stone walls
And houses, shops and factories, fronts erased,
Sag into the bog-ground while light title-deeds

Change hands in the silent communion of commerce.
The city's odd shop-keepers, sour and mean enough,
Clang their rat-trap tills and keep the doors guarded.
For there are those who disregard limb and life
Who blast and bomb with red-eyed, mad-dog malice;
Then again there are those who disregard even that,
Who live only for profit and tomorrow's gain.
If things were different there'd be no buts but
Life goes on, has, and somehow always will,
Despite the bombs and assassinations.
We are successful in ignoring these things,
And carry on, forming – from the old twin cultures –
Some new kind of human resistance and bloody-minded calmness.
In a hundred years it will warrant a paragraph
In some history book: the common people they'll call us,
(Our fathers, they'll note, paid a shilling for a rat,
And ate quartered dogs to live), and they'll not know
Or not reckon the fear in pubs, in shops,
The daily bumping over ramps, the body-searches,
The tension of fire-sirens singing in darkness.

FRANCIS STUART

READING KEATS IN DERRY CITY

September deepens and the nights are long
And noisy; through this autumn damp with blood
There glows the other autumn of his song,
There falls the shadow of the old oak wood
Over the broken, dusty streets that lead
Us on to death's steep brink. And there is still
That spot where the sun slants across the hill
Burning the leaves as though the branches bleed.

My childhood's magic moments shone between
These ancient walls; I will return once more,

One evening late and weary I will lean
Against that gate or knock upon that door
To find again the dusky littered room
Where the oil lamp smokes and the curtains smell of home.

CAROL RUMENS

PASSING A STATUE OF OUR LADY IN DERRY

She appears tired, though dressed in fresh, white stone,
And bows the bandaged snowdrop of her head -
Pleadingly to the bus – which hurries on
And leaves her stranded in my childhood,

Mother of small contritions, great hopes
And the lyric boredom of the rosary
When miracles seemed at our fingertips:
She is much younger now than formerly,

And in her narrow, girlish hands, she weighs
Not holiness, but a frail, human idea
That might accomplish anything – dismiss
An army – or, like childhood, disappear.

SAM BURNSIDE

GRAVEYARDS

We could plunder through burial grounds for ever
Making safe stepping stones of the fallen stones
Scraping moss out of each incised line of evidence.
In the autumn of the year in such places
The slightest breath of air sets leaves whispering;
The sap gone out of them now, they are fussy,

They strive to protest in the face of life,
Snapping spitefully before the fact of life.
Children and lovers delight to kick them aside;
In their state, they have no mind for the departed,
They have no bone to pick with sad martyrs.

JOSEPH BRODSKY

BELFAST TUNE

Here's a girl from a dangerous town.
　　She crops her dark hair short
so that less of her has to frown
　　when someone gets hurt.

She folds her memories like a parachute.
　　Dropped, she collects the peat
and cooks her veggies at home: they shoot
　　here where they eat.

Ah, there's more sky in these parts than, say,
　　ground. Hence her voice's pitch,
and her stare stains your retina like a gray
　　bulb when you switch

hemispheres, and her knee-length quilt
　　skirt's cut to catch the squall.
I dream of her either loved or killed
　　because the town's too small.

PADRAIC FIACC

GOODBYE TO BRIGID/AN *AGNUS DEI*

I take you by the hand. Your eyes,
Mirroring the traffic lights,
Are green and orange and red.

The Military lorries by our side
Drown out your child-heart
Thumping tired under the soot

-black thorn trees these
Exhaust-fumed greasy mornings.

My little girl, my Lamb of God,
I'd like to set you free from
Bitch Belfast as we pass the armed

-to-the-back-teeth barracks and
Descend the road into the school
Grounds of broken windows from

A spate of car-bombs, but
Don't forgive me for not.

JOHN MONTAGUE

CAVE

The rifled honeycomb
of the high-rise hotel
where a wind tunnel moans.
While jungleclad troops
ransack the Falls, race
through huddled streets,

we lie awake, the wide
window washed with rain,
your oval face, and tide
of yellow hair luminous
as you turn to me again
seeking refuge as the
cave of night blooms
with fresh explosions.

JANICE FITZPATRICK

A FOREIGN LOVE STORY AT PORTMUCK

Now, let me name you
and you might settle in,
take a quiet place in this unquiet heart:
Portmuck, little pig of the Irish Sea.
Ulster, what happens here.

I saw you before I saw you
and though I clutched your open palm
I might have turned away
thinking that love wasn't enough.
It was dark and you talked to me
long into passing nights.

Forgive me then, I noticed
the colour of spring gentian,
and your winter nights –
darker than any I've known.
There is my pumping heart
and this old blood between us.
I was afraid, I am sometimes still afraid

of this: the way a single voice will break
an evening's horizon over the Irish Sea,
and how in the shallows grey water laps grey rock

dull as the dullest houses in Belfast
where children carry petrol bombs like frisbees
and mark each anniversary with burnt tyres.

Another ending day in quiet Ulster.
The sun descends calling up the summer stars
and a moon so thin and light-sharpened
that house cats can hunt behind every garden,
take delight at their puzzled victims' blink and start.

This past summer the ragged clouds
dragged across the Plough;
rare and warming winds streamed
off lough waters and shook the leaves of occasional oaks
planted long ago amid the roadside hedges.
It's years of weather that creates this complexity.

The pig is sleeping in my harbour,
and days have gone by
since the last crude bomb killed a baby.

In this beautiful countryside
it's no natural disaster that singles out its victims.

This is a love poem – believe me.
I am trying to tell you only about this:
the quirky ways the heart might heal.
And isn't this late love understanding?
Don't we try to admit each other; don't we acknowledge
how close we are and how different we can be?
Listen to the sharp cries of kittiwakes,
hear the healing slap of water against your tired body –
the power indefatigable and upborne as that osprey
who yesterday, holding his body against the wind,
hovered between seacliff and harbour waves.

PAUL MULDOON

THE FIELD HOSPITAL

Taking, giving back their lives
By the strength of our bare hands,
By the silence of our knives,
We answer to no grey South

Nor blue North, not self defence,
The lie of just wars, neither
Cold nor hot blood's difference
In their discharging of guns,

But that hillside of fresh graves.
Would this girl brought to our tents
From whose flesh we have removed
Shot that George, on his day off,

Will use to weight fishing lines,
Who died screaming for ether,
Yet protest our innocence?
George lit the lanterns, in danced

Those gigantic, yellow moths
That brushed right over her wounds,
Pinning themselves to our sleeves
Like medals given the brave.

CIARAN CARSON

THE KNEE

His first bullet is a present, a mark of intelligence that will
End in the gutter behind The Clock Bar, since he keeps on doing what
He's not supposed to. The next one is for real, what we've just talked about.

It seems he was a hood, whatever, or the lads were just being careful.
Two and two were put together; what they added up to wasn't five.

Visiting time: he takes his thirteen-month-old son on his other knee.
Learning to walk, he suddenly throws himself into the staggering
Distance between his father and his father's father, hands held up high,
His legs like the hands of a clock, one trying to catch up on the other.

FRANK ORMSBY

KING WILLIAM PARK

The mountains must have watched it, the startled eyes
of swamp-life and the long-shinned estuary birds:
that tidal glitter curling out to sea
for the last time, abandoning its mud.
Then centuries of minute adjustments, rivers
changing their beds,
the shifting work of sloblands under the sky
and fibrous growths toughening, holding their own.

Fowlers, fishers and settlers, intricate drains,
channels and cargoes, chimneys, streetlamps and trams;
but always the brickwork tilting, buildings on stilts,
the tide-swell echoes creeping out of the ground
yearly to meet the rainfall and shaping themselves
to crests and troughs in the tarmac, undulant cobbles.
Or pouring their excess out of sudden wounds
in streets miles inland.

Here, where the park is, breakers found a shore
to bury shells, jetsam a place to lie.
Daily the winos spend their bleary rage
in squabbles among the benches,
or sing their hearts out searching for a song
on a green patch with trees beside a junction.

316

And knee-capped boys on crutches raise their heads
to follow us past the railings,

wintry eyes asking how far we have come
and where we are going. A terraced marsh away,
sludge-pumps have sucked a resting-place for stone:
the blocks of a new hospital are hauled
through scaffolding, past windows where the sun
flames in the evening gloriously, or the rain
drifts into soundless networks on its way
to the earth-clogged ears in the groundwork, the listening shells.

FLEUR ADCOCK

THE BULLAUN

'Drink water from the hollow in the stone . . .'
This was it, then – the cure for madness:
a rock with two round cavities, filled with rain;
a thing I'd read about once, and needed then,
but since forgotten. I didn't expect it here –
not having read the guidebook;
not having planned, even, to be in Antrim.
'There's a round tower, isn't there?' I'd asked.
The friendly woman in the post office
gave me directions: 'Up there past the station,
keep left, on a way further – it's a fair bit –
and have you been to Lough Neagh yet?' I walked –
it wasn't more than a mile – to the stone phallus
rising above its fuzz of beech-trees
in the municipal gardens. And beside it,
this. I circled around them,
backing away over wet grass and beechmast,
aiming the camera (since I had it with me,
since I was playing tourist this afternoon)
and saw two little boys pelting across.
'Take our photo! Take our photo! Please!'

We talked it over for a bit –
how I couldn't produce one then and there;
but could I send it to them with the postman?
Well, could they give me their addresses?
Kevin Tierney and Declan McCallion,
Tobergill Gardens. I wrote, they stood and smiled,
I clicked, and waved goodbye, and went.
Two miles away, an hour later,
heading dutifully through the damp golf-course
to Lough Neagh, I thought about the rock,
wanting it. Not for my own salvation;
hardly at all for me: for sick Belfast,
for the gunmen and the slogan-writers,
for the poor crazy girl I met in the station,
for Kevin and Declan, who would soon mistrust
all camera-carrying strangers. But of course
the thing's already theirs: a monument,
a functionless, archaic, pitted stone
and a few mouthfuls of black rainwater.

SEAMUS HEANEY

from THE CURE AT TROY

Human beings suffer,
They torture one another,
They get hurt and get hard.
No poem or play or song
Can fully right a wrong
Inflicted and endured.

The innocent in gaols
Beat on their bars together.
A hunger-striker's father
Stands in the graveyard dumb.
The police widow in veils
Faints at the funeral home.

History says, *Don't hope*
On this side of the grave.
But then, once in a lifetime
The longed-for tidal wave
Of justice can rise up,
And hope and history rhyme.

So hope for a great sea-change
On the far side of revenge.
Believe that a further shore
Is reachable from here.
Believe in miracles
And cures and healing wells.

Call miracle self-healing:
The utter, self-revealing
Double-take of feeling.
If there's fire on the mountain
Or lightning and storm
And a god speaks from the sky

That means someone is hearing
The outcry and the birth-cry
Of new life at its term.

FRANK ORMSBY

INCURABLES

Plaques and a marble silence about the door
of the Ulster Cancer Foundation, the air a tissue
shredding between the chimneys and the moon.
We eavesdrop on police cars, the shift and crackle
of ice in the wavelengths.
Our charts are frosty promises. Their troughs
may suck us down forever and who will know
or care what perished.

Or children may have the peace
to say of us: 'They lived in troubled times.
They stayed afloat and somehow kept their warmth.'
For now, we are grateful that our breath still wreathes
east of the City Cemetery, numinous skies
between us and the troubled distances.
The blinds are lit, the moon is finding gold
in every street's mouthful of worn cobbles.

JOHN HEWITT

THE SCAR
for Padraic Fiacc

There's not a chance now that I might recover
one syllable of what that sick man said,
tapping upon my great-grandmother's shutter,
and begging, I was told, a piece of bread;
for on his tainted breath there hung infection
rank from the cabins of the stricken west,
the spores from black potato-stalks, the spittle
mottled with poison in his rattling chest;
but she who, by her nature, quickly answered,
accepted in return the famine-fever;
and that chance meeting, that brief confrontation,
conscribed me of the Irishry forever.

Though much I cherish lies outside their vision,
and much they prize I have no claim to share,
yet in that woman's death I found my nation;
the old wound aches and shews its fellow-scar.

GERALD DAWE

SOLSTICE
for my daughter

You arrived that bad winter
when I was like a man
walking in a circle no one else was near.

The lakes behind had frozen,
from the dump gulls came and went
and the news was all discontent,

of *Sell-Out* and blame for the dead
country-boy faces that already were
fading from church wall and gate,

but the seas tightened their grip
when you faced the light and let rip
a first cry of bewilderment

at this beginning, the snow
buttressed against brilliant windows,
and where they washed you clean

I saw the ice outside fall
and imagined the fires burning
on the Hill of Tara ring

across the concealed earth
towards a silent hospital
and our standing still

all around you, Olwen,
transfixed by your birth
in such a bitter season.

MICHAEL KINGHAN

LIFE ON MARS

Just before tea
I take my walk again.
I have been neglectful of it lately.
I must see to it
that my glen has not been bulldozed,
that my rocks do not forget me,
that the name in my tree
has not been carved over
by another lover
of trees.

I cannot believe a man I love
is a candidate for death.
Belfast Lough is tranquil.
Belfast looks romantic under its smog.
It makes you think of the breath of industry.
Human beings are fearlessly walking dogs.

By this time
I ought to have adjusted myself
to the climate of death's democracy.
I ought to have learned to believe death's laws.
I ought to have taken up death's cause
poetically.
I ought to have stopped talking
to rocks and trees
long ago.

But I don't.
And Supremo after Supremo sails up the Lough
in a convoy of bubbles
agreeing with me.
I will make myself something exotic for my tea,
and tune my radio

to the BBC's Mars Service
where men are talking sense incessantly.

MARTIN MOONEY

RADIO FREE NOWHERE

We broadcast on the move,
one day perhaps from an attic
in a derelict terrace,
the next from an old shed
on a disused allotment.

We can set up shop anywhere
and be gone in an hour
leaving things as we found them.
The only risk we run
is to be caught in the act,

our transmissions so short,
so nearly untraceable,
a poem or a manifesto
sandwiched between records
is almost unnoticeable,

its small infiltration lodged
in any ear close to a set
a hair's-breadth of ore
or a fleck of mica
in their acres of soft rock.

ROBERT JOHNSTONE

from NEW INCIDENTS IN THE LIFE OF SHELLEY

Not from our dreams, not from our daft cadres
but from somewhere real, the free enclave we
know inside but can't annex, static or

messages are picked up from the tiny
pirate, Radio Shelley. He reads our odes
over the air, sends reports from countries

claiming to be still at peace, where crops grow
and only the facts are changed to protect
our innocence. At his dangerous modes

of thought valves buzz and blush in our old set
on the cleared tea table. Just to have heard
his programme and talk too loud about it

can cost promotion, yet we grab each word.
We demand contact with that better world.

JOHN MONTAGUE

PROCESSION
I.M. Grandmother Hannah Carney

Hawk nose, snuff-stained apron;
I stand beside you again in
the gloom of your hallway
peering up & down Fintona's
cattle-stained Main Street
some thronged fairday evening.

As you ramble on, like someone
sick or drunk, confessing to
a stranger in a bar, or train;
ignoring my small years while
you spell out your restless pain,
mourn a tormented lifetime.

Frank, your pride, eldest boy,
interrogated again and again,
arrested in your warm kitchen,
bayonets and British voices
bullying him abruptly away
to the barbed wire, the tin

huts of Ballykinler, model
for Long Kesh, Magilligan.
Your youngest son, Tom, then
drills in the old bandroom
to follow him; soon lands
himself into the Curragh prison.

Released, your two internees
were met at the railway station,
cheered and chaired home
with a torchlight procession:
but one half of the town
held its blinds grimly down.

Still hatred and division
stain that narrow acre
from which you sprang.
A half century later
the same black dreams
return to plague your daughter,
their sister, my mother.

A Paisleyite meeting
blared outside her window.
A military helicopter

hovered over the hospital,
a maleficent spider. Her
dying nightmares were of her
sons seized by soldiers!

Across the rough, small hills
of your country girlhood –
the untamed territory of
the Barr, Brougher Mountain –
we brought your daughter home,
yellow car beams streaming;
a torchlight procession.

SEAMUS HEANEY

FUNERAL RITES

I

I shouldered a kind of manhood
stepping in to lift the coffins
of dead relations.
They had been laid out

in tainted rooms,
their eyelids glistening,
their dough-white hands
shackled in rosary beads.

Their puffed knuckles
had unwrinkled, the nails
were darkened, the wrists
obediently sloped.

The dulse-brown shroud,
the quilted satin cribs:
I knelt courteously
admiring it all

as wax melted down
and veined the candles,
the flames hovering
to the women hovering

behind me.
And always, in a corner,
the coffin lid,
its nail-heads dressed

with little gleaming crosses.
Dear soapstone masks,
kissing their igloo brows
had to suffice

before the nails were sunk
and the black glacier
of each funeral
pushed away.

II

Now as news comes in
of each neighbourly murder
we pine for ceremony,
customary rhythms:

the temperate footsteps
of a cortège, winding past
each blinded home.
I would restore

the great chambers of Boyne,
prepare a sepulchre
under the cupmarked stones.
Out of side-streets and bye-roads

purring family cars
nose into line,
the whole country tunes
to the muffled drumming

of ten thousand engines.
Somnambulant women,
left behind, move
through emptied kitchens

imagining our slow triumph
towards the mounds.
Quiet as a serpent
in its grassy boulevard

the procession drags its tail
out of the Gap of the North
as its head already enters
the megalithic doorway.

III

When they have put the stone
back in its mouth
we will drive north again
past Strang and Carling fjords

the cud of memory
allayed for once, arbitration
of the feud placated,
imagining those under the hill

disposed like Gunnar
who lay beautiful
inside his burial mound,
though dead by violence

and unavenged.
Men said that he was chanting
verses about honour
and that four lights burned

in corners of the chamber:
which opened then, as he turned
with a joyful face
to look at the moon.

AN ULSTER TWILIGHT

The bare bulb, a scatter of nails,
Shelved timber, glinting chisels:
In a shed of corrugated iron
Eric Dawson stoops to his plane

At five o'clock on a Christmas Eve.
Carpenter's pencil next, the spoke-shave,
Fretsaw, auger, rasp and awl,
A rub with a rag of linseed oil.

A mile away it was taking shape,
The hulk of a toy battleship,
As waterbuckets iced and frost
Hardened the quiet on roof and post.

Where is he now?
There were fifteen years between us two
That night I strained to hear the bells
Of a sleigh of the mind and heard him pedal

Into our lane, get off at the gable,
Steady his Raleigh bicycle
Against the whitewash, stand to make sure
The house was quiet, knock at the door

And hand his parcel to a peering woman:
'I suppose you thought I was never coming.'
Eric, tonight I saw it all
Like shadows on your workshop wall,

Smelled wood shavings under the bench,
Weighed the cold steel monkey-wrench

In my soft hand, then stood at the road
To watch your wavering tail-light fade

And knew that if we met again
In an Ulster twilight we would begin
And end whatever we might say
In a speech all toys and carpentry,

A doorstep courtesy to shun
Your father's uniform and gun,
But – now that I have said it out –
Maybe none the worse for that.

JOHN HEWITT

THE HILL-FARM

My errand brought me once again
along the steep road, down the lane;
and through the long and stumbling dark
there was no cry, no welcome bark
announced my nearing. All was still
from lamp in glen to star on hill.
The door was shut, but curtained light
thrust muffled challenge to the night.
Then at the porch I stopped and stood
to muster courage to intrude,
for, as I paused, I overheard
the rise and fall of rhythmic word,
a voice, the mother's, giving clear
the rosary, the evening prayer,
and, mumbling on a lower key,
the voices of the family
responding and repeating, each
with adult or with childish speech,
the invocations running on,
with, now and then, a smothered yawn.

At each Hail Mary Full of Grace
I pictured every friendly face,
clenched in devotion of a kind
alien to my breed and mind,
easy as breathing, natural
as birds that fly, as leaves that fall;
yet with a sense that I still stood
far from that faith-based certitude,
here in the vast enclosing night,
outside its little ring of light.

SEAMUS HEANEY

THE OTHER SIDE

I

Thigh-deep in sedge and marigolds
a neighbour laid his shadow
on the stream, vouching

'It's poor as Lazarus, that ground',
and brushed away
among the shaken leafage:

I lay where his lea sloped
to meet our fallow,
nested on moss and rushes,

my ear swallowing
his fabulous, biblical dismissal,
that tongue of chosen people.

When he would stand like that
on the other side, white-haired,
swinging his blackthorn

at the marsh weeds,
he prophesied above our scraggy acres,
then turned away

towards his promised furrows
on the hill, a wake of pollen
drifting to our bank, next season's tares.

II

For days we would rehearse
each patriarchal dictum:
Lazarus, the Pharaoh, Solomon

and David and Goliath rolled
magnificently, like loads of hay
too big for our small lanes,

or faltered on a rut –
'Your side of the house, I believe,
hardly rule by the book at all.'

His brain was a whitewashed kitchen
hung with texts, swept tidy
as the body o' the kirk.

III

Then sometimes when the rosary was dragging
mournfully on in the kitchen
we would hear his step round the gable

though not until after the litany
would the knock come to the door
and the casual whistle strike up

on the doorstep. 'A right-looking night,'
he might say, 'I was dandering by
and says I, I might as well call.'

But now I stand behind him
in the dark yard, in the moan of prayers.
He puts a hand in a pocket

or taps a little tune with the blackthorn
shyly, as if he were party to
lovemaking or a stranger's weeping.

Should I slip away, I wonder,
or go up and touch his shoulder
and talk about the weather

or the price of grass-seed?

ROBERT JOHNSTONE

AT THE END OF THE DAY

*. . . invariably everyone was referring to the reckoning to come when
the ledgers of hate would be balanced and the accounts of history finally
settled . . .*

Padraig O'Malley, *The Uncivil Wars*

Cars process past houses, all purchased
        on the never-never,
the sun drips gold on a pellucid
        blue evening of summer,
calm and full of threat, like the world's end,
        every car is silver
descending Tate's Bridge, each descendant
        tuned to the newscaster
– problems with traffic, X was blasted,
        man dead on his tractor,
and the news that what's been predicted
        has been proved true for sure:
the last trump will, or may, have sounded,

there will be a free cure
for everyone who couldn't afford it
and those caught in crossfire,
the bystanders, the unlucky dead,
will learn that life is fair,
fire chariots will be seen overhead,
the bricks will sag once more,
decisively, back to wobbly mud,
we'll ask, 'What was it all for?'
except a tramp who loathes Jews, whose head
is full of hate, desire
for wine, pain, who sinks back in fetid
clothes, a sated lover:
'It was exciting while it lasted
but I'm glad it's over.'

SEÁN DUNNE

from LETTER FROM IRELAND
for Vincent Buckley

Black sacks flapping on street corners, stiff
　Drummers walk to the Republican plot.
Behind them women in black parade with
　Flags dipped slightly. At the sacred spot
　A sheltered man proclaims a speech – *We will not
Stop struggling until the British leave.
There will be no ceasefire. We give no relief.*

Black sacks on hedges, black sacks on doors,
　Black plastic rustling as black hearses pass.
Fertiliser bags tied to electricity poles
　Signal an anger at the ultimate impasse.
　Refuse sacks, strung and stuffed, have heads to match
Thatcher or Paisley, and across a bridge some hand
Has painted in white: *Remember Bobby Sands.*

Black sacks in the doorway, black sacks in the field,
  Black rifles uncovered on a Donegal strand.
Black border on photographs, black dresses for grief,
  Black berets on coffins, black bowlers and bands,
  Black bullet holes in hallways, black words of command.
Black taxis, black jackets, black bruise and contusion.
Black crepe on a letter box, the Royal Black Institution.

Death stalks the farms of south Tyrone,
  Ruffles its cold clothes and changes
Direction for Armagh, stopping to take home
  A soldier ambushed at greeting's range.
  Nobody seems to think it strange
When Death makes some mistake and takes
As well a girl near a farmyard gate.

No matter how I try, that theme
  Slips in like fog through broken windows,
Settling on everything even if it seems
  Impossibly out of reach. Again, I forego
  My instinct for caution and let go
With rhetoric. Yet who, I ask you, could block
Misery out with the blackbird over Belfast Lough?

Echoes, echoes. That old monk in his cell
  Making from bird's cry a gloss
Is sometimes what I'd like to be, well
  Hidden by woodland, free from dross
  With nothing on my mind but women and the cross,
Watercress, berries, and a fly who'd tell
What page I stopped at in the Book of Kells.

But life is wasted searching for the pure
  Meaning of mountains or the ultimate food,
And nothing annoys me more than the dour
  Misfortunates looking for the perfect good
  In sandals and sea salt, windmills and woods
Where they stalk and tramp for purity yet
Still pause to roll a handmade cigarette.

I love instead more ordinary things
  And prefer to gaze on two women talking
Than on plants that grow as they sense you sing,
    While blokes communing with misty mornings
    Are ditchwater-dull compared to the shrill
Whistle of a train. Stuff joss sticks and ouija:
Van Morrison's worth ten of the Maharishi.

Most of what I love's more harmless and mild:
  Books, chips mixed with curry, fine
Typefaces, hurling, woodcuts, light
    Operas and spices, poker at midnight,
    The inside story of gangland fights.
Not to mention Macaulay's prose and slow
Descriptions of silence by H.D. Thoreau.

In other moods I enjoy pillow-talk, say,
  Lightened by love, or the smell of old
Shops where scales tremble with weights.
    I love deserted docklands and cold
    Suburban streets where anything goes.
Mozart, I suppose, Bob Dylan if in the mood,
Ella Fitzgerald singing 'Solitude'.

My Ireland has no tin whistle wailing
  Against creels and mists on open bogs,
And neither has it place for imitation
    Thatch on houses, or for mock
    Blather to camouflage how dog eats dog.
I have no time for the view that Ireland's
The sum of the scenes at a Munster Final.

My Ireland has no dark clichéd hag
  Toothless in turfsmoke as she cackles.
I have seen the face of a woman dragged
    Through bedrooms screaming, battered
    And bruised until her body blackened.
Deirdre of the Sorrows thrives
Mostly in the home for battered wives.

The theme is changing, my rage revives.
Memory Ireland. They shoot heroin these
Times in streets where Connolly said lives
Were lost in slumland hunger and disease
While gentrified suburbs sat in cushioned ease.
Archaeologists point to our early tribes
Where flatlands shelter fifty thousand lives.

So you see, dear Vincent, the outlook's bad
Though still there's much that compensates.
The country's split in a thousand parts
But old ideas still predominate.
The peasant leaning on his broken gate
Is now a manager screaming for more
Grants as his workers face the lengthy dole.

Sometimes I go to Cobh and stare
For ages at water where emigrants waved
To families on the crowded pier.
In Manhattan or Boston, they saved
Enough to bring another until all were there.
Old drawings depicted a country dying:
Grim men standing, shawled women crying.

The liners they left on are pictured on walls
Of bars and hotel lounges, generations marred
By misery and the need to pour all
Into tickets for White Star or Cunard.
The country wears their going like a scar.
Today their relatives save to support and
Send others in planes for the new diaspora.

On the coast in west Cork once I saw
An Indian woman throwing petals to the waves.
Water dripped from her sari, drenching her small
Feet as she wept into water that made a grave
For her son killed instantly in a bombed plane.
Her prayers poured over the waters gathering
And receding again. She stood in shallow lather.

337

Often I think of her on that rough shore
And leave her with you now as I end,
Her hands filled with flowers and more
Meaning in the gesture than I can comprehend.
Something of what she signifies I send
To you in Australia: her dignity a sign
Sent out in defiance of her place and time.

FRANK ORMSBY

SOLDIER BATHING

The bigger fish have country cousins here.
At their own depth sonaghen and gillaroo
dart in the quiet loughs and are not found elsewhere.

I dry on the shore and imagine the world renewed
cleanly between two islands I cannot name:
as a rounded stone, say, that the ebb left bare,
or light on water the morning after a war.

SEAMUS HEANEY

FROM THE CANTON OF EXPECTATION

I

We lived deep in a land of optative moods,
under high, banked clouds of resignation.
A rustle of loss in the phrase *Not in our lifetime*,
the broken nerve when we prayed *Vouchsafe* or *Deign*,
were creditable, sufficient to the day.

Once a year we gathered in a field
of dance platforms and tents where children sang

songs they had learned by rote in the old language.
An auctioneer who had fought in the brotherhood
enumerated the humiliations
we always took for granted, but not even he
considered this, I think, a call to action.
Iron-mouthed loudspeakers shook the air
yet nobody felt blamed. He had confirmed us.
When our rebel anthem played the meeting shut
we turned for home and the usual harassment
by militiamen on overtime at roadblocks.

II

And next thing, suddenly, this change of mood.
Books open in the newly wired kitchens.
Young heads that might have dozed a life away
against the flanks of milking cows were busy
paving and pencilling their first causeways
across the prescribed texts. The paving stones
of quadrangles came next and a grammar
of imperatives, the new age of demands.

They would banish the conditional for ever,
this generation born impervious to
the triumph in our cries of *de profundis*.
Our faith in winning by enduring most
they made anathema, intelligences
brightened and unmannerly as crowbars.

III

What looks the strongest has outlived its term.
The future lies with what's affirmed from under.
These things that corroborated us when we dwelt
under the aegis of our stealthy patron,
the guardian angel of passivity,
now sink a fang of menace in my shoulder.
I repeat the word 'stricken' to myself
and stand bareheaded under the banked clouds
edged more and more with brassy thunderlight.
I yearn for hammerblows on clinkered planks,

339

the uncompromised report of driven thole-pins,
to know there is one among us who never swerved
from all his instincts told him was right action,
who stood his ground in the indicative,
whose boat will lift when the cloudburst happens.

IAIN CRICHTON SMITH

IN BELFAST

The years' lessons are written on the walls –
No Surrender – Ulster Says No.
I see in the sky a Presbyterian rainbow,

orange and unforgiving, woven of fire.
To tear apart what oneself owns!
The nun strides through the city like a whore.

The present seethes about the Holy Book.
And drums tap on the coffins of the slain.
The tanks will ride tall through Genesis: masked men stalk.

O Rose of Sharon, modest and demure,
when among broken stones will you bloom once more
into an ordinarily guilty future,

among the waste of broken iron, doors.
And men rather than angels greet across fences
the scoured tired eyes of pity and remorse.

ROBERT GREACEN

A WISH FOR ST PATRICK'S DAY

Holy Patrick we need snakecharmers now,
The snakes have crawled back again.

Exorcise the demons of intransigence,
Send your green fire into the frozen branch.

SAM BURNSIDE

SIX LOUGHS

No bird sings on Belfast Lough.
On Carlingford, on Swilly, on Foyle
Silence has settled, like death in a house
Long prepared. Tall rushes, like mourners
Standing in rain, shadow the waters
Of the two Ernes.

After all the fraudulent mouthings
That for so long revised the truths
All our people saw and knew, this is rest.
She consorted with the other sort; his behaviour
Was anti-social; this one was an informer;
We will not tolerate

Criminal elements. In the meantime
On some bare headland there stands a grey-cloaked figure
Still, bell in hand, eying grey swans, waiting
For another Patrick. But we need a long silence
Now; and a good rain-shower to wash away this sense
That words may mean anything.

So, the place must lie fallow,
While wind-storm and rain-cloud curve
In round the Mournes and over the Sperrins,
From the West crossing the Bluestack mountains
To bleach skeletons, to achieve time's ends
On bodies buried with lies

And false justifications, spoken over them,
After the beatings and the hoodings and the shootings
By roadside and by lake and by mountain stream,
In fields of grass and grain stained twice:
Who now could celebrate the miller's loaves
Bequeathed to us.

On Slemish and in Armagh silence reigns.
A silence carried up from deep Newgrange inhabits
Antrim's glens. The very air is thick with it
And bird and beast wait for some ending of it,
For the breaking of it by some fresh word.

JOHN MONTAGUE

RED BRANCH (A BLESSING)

Sing a song for the broken
towns of old Tyrone:
Omagh, Dungannon, Strabane,
jagged walls and windows,
slowly falling down.

Sing a song for the homes
or owners that were here today
and tomorrow are gone;
Irish Street in Dungannon,
my friend, Jim Devlin.

Sing a song for the people,
so grimly holding on,
Protestant and Catholic, fingered
at teabreak, shot inside their home:
the iron circle of retaliation.

Sing a song for the creaking branch
they find themselves upon,
hollow from top to bottom,
the stricken limb of Ulster,
slowly blown down.

Sing an end to sectarianism,
Fenian and Free Presbyterian,
the punishment slowly grown
more monstrous than the crime,
an enormous seeping bloodstain.

Sing our forlorn hope then –
the great Cross of Verdun,
Belfast's Tower on the Somme –
signs raised over bloody ground
that two crazed peoples make an end.

ROBERT JOHNSTONE

FESTIVAL OF MITHRAS

Our foreign troops on the airport bus
take the word tax, ask who we are,
where we've been and where we're going.
We answer box by box.

Where I've been great refineries
ran right through the winter solstice,
burning wealth in the longest nights,
brighter than English cities.

Where I'm going is coming home
where all words wait to be remembered.
I picked some up and left them here
and they became my own.

I tell friends of overgrown gardens
where a hundred flowers might bloom,
predict folk-tales of now, turf-stacks
beside each dwelling,

a street next year where masked children
offer a penny for your thoughts
or cadge good words at every door
to pile high on waste ground.

Perhaps our litter never gets lost.
For unwrappings, for blowing up things,
we link arms and warm our faces
at the flames of our past.

And out rockets the word Peace,
exploding in stars that make day
until they're consumed utterly
and fall on our heads like nothingness.

MICHAEL LONGLEY

PEACE
after Tibullus

Who was responsible for the very first arms deal –
The man of iron who thought of marketing the sword?
Or did he intend us to use it against wild animals
Rather than ourselves? Even if he's not guilty
Murder got into the bloodstream as gene or virus
So that now we give birth to wars, short cuts to death.
Blame the affluent society: no killings when

The cup on the dinner table was made of beechwood,
And no barricades or ghettos when the shepherd
Snoozed among sheep that weren't even thoroughbreds.

I would like to have been alive in the good old days
Before the horrors of modern warfare and warcries
Stepping up my pulse rate. Alas, as things turn out
I've been press-ganged into service, and for all I know
Someone's polishing a spear with my number on it.
God of my Fathers, look after me like a child!
And don't be embarrassed by this handmade statue
Carved out of bog oak by my great-great-grandfather
Before the mass-production of religious art
When a wooden god stood simply in a narrow shrine.

A man could worship there with bunches of early grapes,
A wreath of whiskery wheat-ears, and then say Thank you
With a wholemeal loaf delivered by him in person,
His daughter carrying the unbroken honeycomb.
If the good Lord keeps me out of the firing line
I'll pick a porker from the steamy sty and dress
In my Sunday best, a country cousin's sacrifice.
Someone else can slaughter enemy commanders
And, over a drink, rehearse with me his memoirs,
Mapping the camp in wine upon the table top.

It's crazy to beg black death to join the ranks
Who dogs our footsteps anyhow with silent feet –
No cornfields in Hell, nor cultivated vineyards,
Only yapping Cerberus and the unattractive
Oarsman of the Styx: there an anaemic crew
Sleepwalks with smoky hair and empty eye-sockets.
How much nicer to have a family and let
Lazy old age catch up on you in your retirement,
You keeping track of the sheep, your son of the lambs,
While the woman of the house puts on the kettle.

I want to live until the white hairs shine above
A pensioner's memories of better days. Meanwhile
I would like peace to be my partner on the farm,

Peace personified: oxen under the curved yoke;
Compost for the vines, grape-juice turning into wine,
Vintage years handed down from father to son;
Hoe and ploughshare gleaming, while in some dark corner
Rust keeps the soldier's grisly weapons in their place;
The labourer steering his wife and children home
In a hay cart from the fields, a trifle sozzled.

Then, if there are skirmishes, guerilla tactics,
It's only lovers quarrelling, the bedroom door
Wrenched off its hinges, a woman in hysterics,
Hair torn out, cheeks swollen with bruises and tears –
Until the bully-boy starts snivelling as well
In a pang of conscience for his battered wife:
Then sexual neurosis works them up again
And the row escalates into a war of words.
He's hard as nails, made of sticks and stones, the chap
Who beats his girlfriend up. A crime against nature.

Enough, surely, to rip from her skin the flimsiest
Of negligées, ruffle that elaborate hair-do,
Enough to be the involuntary cause of tears –
Though upsetting a sensitive girl when you sulk
Is a peculiar satisfaction. But punch-ups,
Physical violence, are out: you might as well
Pack your kit-bag, goose-step a thousand miles away
From the female sex. As for me, I want a woman
To come and fondle my ears of wheat and let apples
Overflow between her breasts. I shall call her Peace.

ACKNOWLEDGEMENTS

Grateful acknowledgement is made to:

Anvil Press Poetry for permission to reprint the following poem by Thomas McCarthy: 'Counting the Dead on the Radio, 1972' from *The Non-Aligned Storyteller* (1984)

Blackstaff Press for permission to reprint the following poems by Norman Dugdale: 'Some Notes for Impartial Observers', 'Night-Ferry' and 'Ithaca' from *Corncrake in October* (1978); 'Provincia Deserta' and 'Small Hours' from *Running Repairs* (1983); for permission to reprint the following poems by Paul Durcan: 'Ireland 1972' and 'In Memory: The Miami Showband: Massacred 31 July 1975' from *The Selected Paul Durcan* (1982); for permission to reprint the following poems by Padraic Fiacc: 'The Hero' (extract), 'Sanctus', 'Station/An Ordo', 'More Terrorists', 'Requin', 'Intimate Letter 1973', 'The British Connection', 'Enemy Encounter', 'Tears/A *Lacrimosa*' (extract), 'St Coleman's Song for Flight/An *Ite Missa Est*' and 'Goodbye tō Brigid/An *Agnus Dei*' from *Missa Terribilis* (1986); for permission to reprint the following poems by John Hewitt: 'Once Alien Here', 'The Colony', 'The Irish Dimension', 'Encounter, Nineteen Twenty', 'The Coasters', 'Bogside, Derry, 1971', 'The Green Shoot', 'From the Tibetan', *Freehold* (extract), 'Ulster Names', 'Postscript 1984', 'Neither an Elegy nor a Manifesto', 'A Belfastman Abroad Argues with Himself', 'The Dilemma', 'An Irishman in Coventry', 'The Search', 'The Scar' and 'The Hill-Farm' from *The Collected Poems of John Hewitt* (1991); for permission to reprint the following poems by Robert Johnstone: 'New Incidents in the Life of Shelley' (extract), 'As If It Never Happened' and 'Festival of Mithras' from *Breakfast in a Bright Room* (1983); 'Me as Moses', 'Eden Says No', 'Occasions of Love', 'At the End of the Day' and 'The Fruit of Knowledge' from *Eden to Edenderry* (1989)

Bloodaxe Books for permission to reprint the following poems by Brendan Kennelly: 'Our Place,' 'In the Sea', 'A Wound', Offenders' and 'It is the Nearness That Kills' from *Cromwell* (1987); for permission to reprint the following poems by Peter McDonald: 'Totalled', 'Sunday in Great Tew' and 'Count Dracula Entertains I' from *Biting the Wax* (1989)

Sandra Buchanan for permission to reprint the following poems by George Buchanan: 'Revolutionary Revolution' and 'Lyle Donaghy, Poet, 1902–1949' from *Minute-Book of a City* (Carcanet Press, 1972); 'A Speaker in the Square' *(Inside Traffic*, Carcanet Press, 1976)

Simon Campbell for permission to reprint the following poem by Joseph Campbell: 'The Planter' from *The Poems of Joseph Campbell* (1963)

Carcanet Press for permission to reprint the following poem by Eavan Boland: 'Child of Our Time' from *Selected Poems* (1989); for permission to reprint the following poem by Iain Crichton Smith: 'In Belfast' from *The Village and Other Poems* (1989); for permission to reprint the following poem by Donald Davie: 'Belfast on a Sunday Afternoon' from *Selected Poems* (1985); for permission to reprint the following poems by Andrew Waterman: 'From the Other Country' and 'Summer Truce' from *From the Other Country* (1977); for permission to reprint the following poem by Paul Wilkins: 'A Graveyard in Ulster' from *Pasts* (1979)

Conor Carson for permission to reprint the following poem: 'Marie Wilson'

Kerry Carson for permission to reprint the following poem: 'Mourne'

Chatto and Windus for permission to reprint the following poem by Carol Rumens: 'Passing a Statue of Our Lady in Derry' from *Selected Poems* (1987)

Maurice James Craig for permission to reprint the following poem: 'Ballad to a Traditional Refrain'

Gerald Dawe for permission to reprint the following poems: 'Count' and 'Names' from *Sheltering Places* (Blackstaff Press, 1978)

Dedalus Poetry Press for permission to reprint the following poems by John F. Deane: 'On the Killing in South Armagh', 'Le Dormeur du Val: Antrim' and 'Remembrance Day' from *The Stylized City: New and Selected Poems* (1991); for permission to reprint the following poem by Patrick Deeley: '1969' from *Names for Love* (1990); for permission to reprint the following poem by John Ennis: 'Londonderry' from *In a Green Shade* (1991); for permission to reprint the following poem by Robert Greacen: 'A Wish for St Patrick's Day' from *Carnival at the River* (1990)

Norman Dugdale for permission to reprint the following poem: 'Reasons of State' from *A Prospect of the West* (Barrie and Jenkins, 1970)

Seán Dunne for permission to reprint the following poem: 'Letter from Ireland' (extract)

Faber and Faber for permission to reprint the following poems by Seamus Heaney: 'Requiem for the Croppies' and 'Bogland' from *Door into the Dark* (1969); 'Traditions', 'The Tollund Man', 'The Other Side' and 'Servant Boy' from *Wintering Out* (1972); 'Singing School' (extracts), 'Act of Union', 'Funeral Rites', 'Viking Dublin: Trial Pieces' (extract), 'Punishment', 'Exposure' and 'Hercules and Antaeus' from *North* (1975); 'Triptych', 'The Toome Road', 'The Strand at Lough Beg', 'A Postcard from North Antrim', 'Casualty', 'The Harvest Bow' and 'In Memoriam Francis Ledwidge' from *Field Work* (1979); 'Chekhov on Sakhalin', 'Sandstone Keepsake', 'An Ulster Twilight', 'Station Island' (extracts) from *Station Island* (1984); 'From the Frontier of Writing' and 'From the Canton of Expectation' from *The Haw Lantern* (1987); and 'Chorus' from *The Cure at Troy* (1990); for permission to reprint the following poem by Philip Larkin: 'The Importance of Elsewhere' from *The Whitsun Weddings* (1964); for permission to reprint the following poems by Louis MacNeice: 'Carrickfergus', 'Autumn Journal' (extract), 'Belfast' and 'Valediction' from *The Collected Poems of Louis MacNeice* (1966); for permission to reprint the following poems by Paul Muldoon: 'The Field Hospital' and 'The Indians on Alcatraz' from *New Weather* (1973); 'Lunch with Pancho Villa' from *Mules* (1977); 'Anseo', 'The Weepies', 'The Boundary Commission' and

'Sheepman', 'Floods' and 'Aftermath' from *A Store of Candles* (1986); 'The War Photographers', 'Apples, Normandy, 1944', 'Home', 'King William Park', 'Incurables' and 'Soldier Bathing' from *A Northern Spring* (1966); for permission to reprint the following poems by W.R. Rodgers: 'Home Thoughts from Abroad' and 'Epilogue to "The Character of Ireland"' from *Collected Poems* (1971); for permission to reprint the following poems by James Simmons: 'For Jan Betley', 'Claudy', 'From the Irish', 'Lament for a Dead Policeman', 'Ulster Says Yes' and 'An Irish Epiphany' from *Poems 1956–1986* (1986)

Goldsmith Press for permission to reprint the following poem by Desmond Egan: 'Poems for Northern Ireland' (extract) from *Collected Poems* (1984)

Michael Kinghan for permission to reprint the following poem: 'Life on Mars'

Johnston Kirkpatrick for permission to reprint the following poem: 'Catholics'

Lapwing Poetry Pamphlets for permission to reprint the following poem by Howard Wright: 'Yahoo' from *Yahoo* (1991), © Howard Wright

Wes Magee for permission to reprint the following poem: 'No Surrender!' from *No Man's Land* (Blackstaff Press, 1978)

Roy McFadden for permission to reprint the following poems: 'Those Glorious Twelfths' from *The Garryowen* (Chatto and Windus, 1971); 'Reunion' from *Letters to the Hinterland* (Dedalus, 1986); 'Kew Gardens' from *The Selected Roy McFadden* (Blackstaff Press, 1983)

Arthur McVeigh for permission to reprint the following poem: 'Thought on the Derry Riots'

John Montague for permission to reprint the following poems: 'Heroics', 'Falls Funeral' and 'Cave' from *A Slow Dance* (1975); 'Procession' and 'Red Branch (A Blessing)' from *The Dead Kingdom* (1984)

Martin Mooney for permission to reprint the following poem: 'Radio Free Nowhere'

Oxford University Press for permission to reprint the following poems by Fleur Adcock: 'The Bullaun' and 'Please Identify Yourself' from *The Scenic Route* (1974, also in *Selected Poems* [1983]); for permission to reprint the following poems by Derek Mahon: 'Glengormley', 'Ecclesiastes', 'Poem Beginning With a Line by Cavafy', 'As It Should Be', 'The Spring Vacation', 'Rage for Order', 'The Snow Party', 'In Carrowdore Churchyard', 'Afterlives' and 'The Last of the Fire Kings', from *Poems 1962–1978* (1979); 'Courtyards in Delft', 'Derry Morning' and 'Rathlin Island' from *The Hunt by Night* (1982); for permission to reprint the following poem by Craig Raine: 'Flying to Belfast, 1977' from *A Martian Sends a Postcard Home* (1979)

Peterloo Poets for permission to reprint the following poem by Victor Price: 'England' from *Two Parts Water* (1980)

Peters Fraser and Dunlop for permission to reprint the following poem by Tony Harrison: 'The Act'; for permission to reprint the following poem by

Roger McGough: 'The Identification' from *GIG* (Jonathan Cape, 1973); for permission to reprint the following poem by Andrew Motion: 'Leaving Belfast' from *Dangerous Play: Poems 1974–1984* (Penguin, 1985)

Random House, Inc. for permission to reprint the following poems by Robinson Jeffers: 'Shane O'Neill's Cairn', 'Antrim' and 'The Broadstone' from *The Selected Poetry of Robinson Jeffers* (1938)

Salmon Publishing for permission to reprint the following poems by Sam Burnside: 'Six Loughs', 'In and Out of Derry', and 'Graveyards' from *Walking the Marches* (1990); for permission to reprint the following poem by Rita Ann Higgins: 'H-Block Shuttle' from *Philomena's Revenge* (1992)

Martin Secker and Warburg for permission to reprint the following poems by Michael Longley: 'On Slieve Gullion', 'Wounds', 'Wreaths', 'Kindertotenlieder', 'Fleance', 'Altera Cithera', 'The War Poets', 'Peace' and 'Letters' from *Poems 1963–1983* (1991); 'The Butchers' from *Gorse Fires* (1991); for permission to reprint the-following poems by William Peskett: 'The Inheritors' from *The Nightowl's Dissection* (1975); 'From Belfast to Suffolk' from *Survivors* (1980)

Sidgwick and Jackson for permission to reprint the following poem by Patrick Williams: 'Trails' from *Trails* (1981)

Francis Stuart for permission to reprint the following poem: 'Reading Keats in Derry City'

Wolfhound Press for permission to reprint the following poem by Seán Lucy: 'Men of Action' from *Unfinished Sequence* (1979)

Yevgeny Yevtushenko for permission to reprint the following poems: 'Pushkin in Belfast' and 'Ulster Safari'

The Blackstaff Press Limited regret they have not been successful in tracing all copyright holders. They apologise for any errors or omissions in the above list and would be grateful to be notified of any corrections that should be incorporated in the next edition or reprint of this volume.

354

INDEX OF FIRST LINES

357